A Fine-Looking Lot of Ball-Tossers

To my friend Bill Aylward, as well as to Jack Porter, Garrett Coey, Ed Millhoff, Jack Klein, Heinie Bolka, Ernie Kusnyer, Tony Sams, and all the other old-time ballplayers of Akron, living and dead, who were generous enough to make me a part of their very special fraternity

A Fine-Looking Lot of Ball-Tossers

The Remarkable Akrons of 1881

RICHARD L. MCBANE

McFarland & Company, Inc., Publishers
Jefferson, North Carolina, and London

LIBRARY OF CONGRESS CATALOGUING-IN-PUBLICATION DATA

McBane, Richard.
    A fine-looking lot of ball-tossers : the remarkable Akrons of 1881 / Richard L. McBane.
       p.   cm.
    Includes bibliographical references and index.

    ISBN 978-0-7864-2056-8
    softcover : 50# alkaline paper

    1. Akron Akrons (Baseball team : 1879–1881).   2. Baseball—Ohio—Akron—History.   I. Title.
GV875.A53M33   2005
796.357'64'0977136—dc22   2004030532

British Library cataloguing data are available

©2005 Richard L. McBane. All rights reserved

No part of this book may be reproduced or transmitted in any form or by any means, electronic or mechanical, including photocopying or recording, or by any information storage and retrieval system, without permission in writing from the publisher.

Cover photograph: Tony Mullane (National Baseball Hall of Fame Library, Cooperstown, N.Y.)

Manufactured in the United States of America

McFarland & Company, Inc., Publishers
  Box 611, Jefferson, North Carolina 28640
    www.mcfarlandpub.com

Acknowledgments

The seed that has grown into this book was planted in 1998 when I first read three sentences in Harold Seymour's classic *Baseball: The Early Years*. They were: "Spink brought in other clubs, ranging from 'prairie' teams like Dubuque and pickup nines from Chicago to the famous Brooklyn Atlantics and the Akron team, regarded as the strongest non-League club in the country. Louisville, too, was keen for baseball. A record crowd of 7,000 fans turned out the same year for a game with the Akrons."

Naturally, I yearned to know more about that Akron team. The watering and cultivation of the seed began with a resort to the microfilm of the *Summit County Beacon* at the Akron Public Library. That started me down the road of identifying the players whose skill on the diamond made the Akrons one of the premier independent town baseball teams in the country in 1881.

The seed, however, might never have germinated had it not been for fertilization from two sources. The first came from Mark Heppner, curator of Stan Hywet Hall & Gardens in Akron, who invited me to address the convention of the Vintage Baseball Association. It was an invitation that added a note of urgency to the initial task of identifying the principal players, and so pushed along the beginning research which otherwise might have suffered a years-long drought. The second came from two of my former *Akron Beacon Journal* co-workers, Chuck Ayers and Russ Musarra, who urged me to turn the Vintage Baseball Association talk into a book.

I protested that it would take too much time and effort. The seed, however, was determined to grow, so I have many other individuals and organizations to acknowledge for their assistance in nurturing the growth. It is impossible, of course, to compile an acknowledgment without overlooking or omitting someone I should remember. My apologies for that in advance.

First, my thanks to the Society for American Baseball Research's Nineteenth Century Committee in general. The collective expertise of that group is invaluable. Special recognition, however, is due to Richard Malatzky, Reed Howard, Joe Simenic, Vern Luse and Peter Morris for the work in identifying James F. Green. Likewise, Robert L. Tiemann was a great help in providing research on the Akrons' games in St. Louis, as was Priscilla Astifan on coverage of Charlie Morton and Sam Wise during the parts of their careers in Rochester, New York.

Jared Oldaker researched the Mansfield, Ohio, newspapers for me, and Mark Taflinger, reference librarian of the Louisville *Courier-Journal*, provided the coverage of all the Akrons' games in that city.

My thanks is also due to Tim Wiles, director of research at the National Baseball Hall of Fame and Library, and to his staff members, Russell Wolinsky and Rachel Kepner, in addition to W.C. Burdick of the Hall of Fame's photo department. Great help also was provided by John V. Miller Jr. and Stephen H. Paschen at the University of Akron Archives, and by the unfailingly helpful and courteous staff of the Ohio Historical Society Archives in Columbus.

Special mention must be made of my old friend and fellow SABR member Ted Lukacs, and of my friend and former editor at the Akron *Beacon Journal* Michele Lecomte, who each read early versions of the manuscript and made perceptive and helpful suggestions. Of course, I dare not forget my loving wife, Marilynn, my helpmeet and chauffeur, who patiently endured trips to Cooperstown, New York, Columbus, Ohio, and Mercer, Pennsylvania, as well as the countless hours I ignored her when I retreated to my time machine, otherwise known as a microfilm reader.

One note about the photographs: No photographs of the Akrons teams were discovered, so the images that appear are from the players' last years.

For readers who want to enjoy 1860s-era ball, take a trip to the Stan Hywet Hall & Gardens in Akron. Teams play an old-fashioned game in spring and summer. Call (330) 836-5533 or go to www.stanhywet.org.

Finally, any errors which appear in the finished work are entirely my own, but the growth and flowering of the seed planted so long ago, from beginning to end, is due entirely to the providence of God. To Him be the glory.

Richard L. McBane
December 2004

Contents

Acknowledgments	v
Introduction: A Few Words About Nineteenth Century Baseball	1
1. The Original Akrons	9
2. A Fresh Incarnation	14
3. The Reputation Grows	20
4. The Strongest Non-League Club in the Country	32
5. Bid McPhee Comes to Akron	37
6. The Matinee Idol	45
7. That Man Swartwood	52
8. The Most Remarkable Game	60
9. The Home Town Boy	65
10. From Louisville to Limbo	76
11. Art, Music, Literature and Left Field	82
12. The Streak Continues	87
13. A College Boy	92
14. Some Country Hardball	99
15. Into the Mist	107
16. And Into the Darkness	117
17. Toward the Light	126
18. A Dawn of Fresh Glory	135
Appendix A: 1881 Calendar of Scores	141
Appendix B: Box Scores of the Akrons	143
Appendix C: 1881 Akrons Stats	163
Chapter Notes	165
Bibliography	175
Index	177

Introduction: A Few Words About Nineteenth Century Baseball

Unlike the goddess Minerva, who sprang fully formed and armed with a sword and shield from the brow of Jupiter, baseball did not emerge fully formed, unique and popular from the brain of Abner Doubleday in Cooperstown, New York, in 1839. Almost from the earliest days of European colonization in North America, folk ball playing existed in various forms. Whether it was one, two or three old cat, rounders, or various forms of town ball, bat and ball games had more than 200 years to spread and mutate to meet local conditions and tastes before the advent of the New York Knickerbockers and similar clubs in the eastern urban centers.[1]

The group of young men that was to become the Knickerbocker Base Ball Club of New York began playing in 1842 and adopted a set of playing rules formulated by Alexander Cartwright in 1845. This baseball club was indeed a club, a fraternal organization formed not just to play ball but to be an exclusive social association. Harold Seymour in his *Baseball: The Early Years* likened them to what country clubs represented in the 1920s and 1930s, "before they became popular with the middle class in general." The relatively exclusive nature of the early baseball clubs is reflected in the fact that members were supposed to have some social standing, to pay dues, to buy their own uniforms, and to uphold genteel standards of behavior.[2]

Thus, a ball game was recreation and a polite social gathering for the Knickerbockers and the similar clubs that quickly sprang up. Often the convivial dinner that followed a game was the more important of the two events. While every game, by its nature, involves competition, it was the socializing rather than competitive success that was important. Moreover, until the early 1850s, the Knickerbockers played nearly all their games among themselves. Naturally, the other clubs reflected the Knickerbockers both in organization and in the playing rules used. As these clubs grew, matches against other clubs were arranged by formal invitation and the host club was expected to make each match a social occasion.[3]

Although the Knickerbockers dominated the early years of baseball, and it was their rules that established the "New York" game that spread over the country, by 1854 the team had ample local competition with the Gothams, Eagles, and Empires in New York, and the Excelsiors, Putnams, Eckfords, and Atlantics in Brooklyn. Before the advent of the Civil War, about 60 clubs had been created, including the Philadelphia Athletics, as well as teams in Cleveland, Detroit, Chicago and St. Louis. The growth of clubs was such that the National Association of Base Ball Players was established in 1858 to provide guidelines for the new clubs and to assure uniformity in the rules.[4]

It would be a mistake, however, to think that the Knickerbocker rules provided uniformity. They were a pattern, but there was little real uniformity, and the rules themselves changed from year to year as efforts continued to balance the roles of the batter and pitcher, particularly with the advent of the professional game after the Civil War. In the beginning, the pitcher was a "feeder" who was to throw the ball where the batter could hit it and put it into play. Batters, usually called "strikers," could call for low or high pitches. Soon pitchers found ways to fool batters. The pitching distance was changed several times. Various restrictions were placed on pitchers' deliveries. The positioning of infielders also gradually changed based on game experience so that the game in the 1850s was substantially different from that of the 1880s, which was itself substantially different from that of the twentieth century. The Knickerbocker game of the 1850s, if watched by a twenty-first century fan, would be recognizable but would appear to be a version of slow-pitch softball, with its emphasis on participation rather than on spectator entertainment. Most of the rule changes over the years were made to enhance the level of competition, a motivation which itself had a genesis in the desire to attract spectators who very quickly were turned into paying customers.

At the start, all players did without gloves. The catcher, generally positioned far behind the batter, was often referred to as the *behind*. The catcher's mask was developed in the 1870s, and by that time catchers also had taken to wearing gloves, usually tight-fitting kid gloves, to protect their hands. The chest protector and overstuffed catcher's mitt were developed by the late 1880s. Gloves for infielders and outfielders also began to appear by that time. The treatment of fly balls and foul balls changed over the years in part owing to the development of fielding gloves. Initially, fly balls caught on the first bounce were outs. The same was true of foul balls, and the foul bound rule persisted into the 1880s, although it was abolished earlier in the National League. Also, the visiting club did not always bat first, and the home team last. Instead, a coin toss was conducted at the start of the game, and the winner of the toss could elect to bat first or second. Clubs also had to agree on an umpire for each match, a situation that sometimes resulted in lengthy delays if the teams could not agree. And, the starting nine players were expected to complete each match. Substitutes were allowed only if a player was physically unable to continue.

There were numerous contributing factors in the rapid spread of the "New York" form of baseball, including its immense popularity with participants and spectators. The popularity was likely because the Knickerbocker rules and their various permutations provided for a more genteel and better organized game than the various folk versions of ball, required fewer players, and eliminated one important element of violence, namely the practice of "soaking," or retiring a batter or base-runner by hitting him with the ball. But the games' direct descent from various forms of folk ball also meant that most adults understood the game because they'd played some form of it as children. Besides, there was plenty of vacant land for ball grounds, and acquiring a bat and ball was relatively inexpensive.

Moreover, America had begun to change from a rural, agrarian society to an urban industrial one in the decades preceding the Civil War. Travel became easier, first with the development of the canal system, and then with the development of railroads. There was an increase in commerce and in newspapers and periodicals. The advent of the telegraph along with improvements in postal service stimulated the more rapid spread not only of news, but of developments in business and entertainment. It was simply easier for people to know what was happening elsewhere and to get together over longer distances.

Indeed, it was the railroad system that made possible what Harold Seymour called "the first great baseball tour," the trip of the Excelsior Club in 1860, which helped arouse baseball fever along the route and led to the formation of many clubs.[5]

The Civil War spurred rather than hindered most of these developments. Baseball was played in the camps of the Union and Confederate armies, and many veterans returned home with a passion for the game. In 1865, 91 baseball clubs belonged to the National Association. But when the association held its convention in 1866, the sport's craze was illustrated by the fact that 202 clubs from 17 states and the District of Columbia were represented, including 15 members of a North Western Association that extended from Kenyon College in Ohio to Dubuque on the banks of the Mississippi River. A year later representatives from more than 300 clubs appeared at the convention, including members of nine clubs in Des Moines, Iowa, and several from towns in Minnesota. Remember that at the time, both states were still on the western frontier. By 1869 *The New York Times* was estimating that more than 1,000 clubs were active.[6]

The very popularity of the game with the continuing proliferation of teams brought new problems and exacerbated those that existed. Seymour observed, "A game can remain amateur only as long as a privileged minority plays it as an aristocratic diversion." In his analysis in the Seymour Medal-winning *Early Baseball and the Rise of the National League*, Tom Melville added, "Clubs began to establish reputations based upon their competitive success or failure, which in turn began to refocus club purpose more on competitive results than simply recreational enjoyment."[7]

Particularly in the New York City urban area, where the clubs were closer together, more highly skilled through long practice and more competitive, the better players began to move freely from one club to another based on their ball playing expertise. The top talent congregated with the more competitive clubs, and domination by a few clubs began to be viewed with concern, if not with alarm. Matches that were once viewed as social events where competition was secondary now were invested with championship implications of the semiofficial superiority of one club over another. Even the insistently amateur Knickerbockers had a "first nine" for important matches.[8]

Clubs that wished to be at the top of the competitive heap began to offer inducements to top players, including paying a few of the most talented. Melville, in *Early Baseball and the Rise of the National League*, characterized this as a vertical dynamic "with some communities always trying to work up to baseball's highest recognized competitive level, while others were always falling back to a lower competitive status."[9]

While the practice of luring top players from one club to another originated in the urban East, it spread rapidly to the West, particularly when the newer western clubs found themselves at a distinct competitive disadvantage against the more highly developed and experienced Easterners. But there were other social dynamics at work besides simply competitiveness. One of these was commercialism. Clubs that remained putatively amateur began charging admission and using the gate receipts to attract the best players, regardless of who they were or where they came from. Besides the promoters, who often saw, or thought they saw, an opportunity for a quick profit, businessmen also began to look at the game from a commercial standpoint. The publicity value of a good team often was sufficient for them to provide jobs for talented ball players.

This motivation mixed easily with the social dynamic of civic pride.

A top-notch baseball team was easily equated with a top-notch or up-and-coming community. It was a dynamic that worked in all localities, East and West, large and small, after the Civil War. Having a winning team was more important than having a team of local amateur talent. Thus, in the predawn of professional baseball, the original amateur social ball clubs had quietly become semipros with some salaried players and others who were provided jobs with local businesses.[10]

All of these developments heightened the contrasts and tensions between the older purely amateur social clubs and the newer clubs and town teams, which desired the revenue to attract the best players they could afford for scaling the competitive heights. Enclosed fields became a necessity to have paying customers, but the baseball organizations also had to change from social organizations into more business, or revenue-centered operations—an amusement business. From an organizational standpoint there was a recognized distinction between clubs operated as joint stock companies and those operated as co-operatives. Initially both retained some appearance of being a club.

With a joint stock operation, the club members generally subscribed or paid a fee to buy a share of stock in the company. Depending upon the size of the community and the state of the local economy, the number of shares offered and the price would vary but usually would be $5 or $10 per individual. The funds subscribed would provide the initial cash to organize and operate a team for a season, with additional funds coming from admissions. Such clubs generally were operated by a board of directors. Only later did the baseball team as a closed corporation, controlled by a few wealthy individuals, appear. In contrast, the co-op clubs sometimes had a similar organization but instead of paying their players a salary simply allowed them to split gate receipts. Players themselves sometimes formed co-operatives or combines, particularly to play in the South after the close of the regular baseball season.[11]

The dawn of fully professional baseball came up like thunder over Cincinnati in 1869. The early history of baseball in the city mirrored all the developments already noted. It began as a gentleman's game, imported by a pharmacist from upstate New York in 1860. Various professional groups, among them bankers and lawyers, formed clubs, and in 1866, a group of lawyers formed the Cincinnati Base Ball Club. They erected a grandstand at their field, Union Grounds, in 1867 and began to charge admission. That same season the Washington Nationals, touring the West, easily defeated the local clubs. That ignited the desire to field a team that could challenge the top Eastern clubs.

The Cincinnati Base Ball Club, originally known as the Resolutes, and their chief local rival, the Buckeyes, hired some players from the East for the 1868 season. That fall, the directors of the Cincinnati club, under president Aaron Champion, decided to recruit the best players they could from around the country and to pay them salaries. It already had Harry Wright, one of the best players in the country, who had been hired as a pro by the Union Cricket Club of Cincinnati in 1865. He captained the Cincinnati baseball club in 1866 and thereafter, and took over the day-to-day management of the first fully professional club in 1869. It turned out to be a *tour de force* as the team, now known as the Red Stockings, stunned the baseball world, toured from the Atlantic to the Pacific, attracted more than 100,000 paying customers, and posted a record of 57 wins, no losses, and one tie.[12]

Cincinnati's achievement revolutionized the baseball world to such a degree that the club found itself in a completely different competitive environment in 1870. Nevertheless, the Red Stockings won their first 27 games before being defeated by the Brooklyn Atlantics 8–7 in 11 innings. The Red Stockings finished the 1870 season with 67 wins and six losses, but no teams played fixed schedules in a closed league, and under the prevailing rules they were denied championship status. Moreover, both the team and the management were wracked by dissention and subjected to acute newspaper criticism. Plus, the club had financial difficulties. It was organized as a joint stock company in which club members, not players, subscribed to the stock. The club was always undersubscribed, and when the directors attempted to bolster income in 1870 by doubling membership fees from $5 to $10, the move backfired. Membership dropped from 490 to 150. In November 1870, after fruitless salary negotiations with key players, the directors announced that the club would be fully amateur again in 1871.[13]

This, too, was a typical development of the era. When a club failed, either competitively or financially, it didn't necessarily disband but simply reverted to a local, amateur, or non-competitive status. This happened not only to the original Red Stockings but to other early professional clubs. While Cincinnati was an example of success and failure, it was the success rather than the failure that attracted the attention of towns and cities around the country. At least five teams were fully salaried by the end of 1870, and the number continued to grow, creating a crisis for the old, supposedly amateur National Association of Base Ball Players. In the resulting confrontation between amateur and professional clubs it was no surprise that the Knickerbockers were the first to walk away from the association when it recognized the professionals. The result was that the professional clubs formed a new association in March 1871, the National Association of Professional Base Ball Players.[14]

The new organization, recognized as the first professional league and usually referred to simply as the National Association, really wasn't a "league" in modern terms. It wasn't a closed circuit; any club willing to put up the money could join. There was no set schedule as the "championship" was still determined by matches, series of games arranged between the clubs. Many clubs played only a few "league" games before folding, and clubs were free to play whichever clubs they pleased, whenever they pleased. The organization also proved incapable of disciplining its members so that rowdyism and dishonesty, including game fixing, tainted the professional game. Gambling was frequent, and in some venues liquor was sold on the ball grounds. Nevertheless, the professional National Association, in five years of existence, prepared the way for the formation of the National League before the 1876 season.[15]

In large part the new National League of Professional Baseball Clubs was the brainchild of William Hulbert of Chicago, who carefully laid the groundwork for it following the 1875 season. His plan was revealed before carefully selected representatives from Boston, Hartford, New York and Philadelphia at a February 1876 meeting in New York. For the first time professional baseball had a closed league with a set schedule; a league that placed administrative responsibilities with club owners and that had disciplinary authority over both teams and players. In a shrewd public relations move, the owners also promised to restore the reputation of the professional game to that of its gentlemanly past.

It was a promise calculated to recapture public respect and patronage, and, at least in part, it was fulfilled during the early years through the expulsion of several teams for violating league rules. The New York Mutuals and the Philadelphia Athletics failed and were expelled in 1876. St. Louis and Louisville were the next to go after the 1877 season. Four Louisville players also were expelled and never reinstated because of a game-fixing scandal, and St. Louis had signed three of the four for the 1878 season. Cincinnati also was expelled following the 1880 season, largely for renting its grounds for amateur Sunday games and for selling liquor on the grounds. Of all the actions taken by the fledgling National League, the expulsion of Cincinnati proved to be the most damaging.[16]

Expulsion from the National League was far from being a death sentence. Apart from the National League and the National Association, other leagues and scores of independent professional teams existed during the 1870s, and all of them considered themselves equals as well as rivals of the National League clubs. The New York, Philadelphia, Louisville and Cincinnati clubs did not cease to exist when they were expelled. Indeed, it was Cincinnati that headed the organization of the second professional "major" league, the American Association, in 1882.

In addition, from its inception in 1876 until the 1884 season, National League teams played fewer than 100 league games a season. National League teams, therefore, depended upon games with nonleague clubs to supplement their revenue. This was not a new situation. While still in the National Association in 1873, Boston played half of its 110 games against non–National Association teams. In 1877, the National League's second season, league clubs lost 72 games to nonleague opponents. Eventually, league clubs were accused of avoiding strong independent teams. Perhaps as a result, the National League lost only 31 games to the independents in 1880. The New York Metropolitans were organized as an independent club in the fall of 1880, and in 1881 played 151 games, the greatest number played until that time by any professional club. Sixty were played against league clubs, and the Mets won 18.[17]

The very success of the nonleague independent clubs made them a target for other clubs, particularly league teams attempting to upgrade their personnel. Complaints about raiding and contract jumping were common, and the National League, then in direct competition with the upstart International Association, attempted to kill two birds with one stone in 1877.

Under the title of the League Alliance, the National League offered other clubs a kind of second-class citizenship. The player contracts of clubs that signed up and paid an entrance fee would have their contracts respected by the league. On the other hand, they made themselves subject to National League rules without having any voice in those rules, plus agreed that league teams could play nonleague clubs only on the league's off days and not on league grounds. Besides extending its authority over the subsidiary clubs, the league hoped to destroy, or at least weaken, the International Association by disengaging its strongest clubs and placing them in a subordinate relationship with the league. The plan was denounced as a "heads I win, tails you lose" kind of arrangement. Nevertheless, the league signed up 13 teams in 1877. The Alliance never was popular but limped along until 1883 when the National League, then in serious competition with the American Association, abolished it.[18]

In this dog-eat-dog environment of the early years of professional baseball, some teams thrived, but many others floundered as lofty dreams frequently crashed on the mundane reality of inadequate finances. Success on the field was essential to pull in paying customers, but when payroll outstriped attendance even talented teams could be doomed, particularly if key players discovered that the grass was greener on some other club's ball grounds. This was the world in which the little Ohio canal town of Akron made its baseball debut.

1

The Original Akrons

Civil War veterans returning to their homes in Akron and the other towns and villages of northeastern Ohio, like so many other places in the nation, brought with them a contagious enthusiasm for baseball. The first account of a game was reported in the June 13, 1867, edition of the *Summit County Beacon*, a weekly newspaper. It reported that the Akrons had defeated the Mechanics of Middlebury 41–26 on the Akron grounds in two hours and 45 minutes.[1]

It was no accident that the first recorded game was between a team representing Akron and one from Middlebury. Akron was settled in 1825 as a consequence of the construction of the Ohio and Erie Canal, which linked Cleveland and Lake Erie on the north to the Ohio River at Portsmouth in the south. Middlebury was then a busy commercial center, but it missed out on the canal, which climbed up 17 locks at Akron to get over the heights that separated the Great Lakes watershed from the Ohio Valley watershed. Still, despite the advantage of the canal, Akron continued to play second fiddle to its older and more prosperous neighbor.

In 1860, Akron had a population of 3,520 and had suffered a decline in business during the preceding decade. But the village prospered during the Civil War and grew, topping 10,000 in the 1870 census. By 1872 Akron had absorbed its Middlebury adversary, but rivalry was alive and well on the baseball diamond in 1867.[2]

In May 1879, the Akron *Sunday Gazette*, another weekly newspaper, presented a lengthy retrospective on the "Old Akrons. Reminiscenses of Akron's Famous Base Ball Nine of 1867." The account demonstrated that the factors that contributed to the spread and popularity of the game elsewhere were at work in Akron. The desire for a "crack" nine was such that even at that early date players were recruited to bolster the lineup. Second baseman Ace Hanscom had played a few games with the Forest Citys of Cleveland; first baseman J.W. Hudson had belonged to a Cuyahoga Falls club; shortstop J.D. Buchtel had been a member of the Summits, a club started in 1866; and third baseman Fred Hanford and left fielder Tom Perkins had belonged to the Western Reserves. The organizer, captain, and pitcher was Ed Rawson, identified by the *Sunday Gazette* as the "moving spirit and promoter." Along with Rawson, catcher E.B. Angel, center fielder Will Babcock, and right fielder E.S. Smith had never played before on a "regular" nine.

The Akron ball grounds in 1867 were on the north side of Grace Park near the railroad tracks. Said the *Sunday Gazette* in 1879, "Very few of the houses on that street were then standing and the ground was a very good one. Later there was a high back stop erected back of the catcher's place." It continued, "Once in a while a foul in the right field would send the ball down on the railroad track and still less frequently would some one knock a ball over the brow of the hill, north of the grounds, and then there was no knowing when the ball would stop, until it reached the canal. J.W. Hudson did it in one match game and excited so much enthusiasm in the large crowd attending, that it took fully five minutes for them to quiet down."[3]

The club did not begin practice until the first of June, and the *Sunday Gazette* reported that the team's success was partly due to the regularity of its practices, but the paper attributed the larger part of the success to "the excellent control Captain Rawson always kept over his men." However great that control may have been, it didn't prevent Buchtel and Hanford from running into each other while chasing a pop fly behind third base. Nevertheless, both men were ready for the opening game against Middlebury just a week after the practices began.

The 41–26 victory over the Mechanics as well as the other large scores recorded during the season were common in that era because the pitcher's role was to deliver the ball where it could be hit and because none of the fielders wore gloves. As the *Sunday Gazette* noted, "Heavy hitting was the order of the day."

On June 19, the fledgling Akrons were tested by a visit from the more established Western Reserve club. The Akrons rallied to take a 28–26 lead in the top of the seventh inning, only to have the Reserves regain the lead with 11 runs in the bottom of the inning. Not to be outdone, the Akrons responded with 18 runs in the top of the eighth and went on to a 53–41 victory. On June 29, the Akrons beat the Middlebury Mechanics again 52–37.[4]

The advent of the railroad had certainly added to the prosperity of Akron, and it made baseball matches with representative teams from other communities a possibility. The Akrons' first road trip was a July 10 visit to Mansfield, a community two counties distant. To mark the occasion

1. The Original Akrons

Akron station on the Atlantic & Great Western Railroad, where the Akrons departed for their trips to Louisville and St. Louis (University of Akron Archives).

Akron fans had presented a stand of colors to the team to mark the foul ball line, and a large number of supporters made the trip with the team. They did so with some misgivings, believing that the Mansfield club might be their superior. Also, the Akrons took the field with two of their "second nine" in the lineup. Fears were misplaced. Said the *Sunday Gazette*, "The men were in good trim and batted the ball for all it was worth." The Akrons added a 63–33 victory to their record.[5]

There was, however, still much of the "social club" atmosphere associated with matches, and visiting clubs expected to be well treated, if not entertained. Despite the 30-run victory, the Akrons' treatment in Mansfield was labeled "disgraceful," and the club vowed to never return to Mansfield. Matches were arranged on a home-and-home basis, however, and the rancor probably helped attract an exceptionally large crowd for the visit of the Mansfields to Akron on July 24. The Mansfields, arriving by a special train, were accompanied by 400 fans, and the *Sunday Gazette*, in its retrospective said, "The crowd was numbered by the thousands." The *Summit County Beacon*, reporting closer to the event, contented itself by noting "A very large concourse of persons present." The Akrons pleased the home crowd by pounding out a 46–31 victory which included home runs by Hanford, Hanscom and Rawson.[6]

The spirit of the times was reflected in the fact that the *Sunday Gazette* made special note that: "The Mansfield nine were all gentlemen and their treatment here was entirely gentlemanly." This was also reflected in the fact that while the Akrons also defeated the Cantons twice, that on the Cantons' visit to Akron, "a grand dance was given them at Mazourka Hall."[7]

The Akrons finally met their match when they played the Forest City Club in Cleveland, losing 52–33. Perhaps they were overawed at playing in the big city to the north, or perhaps they just had a bad day. The *Sunday Gazette* said, "The club wobbled fearfully that day and couldn't stop anything or hit a barn door." The Forest Citys made six home runs. Rawson had the only circuit clout for the Akrons. This August game was their only defeat of the season.[8]

During the course of the 1867 season, the *Summit County Beacon* also reported on the Reserve Club of Hudson, the Summit Club of Akron, the Eagle Club of Hudson, the Buckeye Club of Akron, the Lake Club of Uniontown, the Enterprise Club of Hudson, the Star Club of Ravenna, and the Monumental Club of Twinsburg, reflecting the widespread interest in baseball.[9]

The Akrons, however, were the representative club for the city, and although the team was strictly amateur, it did recruit players, and it did have expenses. It was organized on a club basis with its expenses raised by subscription and by electing honorary members to the club. The *Sunday Gazette* called club patronage "very liberal." One indicator of the club's relative standing in the community is that most home games were umpired by Col. George Tod Perkins. The grandson of Gen.

Col. George Tod Perkins, umpire for the original Akrons of 1867, later became president of B.F. Goodrich Co. (University of Akron Archives).

Simon Perkins, one of the founders of Akron, Perkins had enlisted as a private in Company B, 19th Regiment, Ohio Volunteer Infantry at the outbreak of the Civil War, and came home as a colonel. By 1867 he headed the Akron Steam Forge Works, which made locomotive and car axles and shaftings, eye-bars for bridges, and wrought iron specialties. He had close connections with the Atlantic & Great Western railroad, which his father had helped promote. Eventually, he became president of B.F. Goodrich Co.[10]

The original Akrons returned to play in 1868, but with less unbroken success. Support waned, and the Akrons of 1868 faded away.[11]

2

A Fresh Incarnation

When the curtain fell on the original Akrons in 1868, it was not the end of baseball in the city. Other amateur nines filled the landscape, but the relative success of the National League after its formation in 1876 once more whetted the desires of some Akron enthusiasts to compete at a higher level. By April 1879, the Akron *Sunday Gazette* was beating the drum.

It wrote: "Many of us can not even now restrain our enthusiasm as we think of the glorious successes our crack clubs have obtained, of the many victories of the Red Stockings, the Buckeyes, the Blue Stockings, the Akron City's and other nines have pounded out at the end of their clubs, and sometimes got pounded themselves also. We believe the time is not far away when Akron will awake from her base ball lethargy and organize a good paid nine. Such an effort should receive substantial backing and in the right hands prove successful."[1]

Three days later the *Summit County Beacon* noted: "There is some talk of organizing a crack base ball club in Akron for the coming Summer. The project has not yet assumed definite shape, but the boys are determined to make a go if such a thing be possible."[2]

The *Sunday Gazette* weighed in again on April 27, repeating a report from the Cleveland *Leader* that as many as 24 northern Ohio towns might field teams, and citing Garrettsville, Youngstown, Austinburg, Warren and Alliance as communities which had clubs in the field, although the Alliance team represented Mount Union College. Said the *Sunday Gazette*: "This report is about as good a one as could be expected under the circumstances and before the summer is over some other places will organize clubs. There are various reasons why other places have no organizations, some towns have no suitable grounds, as in Akron, and others like Akron again, have had good nines and excited great enthusiasm on the subject which finally died out, while other places never did have any enthusiasm over the game and have taken it second hand from Cleveland and Cincinnati.

"We believe Akron will again sometime possess a good nine but it won't be this year and perhaps not the next. The first thing to be obtained are good enclosed grounds. There are several places near the city which might be used for that purpose. The next thing to be done, is the formation of a stock company with a small capital. Until our best citizens take hold of the thing, there will probably be no revival of the national game in our midst. The attempt must be under the charge of the most respectable elements, or it will be a failure. Lastly, there must be one man, a manager, who will start the ball rolling and push it through to success."[3]

The relatively pessimistic tone of the *Sunday Gazette* was, in part, borne out by the fact that the new Akrons were not born until July, playing their initial game of the season on July 15 at Orrville and posting a 15–10 victory. As initially made up, the club consisted of pitcher William Johnson, catcher Sam Wise, first baseman Abe Glick, shortstop Charles Trowbridge, second baseman E. Darrow, third baseman D. Harrington, left fielder W. Parks, center fielder John Moran, right fielder F. Wiedner, and tenth man C. Porter.[4]

Johnson, also identified as Ed Johnson, was reputed to be a black player. Akron had been a hotbed of abolitionist sentiment before the Civil War. Businesses closed and church bells tolled when John Brown, who had lived in Akron, was executed. It is not surprising that the appearance of a black man as a member of the city's representative ball club occasioned no comment in the *Summit County Beacon* or the *Sunday Gazette*.

John Moran, the middle or center fielder, had played the same position on the Worcester, Massachusetts, team of 1878. The recruiting of Moran from Massachusetts is a sure sign that at least some of the Akron players were paid; although consistent with the general practice in this era, the team was regularly referred to as amateur. As it turned out, Moran gained the distinction of suing the Akron Baseball Association and season ticket holders for $31 in back salary following the 1880 season.

In this unstable period of baseball development, the incident was merely another example of how typical Akron was of the many independent town teams that operated with only a thin margin of financial security. Like the many similar organizations that sprang up all over the country in the 1870s and 1880s, the Akron Base Ball Association was a joint stock company with prominent citizens or businessmen serving as directors, motivated by civic pride and the promise of a return on their investment. With the idea of profit in front of them, the directors put up the cash necessary to get a team organized and playing. If the initial investment was too small, the operating expenses too high, and the paying customers too few, the team was likely to fold if the directors were unable to recruit new investors or unwilling to cover the losses. An independent team with good management and solid support from the business community could flourish in this environment. At times, Akron had both.[5]

After the initial 1879 victory over Orrville, the Akrons immediately challenged the strong team from Garrettsville, a small community in neighboring Portage County. The first of what eventually turned out to be five games with the Garrettsvilles ended with a 7–6 win for the Akrons in a game halted after six innings because the club had to travel by buggy to Ravenna to catch the last train to Akron. On August 2, the Akrons made another trip to Garrettsville, and in a special dispatch to the *Beacon* it was reported that the entire village had turned out to witness the game, which was called "the best ever played here." The Akrons rallied for a 9–6 win by scoring three runs in the seventh and two in the eighth over the Garrettsvilles which had been undefeated in nine games up until their first meeting with the Akrons. Wise, catching for the Akrons in the August 2 game, was hit in the chin in the sixth inning, suffering a bad cut. Said the dispatch: "After binding up the wound he played the balance of the game in fine style. Everybody compliments the Akron men's playing."[6]

A week later the *Summit County Beacon*, picking up snippets from exchange papers, a common nineteenth century practice, quoted the Ravenna *Republican-Democrat* as saying, "The Akron club with the right sort of patronage will make a very strong organization." And, from the Youngstown *Register & Tribune*: "The Garrettsvilles sustained their second defeat at the hands of the Akron 'Mashers,' Saturday, and still they are not happy. They had gotten the idea that they were impregnable, and the two defeats by the newly organized Akronites makes them feel doubly sad, coming, as it does, just before starting on an extended tour throughout the state."[7]

But, after the second victory over Garrettsville, the Akrons went almost three weeks without a game, largely because the club had no home field. It was a problem that wasn't solved until August 19, when the committee charged with securing grounds reported to the club directors that a lot belonging to Jacob Good, between Good Street and Smith's Grove, behind the property of Judge U.L. Marvin, had been secured for the balance of the season, with a conditional promise that it would be available for 1880 if Good did not sell it or build on it. At that meeting, it was announced that family tickets would be issued for $5 and season tickets for $2. Single game tickets were to be 15 cents. Subscriptions to support the team had amounted to $100. It was also announced that the uniforms were to be white, trimmed with brown, the stockings being brown. A committee was appointed to determine what monogram or emblem was to be put on the front of the shirts.[8]

2. A Fresh Incarnation

Even though formation of the club had been delayed until July, and it took another month to procure home grounds, the club itself continued to play well, chalking up a 21–5 win over the previously undefeated Aetnas of Warren in its first home match of the season on August 20. In the kind of comment typical of the era, the *Summit County Beacon* appended to the report of the score, "tickles 'em." The Akrons then played a home-and-home series with the Ashland Anchors, winning 7–4 in Ashland and 11–10 on the new home grounds. The club ran its record to 7–0 on August 29 with an 11–7 triumph over Elyria. The game was noteworthy in that Sam Wise hit a double, a triple, and a home run.[9]

Samuel Washington Wise was a 22-year-old Akron native employed at the Buckeye Mower & Reaper Works. George Myers, writing in *A Centennial History of Akron*, said the Akron team was built around Wise. Initially, he played catcher, a particularly important position in the game of that era, and according to Myers, he also served as team captain. It appears, however, that Wise never was captain of the 1879 nine. At a directors' meeting on August 30, Glick submitted his resignation as captain and as a member of the team. Clarence Knight, editor of the weekly Akron *City Times,* was elected a member of the club and captain. The *Summit County Beacon* reported that Knight "will have full control and disposition of the men, and will hereafter do whatever kicking [arguing with the umpire] is necessary." In addition, C.H. Mathews also resigned his position as manager, but remained secretary and treasurer of the board of directors. Robert. S. Iredell, son of Akron's first mayor, was chosen as manager.[10]

To appreciate the changes, it is necessary to understand nineteenth-century terminology. A captain was, in fact, the on-field manager and director of game strategy and tactics. A manager filled a role more like that of the modern-day general manager and traveling secretary rolled into one. Even when the manager was a player, he was in charge of recruiting and signing players, arranging matches with other clubs, collecting money at the gate and paying bills. Often it was the manager who appointed the team captain.

The fact that these changes at the management level of the association took place between the August 29 victory over the Elyrias and a September 2 win by a 9–4 score over the Sevilles, both on the Akron grounds, is a reflection of the desire of the directors to improve the on-field quality of the club, even though it was still undefeated for the season. It was a desire that was reinforced when the visiting Garrettsville club surprised the Akrons with a 4–2 loss, their first of the season, on September 5. During the balance of the 1879 season, additions to the club included Michael Dorsey at second base, Ed Swartwood at first base, James Green at catcher, Charlie Morton at shortstop, and Jack Neagle at pitcher.

Dorsey had played with teams in Auburn, New York, and Rockford, Illinois. Swartwood had played 29 games with a Detroit club and posted a .319 batting average before coming to Akron. Green and Morton were recruited from Cleveland clubs, and Neagle had pitched for the Cincinnati Reds earlier in the season.

In fact, the club had won another six straight games after the loss to Garrettsville when the *Summit County Beacon* reported, "The Akrons with their new additions are playing a fine game." The streak included a 20–11 win over the Sevilles on September 11, a 22–3 win over the Ravennas on September 12, a 7–1 victory over the Mansfields on September 15, a 15–1 triumph over the Forest Citys in Cleveland on September 18, followed by a 5–0 whitewash of the Forest Citys in Akron the next day, and a 10–5 win over the Garrettsvilles on September 23.[11]

The streak was extended to seven games on September 27 with a hard-fought 16–14 come-from-behind victory over the visiting Western Reserves. While the win gave the Akrons a 15–1 record, the playing was criticized as "the worst exhibition of unadulterated muffing ever seen on these grounds and a more disgusted crowd of spectators could scarcely have gathered. If the Reserves had fielded one-third as well as they batted the Akrons would have been shut out entirely." As sometimes happened in bare-handed game, errors piled up rapidly, and the final tally was 17 misplays by the Akrons and 15 by the Reserves. Every player on the Akrons committed an error, including four by Weidner in center field and three by Green, who played first base, catcher and pitcher during the contest. Errors by the Reserves, however, were more costly than those committed by the Akrons, as 11 of the Reserve errors enabled men to reach base. None of the 30 runs in the game were earned.

Nineteenth-century players were expected to be versatile, but having men playing out of position likely was a contributing factor. Dorsey started the game behind the plate but hurt a finger and moved to first, with Green moving behind the plate. Johnson was the starting pitcher for the Akrons but was replaced by Green after the fifth inning, trailing 14–8. With Green going to the pitcher's box, Wise moved from third to catcher and Johnson went to third. Green's pitching baffled the Reserves over the final four innings while the Akrons rallied for the win.[12]

The Akrons chalked up a 20–2 victory on the road in Garrettsville to set the stage for a pair of back-to-back games on the Akron grounds against Cleveland's National League club on October 7 and 8. An estimated 2,000 people turned out for the first of the two games, a 9–2 Cleveland triumph. The Clevelands won again the next day 12 to 5 before a crowd of about 800. Then the Akrons wrapped up a 17–3 season with a 31–1 victory over the visiting Kents on October 17.

2. A Fresh Incarnation

The *Summit County Beacon* proudly proclaimed the club "The Champion Amateurs of Ohio." After excusing the one loss to Garrettsville as coming on day when the best Akron players were off, the *Beacon* referred to its published list of games and scores. It concluded: "The above list shows up to good advantage for our club and the figures will testify to their abilities. The boys challenge comparison by any club out of the league in Ohio, and modestly claim the championship of the amateur base ball clubs of Ohio."[13]

3

The Reputation Grows

The first signs of spring in northeast Ohio were barely visible on March 20, 1880, when the *Sunday Gazette* posed the question: "Is Akron to have a base ball club next season?" The question was answered by an individual identified only as "a well known gentleman interested in the national game." Said he, "I don't know. I understand there will be a meeting called during the coming week for the purpose of forming an organization. The first business of the organization will be the raising of the necessary subscription stock, and if a sufficient amount is subscribed, we are sure to have a first-class nine in the field for next season."[1]

The organization was initiated during the first week of April with a goal of raising $1,000 in shares of $10 each to fund the club. Said the *Sunday Gazette*, "Only one-third of this amount is needed at the start, however, and the sum raised already covers the required amount." It was projected that Green, Wise, Johnson, Neagle, Dorsey, Morton and Swartwood would return from the 1879 club. John Moran was later added to that number.[2]

The formal organization came on the evening of April 30 at the office of Dr. A.F. Chandler with more than 30 men in attendance. Clarence Knight was meeting chairman and W.H. Carter was secretary. In short order George W. Crouse was elected president of the club with Chandler as vice president, Carter as secretary, and M.R. Haynes as treasurer. According to the *Sunday Gazette,* "The choice of Mr. Crouse as president of the organization was made with the most perfect unanimity, and all the stockholders approved of the selection, deeming it the most appropriate manner of signifying their appreciation of Mr. Crouse's friendly interest in athletic sports in general, and his special interest in the great national game."[3]

Crouse was the kind of man who attracted titles the way a magnet attracts iron filings. He was a businessman, an industrialist, a financier and a politician. At various times during his career he served as county auditor, county treasurer, a county commissioner, an Akron city councilman, a state senator and congressman. In 1870 he was one of the organizers of the Bank of Akron. He also was one of a group of men who loaned money to Dr. B.F. Goodrich, so he could build the first rubber plant in the city. In 1878, Crouse endorsed the promissory notes of the Goodrich company to save it from collapse. By 1880, the 47-year-old Crouse also was president of Aultman, Miller & Co., operator of the Buckeye Mower & Reaper Works in Akron. That meant that he was the employer of Sam Wise, the player around whom the 1879 club had been organized.[4]

George Crouse, president of Buckeye Mower & Reaper, and president of the Akron Base Ball Association (University of Akron Archives).

In addition to Crouse, a board of five directors was chosen. Knight, Haynes and Carter became board members along with D.J. Long and L.K. Jones. Their duties included selection of a "nine" and a manager. It was announced that no selection of playing grounds for the season had been made, but it was expected the choice would be limited to the Good tract used in 1879 or the Buchtel College lot. "These seem to be the only grounds that are at all suitable for the uses of the club and the convenience of the patrons," said the *Sunday Gazette*.

It continued, "There will be no difficulty in filling the season with interesting games. Many of the [National] league clubs, as they pass through the state, and particularly at such times as there may be a spare day between the contests in Cleveland, can be induced to stop off here and give our ambitious nine a whirl. Aside from this, it is altogether likely that a Northern Ohio League will be formed, including clubs from Cleveland, Garrettsville, Warren, Norwalk, Findley [sic] and Elyria. With these clubs in the field, there will be a regular succession of exciting matches from the beginning of the season to the end thereof. Games may be expected, also, with the Western Reserve College Club, of Hudson, but this organization will disband the first week in July (when the college year closes), not to be restored until the coming fall."

Concluded the *Sunday Gazette,* "Now, gentlemen of the directory, the sooner you get your nine in the field the better will the public be pleased."[5]

A week later it appeared that progress was being made. The committee on subscriptions, composed of Knight, Haynes and Morton, was approaching the goal of 100 stockholders. The committee on players, composed of Knight, Iredell, Carter and Jones, was reported "in correspondence with many expert ball tossers." The committee on grounds, composed of Iredell, Carter and Jones, had received propositions from several landowners. It was noted that "the grading and guttering of Good street through the old grounds seems to have put them out of the question." Two weeks later the Akron Base Ball Association had exceeded its 100 stockholder goal and "additions are being made daily." Moreover, the new grounds, at the northwest corner of Perkins and North Union streets, had been selected. Before play began a grandstand to seat 800 had been erected.[6]

The initial game on the new grounds was played on June 15, nearly a month earlier than the opening game of 1879. They Akrons opened the 1880 campaign with a 7–3 triumph over the visiting Elyrias, but it was a financial disappointment. The *Summit County Beacon,* quoting the Akron *Daily Beacon* of a week earlier, reported: "Although the weather was very unfavorable there were at least 200 people present, including a large number of business men. The ground was heavy and proved considerable annoyance to the players. Another bad feature was the darkness which prevailed,

Akron ballpark, at the northwest corner of North Union Street and Perkins Street, taken from an 1882 bird's-eye map of Akron (University of Akron Archives).

frequently hiding the ball so that the players were unable to gauge its proper course."[7]

The Akrons again defeated the Elyrias before a crowd of 400 on the following day, 2–1, in a game called "the best ever played in Akron." The New York *Clipper*, in a brief item, noted that: "Neagle and Osterhout of Syracuse, N.Y., filled the respective positions of pitcher and catcher for the winners, by whom they are engaged for the season." The Elyria catcher in these games was Moses Fleetwood Walker, who in 1884 became the first black professional player in the major leagues with Toledo of the American Association. Morton, who had seen Walker's ability with the Elyrias in 1880, was the Toledo manager in 1884.[8]

The Akrons, of course, had their own black player, Ed Johnson, who was the change pitcher as well as a first baseman and outfielder. The opening line-up for the Akrons was given as Dorsey, second base; Morton, shortstop; Neagle, pitcher; Wise, third base; Osterhout, catcher; Johnson, first base; Snyder, right field; Darrow, left field; and Moran, center field.[9]

The presence of Charlie Osterhout represented the efforts of the Akron Base Ball Association directors to seek out experienced players before and during the 1880 season. Osterhout, who had had a brief tryout with Syracuse of the National League in 1879, was merely the start. By the fourth game of the season, John "Doc" Mansell, the youngest of the three ball-playing brothers from Auburn, N.Y., was added as first baseman.[10]

The Akrons won their third straight, 8–1 over the Warrens, and then on June 30, the Cleveland National League team defeated the Akrons 14–0 on the Akron grounds before a crowd estimated at 800 to 1,000. Mansell was at first base and Johnson had been shifted to left field. The *Summit County Beacon*, quoting from other papers, noted: "The [Cleveland] *Leader* says: Johnson, of the Akrons, is a good fielder." And, quoting the Canton *Repository*: "The Akrons did some fine playing in the field, making a double play in the first inning and another in the third, in the latter inning Johnson took a fly in left field and sent it in home, putting a man out who was trying to make a run." The *Leader* also praised the Akron fielding and noted that "the Clevelands while in the ball field made many friends by their gentlemanly conduct." The Cleveland *Herald* was quoted as calling the Akrons "one of the strongest amateur teams in the country." It added, "some very brilliant plays being made by both sides, and the Clevelands were whitewashed in four innings. The Akrons were generally retired in one, two, three order, although in some innings two men were left on bases, and sometimes very near a score. Notwithstanding the professional team did all the scoring, the game did not drag, but it was interesting to the close."[11]

On July 3, the Akrons won their fourth of the year, 10–3 over the visiting Mutes of Columbus, before a crowd estimated to be almost as large as that which had witnessed the game against the Clevelands. Observed the *Sunday Gazette*, "The fact that the Mutes have secured the reputation of being among the best amateurs in the State had much influence doubtless in bringing together so large a crowd, yet the greatest interest centered in the unfortunate condition of the visiting nine. To play a passable game of ball in these days of highly developed professional skill is a task well worthy a possessor of every faculty, and the sense of hearing is certainly of prime importance. That the Mutes should play a good game, at times a strong one, in opposition to a nine of such acknowledged ability as the Akrons, is a fact which is in itself a credit, despite the issue of the game. The sympathy of the audience was enlisted strongly in behalf of the gentlemanly visitors who received far more well-wishes than usually fall to the lot of foreign competitors."

Johnson pitched for the Akrons and was "welcomed back to his old position by scores of friends." Umpire George R. Walker, said the *Gazette*, "proved eminently successful in conveying his ideas through a gesticular medium, to use no larger words." It added, "The Mutes may not 'talk back' yet they are always able to show their displeasure in an unmistakable manner." After the game it was noted that Ed Swartwood, who had played for the 1879 Akrons, would soon be added to the club.[12]

Four days later, the Troy Haymakers of the National League visited Akron and Johnson again was in the pitcher's box. The New York *Clipper* reported, "The visitors got twelve of their runs off Johnson in the first three innings, after which Neagle did the pitching." It was a 15–2 loss for the Akrons.[13]

That was the first of three straight losses for the Akrons, the second coming on July 12 when the Chicagos paid their first visit to Akron and came away with an 11–4 victory. The game, of course, had been heavily promoted, and the defending National League champions arrived in Akron with a 34–3 record. A crowd of 1,500 turned out for the contest and were not disappointed despite the outcome. The *Summit County Beacon*, as usual quoting the Akron *Daily Beacon,* said: "The contest with the Clevelands and Troys had fortified our boys and caused them to have confidence in their efforts. The result was manifested yesterday. The Akrons played a splendid game, both in the field and at the bat." Osterhout, the Akron catcher, was unavailable for the game, so Ned Williamson of the Chicagos caught for the Akrons. The *Beacon* reported: "The Chicagos were highly pleased with their recent visit and are anxious to repeat it. The fee presented to Williamson for his efficient work behind the bat was a pleasing feature well deserved."[14]

3. The Reputation Grows

At about the same time, the Worcester National League Club was attempting to recruit Dorsey, the Akrons second baseman, to play left field on its club. Tampering with players on other teams was an established if not always an approved way of doing business. The League Alliance, an organization fostered by the National League, was supposed to protect a member club from having others, including National League teams, sign a player who was already under contract. At best, the alliance was ineffective and was dissolved in 1883. Nevertheless, the *Summit County Beacon,* writing both of Dorsey and a proposed membership in the League Alliance, said: "He honorably refused to consider the proposition, and laid the correspondence before the home directors. The union with the League Alliance will do away with anything of the sort in the future." Akron never did join the alliance.[15]

The loss to the Chicagos was followed by a third straight defeat, a 6–5 loss to the Elyrias at the start of a road trip to play other Ohio clubs. Swartwood and Green from the 1879 team returned to the fold at this point. In addition, Knight replaced Iredell as manager and accompanied the team on the road. Knight, who was editor of the weekly Akron *City Times,* soon realized he could not absent himself from his newspaper duties. He remained a director of the association, but on August 10, Morton became manager and remained a player.[16]

The record shows that Charles Hazen "Charlie" Morton may have had less playing ability than some others on the club, but he apparently was endowed with a great ability to identify talent in others. In three years in the major leagues, two in the American Association and one with Detroit in the National League, he played in just 88 games and posted a career .194 batting average. Nevertheless, in 1881 the Louisville *Courier-Journal* said, "Morton, shortstop with the Akrons, can run like a deer. It is probable that nobody in the country can beat him for fifty yards." And, in 1883, he hit .335, fifth best in the Northwestern League, and as a playing manager manned third base while piloting the Toledo team to the league pennant.[17]

Indeed, it was as a manager that Morton excelled, winning four pennants in the minor leagues. When he was named to manage Buffalo in the Eastern League in 1894, a dispatch from that city said, "President Franklin has done wisely in selecting Charles Morton as manager, for a more conscientious and respected man is not connected with base ball. Mr. Morton's relation with the national game has been long and honorable." Indeed, the gentlemanly Morton, who made his home in Akron, capped his career a quarter of a century after leading the 1881 team by playing a key role in organizing the Ohio-Pennsylvania League, for which he served as president for four years.[18]

With his advent as manager of the Akrons, Morton quickly showed his lifelong knack for assembling winning teams. During August 1880, the Akrons secured the services of Tony Mullane, Mike Mansell, Leech Maskrey and Rudy Kemmler. Mullane quickly displayed his great athletic ability and became the number one pitcher. Mansell, one of the older brothers of the Akrons' Doc Mansell, joined the team after being released by the Cincinnati National League team, where he had batted just .193 while playing 53 games in the outfield. Kemmler came to the Akrons after the Kansas City club had disbanded. Never a threat with the bat, Kemmler was an extraordinarily durable catcher in an age when catchers, with only rudimentary protective equipment, were subject to frequent injury. In fact, while playing with Columbus of the American Association in 1883, Kemmler caught more games than any other player in the country. Maskrey, a fine outfielder, who happened to be a cousin of Morton, came from Topeka. Said the *Sunday Gazette* of Maskrey, "It is worth attending a game of ball just to see him judge a fly. He has not been excelled in that respect by a single fielder on the grounds this year."[19]

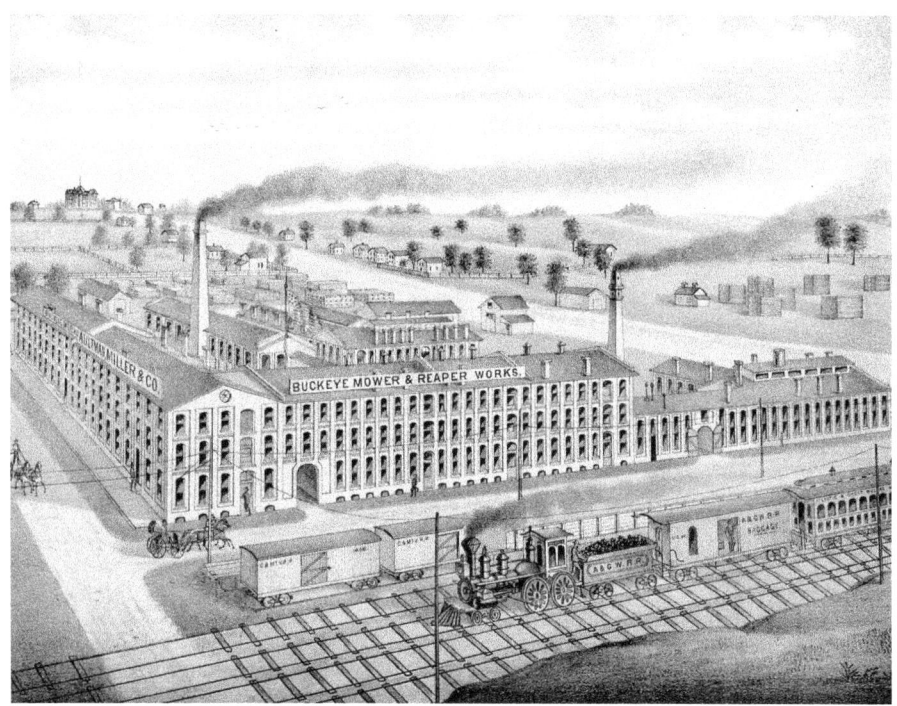

Buckeye Mower & Reaper Works, where Sam Wise was employed (University of Akron Archives).

3. The Reputation Grows

Following the road loss to Elyria, the Akrons began a winning streak with a 12–4 victory over Norwalk followed by a 16–5 win at Findlay over the Nine Spots. Back home they earned a 5–1 triumph over the White Sewing Machine club of Cleveland with all the runs scoring in the first two innings. Some timely hitting by the Akrons in the second inning, coupled with three wild throws by the Whites, accounted for four runs and enabled Neagle to pick up an easy victory. The *Sunday Gazette* praised "the impartial bestowal of applause — a good play from either side calling forth prompt and hearty recognition from the spectators." Then, in the next paragraph it complained: "The score or more of 'kids' who earned their way into the grounds by capturing the ball on foul hits took the game in to the full but were altogether too noisy and demonstrative for the comfort of the masses."[20]

Whatever the relative comfort of the paying customers, at least one Akron fan made his own comfort without paying. On baseball afternoons he'd park his wagon next to the fence along Union Street, set up a step ladder in the wagon, climb to the top, and enjoy the action. "Of course it's hot, but then it has the advantage of cheapness," said the *Sunday Gazette*.[21]

The July 24 victory over the Whites was followed by a 9–7 win over Elyria, back-to-back wins over Norwalk, 4–3 and 4–0, a 5–4 triumph over the Cleveland Grays, and a 39–6 walk-over of the Ravennas on August 6. The previous week the *Summit County Beacon* had reported that Ravenna had organized a strong nine, including three players from the 1879 Garrettsvilles. After the fact the *Sunday Gazette* took a different tact: "The Directors of the Akron Base Ball Association can't afford to try any more experiments like the Ravenna-Akron game last Friday. Most of the spectators took it in good humor, but not a few were disgusted, and some were actually mad."[22]

The winning streak ended with a disputed 1–1 tie against the White Sewing Machine club in Cleveland. Said the *Summit County Beacon*, "It was conceded by the spectators that the Whites were defeated, but the umpire changed the result." The *Sunday Gazette* reported, "The Cleveland nine themselves admit it was a clean victory for the Akron team." Akron had taken the lead in the second inning when Johnson doubled Green home, and the 1–0 lead held up until the top of the ninth. Neagle struck out the first two batters, and the third hit a grounder to Morton at short, who threw to Doc Mansell at first for what should have been the final out. The *Sunday Gazette*, referring to the "snide work" of the "alleged" umpire, explained: "It was a plain case to players and spectators. Coats were immediately thrown on by both nines, everybody supposing that the game was at an end, and the spectators were already beginning to leave their seats.

The alleged umpire mentioned above made himself heard at this juncture and to the amazement of the crowd pronounced the man 'all right.' The game went on and the runner scored. When this half of the ninth had been finished it was high time for the Akrons to leave for the train, which was being held for them, and thus the game ended. It was acknowledged a fair victory of 1 to 0, on all hands, and even Nolan himself admitted that he failed to reach first by at least six feet."[23]

Not only did the tie with the Whites end the Akrons' eight-game winning streak but it also set the stage for the club's worst loss of the season. The National League Worcesters shellacked them 19–0 before a crowd of about 800. The only bright spot for the Akrons, such as it was, was that they appeared in new uniforms, which the *Summit County Beacon* declared "nobby." The uniforms were purchased with $125 solicited by "a number of the first society ladies of Akron, who make no secret of their fondness for the national game and their admiration of the record achieved by the home nine," according to the *Sunday Gazette*. The new suits were of white flannel with red stockings, red belt, white hat and red trimmings. Said the *Gazette*, "With each suit is a white blouse, similar to that worn by the Clevelands on their visit here, to be worn when the players are at rest waiting to go to the bat."[24]

The Akrons immediately proved their new uniforms were not a hex by playing a home and home series of four games with the Norwalks, and winning three by scores of 8–2, 13–3 and 4–3. The lone loss was in Norwalk by a 4–1 score. The final two victories of the series, back in Akron, were the precursor to their next match with a National League team, a second appearance by the Clevelands on the Akron grounds on August 27. It was also about this time that the last of the roster changes were made for the season. Johnson and Snyder were released, and Osterhout went home to be with his sick wife. Mullane and Maskrey were already on hand, and Kemmler arrived before the Cleveland game and impressed the local cranks with his work behind the bat in what turned out to be a 9–6 loss before a crowd of about 1,000. The game was tied in the eighth inning before the Clevelands rallied for five runs.[25]

On August 30, the Akrons lost 11–2 when the visiting Bostons scored six runs in the eighth inning. Neagle hit a home run, but the *Summit County Beacon* reported frankly, "Our nine played a poor game." On September 4, however, the Akrons rebounded against the Forest City club of Cleveland with an 18–2 victory that included a nine-run second inning. Neagle and Green combined on a four-hitter, two hits and four strikeouts for each hurler, and the *Sunday Gazette* said, "The Akrons played a fine game all around and did some strong batting, Morton and Doc Mansell leading at the stick." As sometimes happened among clubs in this era, the Akrons loaned Mullane to the short-handed Forest Citys. Mullane played left, right and first in succession, got one of the Forest Citys' four hits, and knocked in one of their two runs.²⁶

On September 1, two days after the lopsided loss to Boston, second baseman Dorsey, apparently disappointed with his poor hitting, had announced his intention to retire. His resignation was accepted, but he continued to play, prompting the *Sunday Gazette* to observe that his retirement "is not yet a settled fact." It added, "Pressure is being brought to bear upon the directors from certain quarters for his retention." Indeed, he was cited for his excellent work at second in the win over the Forest Citys. He had five putouts and four assists without an error. He also had two hits in six at-bats and turned a doubleplay. Then in the September 8 game against the Chicago, he had one of the Akrons' eight hits and finished out the season three weeks later by going five-for-five, accounting for half of the team's hits, in a seven-inning 16–0 walk-over of the Western Reserve College club. Whatever the reason for his resignation, or the source of the pressure to retain him, the situation did not seem to affect either his play or that of the club during the balance of the season.²⁷

John "Doc" Mansell (*New York Clipper*)

Such was the situation on September 8 when the champion Chicagos made their long-awaited return visit to Akron. Since the earlier visit the Akrons had been substantially strengthened, and with Mullane doing the pitching may well have taken Cap Anson's team by surprise. At a time when batters could still call for high or low pitches, the fact that Mullane hurled a two-hitter against the National League champions is significant. Also notable was that the Akrons had only two outfield putouts and that Mullane had 11 fielding assists as pitcher. According to the box score, Mullane also had 22 called strikes, while Anson and Ned Williamson, who did the pitching for Chicago, combined for just six called strikes. The only conclusion to be drawn is that the Chicagos were badly fooled by Mullane's delivery, were taking balls over the plate and were hitting weak grounders back to the pitcher. Akron scored two runs in the second inning with Anson pitching and two more in the fifth with Williamson pitching and hung on for the 4–3 victory. The crowd of about 800 saw one of the best ball games ever played in Akron.[28]

If ever a single game established a national reputation for a club, this game did so for the Akrons, although news of the outcome was slow to spread. The Cincinnati *Enquirer* was able to boast that it was the only paper in the country to publish the defeat of the Chicagos by the Akrons. As quoted by the *Sunday Gazette,* the *Enquirer* bragged, "The *Enquirer* even carried the news to Chicago, else the good people up there had never known how their big men had been walloped by backwoods scrubs."[29]

In response, the *Sunday Gazette* noted, "'Backwoods scrubs' can be taken with mighty good grace from a paper that has been devoting all its energies this season to propping up the decaying fortunes of its 'Bucktown' nine — the 'rag tag and bob tail' of the league." The Cincinnati club finished last in the National League with a 21–59 record in 1880. In regard to the game itself, the *Gazette* called Mullane's pitching simply magnificent. It said, "He slugs them in a way that must be decidedly warm for the catcher, but it worries the batter in a style that leaves nothing to be desired." Strangely enough, the *Summit County Beacon* summed up the game in just two sentences: "Last Wednesday afternoon the Akrons defeated the Chicagos, the League Champions, by 4–3. The contest was a fine one." Perhaps it was merely coincidence, but Anson's Chicagos never returned to Akron.[30]

The great victory over the Chicagos was followed on September 11 by a disappointing 3–2 loss to the Cleveland Whites before a sparse crowd of 300 on the Akrons' grounds. Neagle pitched well but was unable to hold a 2–1 lead in the sixth inning. Neagle allowed the first Whites run to score on a wild throw. The go-ahead run for the Whites came in the eighth when Daniel "Link" Sullivan, who joined the Akrons in 1881, tripled and scored on a passed ball by Kemmler. It was Akron's first loss at home to an amateur squad. It also was the first in a four-game losing streak as the Akrons then proceeded to lose to Cleveland, Cincinnati and Buffalo, all of the National League, as the season approached its end.

But the season was not to end on a sour note. On September 25 the Akrons played the Whites a final time on the Cleveland League grounds. This time, with Mullane pitching, the Whites were held to just three hits, one of them a triple by Sullivan, and the Akrons pounded out a 21–2 victory. It included a double by Neagle, who played center, triples by both Doc and Mike Mansell as well as by Morton, and a Wise home run.

3. The Reputation Grows 31

The final contest, a meaningless benefit game, played in the rain and witnessed by a scant 100 spectators on September 29, was a 16–0 walk-over of the Western Reserve College team. The match was halted after seven innings, but Mullane pitched a no-hitter and would have had a perfect game had it not been for four Akron errors. The Akrons had 10 hits, five of them by Dorsey, and were aided by 16 Western Reserve errors. Of greater note, the Reserves' lead-off man and catcher was Ed Andrews. In three at-bats against Mullane, Andrews reached base twice on errors, and both times advanced to third base because of his superior base-running. In fact, he was the only man to reach base for the Western Reserve Club.[31] Morton never forgot a good ball player. He recruited Andrews for the 1881 Akrons.

Col. David W. Thomas paid off the back salary of John Moran in 1881 (University of Akron Archives).

4

The Strongest Non-League Club in the Country

Despite the four-game losing streak that preceded the final two victories of 1880, enthusiasm ran high among Akron baseball fans at the close the season. Indeed, the club had posted a 19–12–1 record for the year against substantially tougher competition than had been faced in the 17–3 season of 1879. Rather than just two losses, both to the National League Clevelands in 1879, the 1880 record included ten games, and a 1–9 record against National League opponents: three games with Cleveland, two with Chicago, and one each with Troy, Worcester, Boston, Cincinnati and Buffalo.

Leaving the National League games aside, the record had been 18–3–1, with the tie and one of the losses against the strong White Sewing Machine club of Cleveland, and the late season 3–2 loss to the Whites, the Akrons' only loss at home was to an "amateur" club. Certainly the 4–3 victory on September 8 over the National League champion Chicagos gave the club an aura of success that the subsequent losses did not diminish. Moreover, the club's final 1880 roster also was substantially stronger than it had been at the start of the campaign.

No wonder the *Summit County Beacon* reported, "The question has been frequently asked why Akron could not join the [National] League. According to the rules of the association only cities with a population of 75,000 can belong to it, consequently Akron is barred. But then, Akron will be so situated that she will have nearly all the advantages of a league club." Even by the National League standards of the era, Akron was still just a small town playing in fast company. But it also was a growing, prosperous community, and the 1880 census showed it with a population of 16,517, an increase of 50 percent from 1870. Besides, it had been challenging major league teams since 1879. It was feeling its oats.[1]

The assertion that Akron would have the benefits of a National League club was buttressed because John B. Sage, president of the Buffalo team, had been in Akron with his team and had told the directors of the Akron Base Ball Association that the National League would arrange its schedule for 1881 so as to give every team open dates in Cleveland. Said the *Beacon*, "This will give all the league clubs an opportunity to visit Akron, and thus provide our people with none but first-class games, and at very reasonable admission fee." The fact that the National League even contemplated such a move for the 1881 season is a testimony to the strength of the Akrons, but the visit of National League teams to Akron during the 1880 season also was eased in part by the fact that the Valley Railroad, linking Cleveland, Akron and Canton, had been opened on January 28, and the Cleveland-to-Akron-to-Canton run of 59 miles could be completed in two hours.[2]

Despite the cited advantages, the Akrons, like almost all independent joint-stock clubs of the era, were still operating on a very thin financial margin. Signs of this surfaced from time to time. In July, when the Akrons made their road trip to Elyria, Norwalk and Findlay, one of the Elyria games was rained out. Akron's guarantee for the game was to be half of the gate receipts, rather than a set amount. With no game, there were no receipts. Observed the *Sunday Gazette*, "This is a misfortune much to be regretted. The efforts of the Akron Directors are certainly deserving of the fullest success, and it is to be hoped that the deficit will be made up by good luck during the remainder of the season."[3]

Instead, the Akrons experienced the opposite side of the same coin when the Forest City club came to Akron in August on a set guarantee and the game was washed out in the first inning by a driving rain storm. The Forest Citys got their money and the Akron directors again were soaked in the pocketbook. By this time, the *Sunday Gazette* was looking forward to the 1881 campaign. It reported, "A guaranty fund of $2,500 with some of Akron's foremost business men as backers, and a club which will get away with any amateur nine in the country are among the probabilities for next season."[4]

The fact that the directors had added a roof to the grandstand, and had continued to upgrade the roster, particularly after Morton became the manager in August, undoubtedly contributed to the financial crunch. That the directors were looking for extra sources of cash is revealed through plans to convert the ball grounds into a skating rink during the winter, as was done with the league grounds in Cleveland. At the end of August the *Sunday Gazette* reported, "If Akron's water works is in successful operation by that time, Base Ball Park will be utilized next winter as a skating park." About a month later the *Summit County Beacon* not only confirmed the plan, but reported other proposed improvements. It said, "The feasibility of converting the base ball grounds into a skating rink this winter is to be a reality. The Water Works will supply the water. It is the intention to provide the necessary dressing rooms, and make such other changes as are necessary. The diamond will be sodded and grass seed sown, so that next season the grounds will be in better shape than ever. The grounds will be lighted by the Electric Light."[5]

The mention of the "Electric Light" deserves a word of explanation. It was not a nineteenth-century scheme for night baseball. Electric lights first came to Akron in October 1880 when George Crouse, president of the Akron Base Ball Association and the Buckeye Mower & Reaper Works, had lights installed at the plant to aid his workers. The "Electric Light," however, was a scheme to entirely illuminate the city. Four arc lights of 2,000 candlepower each were mounted on a 208-foot mast at Market and Howard streets, then the heart of downtown. Another 60-foot mast with four more lights was placed on top of the Buchtel College building. Together, they were supposed to completely bathe the city in light. They didn't, and by 1883 the city was out of the electric light business.[6]

Even if Crouse and the other directors had considered night baseball, they were in no position to pursue that dream. The nature of the association's finances was revealed in the published account of the meeting of the association in March 1881. While the columns of receipts, disbursements and unpaid bills do not add up, the report included $1,505.02 for salaries and showed $336.11 of that amount unpaid from the 1880 season. With receipts totaling $4,023.15 for 1880, the association showed a net loss of $925.29 for the season.[7]

Nevertheless, expectations for the 1881 season remained high, and with the exception of Dorsey all the regular players from the club that closed the season were expected to return. As it turned out, Dorsey's replacement in 1881 was Bid McPhee, who the next year went from the Akrons to Cincinnati where he starred for 18 seasons as a second baseman. The last major leaguer to play without a glove, he led the American Association in fielding six times and the National League in fielding twice. He hit .277 for his career and was elected to the National Baseball Hall of Fame in 2000. After eleven of those seasons, it was said of him that he was "rated as one of the most honorable men, as well as one of the best players in the profession."[8]

More volatile than McPhee, another player who turned out to be a major attraction as well as a key performer for the Akrons was Mullane. Often referred to as "The Count," Mullane left the Akrons to join the Detroit Wolverines of the National League in August 1881. Born in Ireland, he grew up in Erie, Pa., and, according to an item in *The Sporting News* in 1886, "would run away from home and play ball. He wouldn't learn a trade. He imagined that he was cut out for a ball player and he undoubtedly was. He filled the box in several amateur games at Erie, and then became discontented because no pay was attached." He signed his first professional contract with the Geneva, Ohio, team in 1876, for a dollar a day plus room and board. It is likely that he had drifted to other clubs in eastern Ohio and western Pennsylvania before joining Akron in 1880, where he is sometimes credited with beginning his professional career.[9]

Mullane, who won a total of 284 major league games over a 13-year pitching career, won few friends along the way. As early as 1885 it was reported, "He is cordially detested by all the base ball magnates as well as many players." Two years later, during a salary dispute, it was reported, "Anyone acquainted with Mullane's past record will not be surprised at his action. He has always had the reputation of being the most avaricious and ungrateful player in the profession."[10]

While it was remarkable that a small town club like the Akrons could attract a pair as talented as McPhee and Mullane, they were far from alone on the club from a talent standpoint. Of the 19 players who played all or part of the 1881 season with the Akrons, 14 played in either the American Association or the National League in 1882. Even more significant than the number is that several of the Akrons had significant and, in some cases, distinguished major league careers.

Sam Wise, Akron's home-town hero, played in the majors for 12 years. He was Boston's starting shortstop for six seasons, their first baseman for one, and the starting second baseman for three seasons with Washington and Baltimore. Ed Swartwood played in the majors for nine years, seven of them as a starting outfielder or first baseman and had a career .310 batting average. He led the American Association in batting with a .357 mark in 1883. Leech Maskrey was a starting outfielder for Louisville for four seasons. Among Akron newcomers in 1881, Ed Andrews was a starting outfielder with Philadelphia for five seasons with a total of eight major league years. He led the National League with 56 steals in 1886. Blondie Purcell spent 12 years in the majors, ten as a starting outfielder, and also started 57 games as a pitcher. Frank Mountain pitched in the majors for seven years, and in two seasons with Columbus of the American Association (1883–84) made 100 starts and pitched 863 innings.[11]

Aside from playing 12 game against National League opponents in 1881, the Akrons also played ten games on the road with the well-respected independent Louisville Eclipse and another six with the independent St. Louis Brown Stockings. They won eight with a loss and a tie in Louisville and split six games in St. Louis at the end of the season after Mullane had gone to Detroit.

When the American Association was formed in 1882 as a second major league, Louisville and St. Louis were among the initial six teams. In that era it was common for teams to carry only ten or 11 players at a time on their rosters. In comparison with the Akrons, seven members of the 1881 Louisville Eclipse played in the major leagues in 1882, five of them with Louisville. Similarly, five members of the 1881 Brown Stockings played in the major leagues in 1882, four of them with St. Louis.[12]

Civic pride could justify the *Summit County Beacon* calling the Akrons "the champion amateurs of Ohio" in 1879. The same could be said of the *Sunday Gazette* in 1880 when it implied championship status for the club, writing, "Only three defeats outside the League. Where are the Elyria 'Champions'?"

Of course, the club wasn't amateur, and in 1881 the accolades came from other sources, including fans who turned out in droves in Louisville and St. Louis for a look at the Akrons. In Louisville, a crowd estimated at 7,000 turned out for one of the games, prompting the *Courier-Journal* to report "a game of base ball was never witnessed before in Louisville by such a vast concourse of spectators." Later, in St. Louis, a crowd estimated at between 5,000 and 6,000 patronized a game. The *Globe-Democrat* said, "There never was a larger crowd at the Grand Avenue Park." The rival Missouri *Republican* reported, "The crowd out to see the game numbered, by actual count, 6,500."[13]

These were eye-popping attendance figures for a game at the time, but no official attendance records were kept during the 1880s, so true comparisons are impossible. The New York Giants were credited with a record crowd of 20,709 in New York City in 1886, but it appears that as late as 1889 the Giants averaged only about 3,200 per game. During the 1890s, the average major league attendance was estimated at 2,000 to 3,000 a game.[14]

Local newspapers were always partisan for the home team, so plaudits for the visiting club were hard-earned. On the Akrons' first visit to Louisville in June the *Courier-Journal* said they were "powerful batters and superb fielders." By August, the *Courier-Journal* called them "the Champion Akrons," and by the time the Akrons made their final visit to the Eclipse in September they were refered to as "the Invincible Akrons," and "unquestionably the strongest non-league team in the country." As early as July 23, the Cleveland *Leader* had said of the Akrons, "It is today the strongest non-league club in the country." The phrase was later picked up by Harold Seymour in his classic *Baseball: The Early Years*. The St. Louis papers were a bit more restrained. The Missouri *Republican* calling the Akrons' base running "simply superb, and their batting a perfect wonder." Said the *Globe Democrat*, "They are as fine a looking lot of ball tossers as are likely to be seen."[15]

5

Bid McPhee Comes to Akron

When the directors of the Akron Base Ball Association met on March 29, 1881, that fine-looking lot of ball tossers had yet to be assembled. Hopes for the coming season were high, but tempered by reality. On one hand, the grounds were in good enough shape they could be "used right away if desired." On the other hand, part of the backstop had been blown down, although the Summit *Weekly Beacon* offered the opinion, "It would have probably been removed any way as it is proposed to erect a ladies' stand." On one hand, the directors were receiving applications from players. On the other hand, the association had a deficit of more than $900 from the 1880 season, including $336.11 in unpaid salaries, and a committee was appointed to solicit subscriptions at $10 each.[1]

One consequence of the unpaid salaries from 1880 was that John Moran, who had played center field on the 1879 and 1880 clubs, filed a lawsuit against the association and season ticket holders to recover $31 in back salary. In July 1881, while the team was being reorganized, and an hour before a hearing on the case was to begin, Moran received his money from Col. D.W. Thomas. Thomas was an owner of Miller, Thomas & Co., which operated a planing mill, dealt in lumber, manufactured windows and doors, and eventually was listed as a building contractor.[2] While he is not identified as a member of the association, he clearly was a backer of the team and likely involved in the reorganization.

Although there was no public discussion of the makeup of the 1881 club at the time of the March meeting, it soon became clear that most of the regular players from 1880 would be returning, including Sam Wise, Charlie Morton, Leech Maskrey, Doc Mansell, Jim Green, Jack Neagle, Rudy Kemmler and Ed Swartwood. That meant that the key position to fill was that of the departed Michael Dorsey at second base.[3]

The search for a second baseman eventually led Morton to 21-year-old John Alexander McPhee, who was working as a dry goods clerk in Denver. The story, as related some dozen years later by W.E. Rockwell, who was then president of the Pacific Northwest League, is that McPhee and his widowed mother had moved to Keithsburg, a little river town in western Illinois. Rockwell, who also lived in Keithsburg, had begun to earn a reputation as a pitcher, and in 1876 he and the 16-year-old McPhee formed a battery with McPhee as the catcher. In the spring of 1877 the inevitable happened. Catchers had no protective equipment at the time, and a foul tip struck McPhee in the face and broke his nose. McPhee then became a second baseman.[4]

An additional sidelight on McPhee's broken nose was revealed in 1899 when McPhee had a brief reunion with boyhood friend and former ball-playing buddy Tom Marshall. They met at the Cincinnati Gun Club, and Marshall, two-time winner of the Grand American Handicap of trap shooting, recounted the Keithsburg game in which McPhee had been struck by the foul ball. "While we were patching him up," recalled Marshall, "I heard one girl in the crowd say: 'Oh, it didn't hurt him any. He's a professional.' That remark became a club standby, and whenever anybody had a finger knocked out we used to spring the estimate of that fair fan, who imagined that a professional couldn't get hurt."[5]

As recounted in the Seattle *Post-Intelligencer*, McPhee and Rockwell went together in the fall of 1877 to play on the Davenport, Iowa, club and remained at Davenport through the 1878 season. There they became acquainted with Leech Maskrey, who also played on the Davenport team in 1878. Rockwell went to Chicago in 1879 to work for the *Times,* but McPhee stayed in Davenport for another season before he went west to the job in the dry goods store. According to Rockwell's story, Maskrey pointed Morton in McPhee's direction, and Morton wrote to Rockwell in Chicago to ask his opinion. Of course, Rockwell gave a good recommendation.[6]

A Cincinnati baseball enthusiast named Al Dreyfoos also claimed a part in setting McPhee on the road from Denver to Akron, and then to Cincinnati. According to a story in the Cincinnati *Times Star*, Dreyfoos and McPhee were in Denver in the early 1880s. At that time McPhee was a member of a semiprofessional team in the Colorado League, and he received offers from Colorado Springs and Akron. The offer from Colorado Springs apparently was somewhat better, and McPhee was hesitating between the two. Dreyfoos said he counseled McPhee to go to Akron, saying, "You'll make a ball player, and it is only a step from Akron into fast company." The *Times Star* concluded, "And so, 'Bid' McPhee left Denver for Ohio and stepped into a higher class, with Tony Mullane and Sam Wise."[7]

But McPhee's translation from dry goods clerk to star second baseman was not altogether smooth, as Rockwell also related while giving some additional insight into how the Akron club was operated. Said Rockwell:

> However, it was not on the diamond alone that the members of the Akron team earned their money. Each was given a position with some business establishment according to his abilities, and was given a lay-off when a ball game was to be played. McPhee, who is an expert penman, was installed as bookkeeper for a lumber company. His work on the ball field at the start was anything but a success. In fact, he was rated as a dead failure and his release was decided upon. But Leech Maskrey, with the true spirit of companionship and mindful of the boy's fine work at Davenport, urged that he be kept, telling the management that there would be no cause to regret the step. It did not take long to prove the wisdom of his words. "Biddy" was given another chance and in a short time "owned the town" by his splendid play.[8]

Indeed, by the time the Akrons traveled to Louisville in June for their big series with the Eclipse club, the Louisville *Courier-Journal* reported, "McPhee's playing at second yesterday was faultless. He captured the crowd completely."[9]

When McPhee signed with the new Cincinnati club in the American Association for the 1882 season, he began an 18-year major league career in which he quietly assembled a record that eventually led him to the Hall of Fame in 2000. The numbers are persuasive: he hit .277 with 2,313 hits over his career and also walked 983 times for a career .355 on-base average. Despite his slight build, 5-foot-8 and 152 pounds, he also could drive the ball and led the American Association with eight homeruns in 1886 and 19 triples in 1887. He also stole more than 568 bases. His exact total is unknown because the stolen base records were not kept before 1886.[10]

Bid McPhee (**National Baseball Hall of Fame Library, Cooperstown, N.Y.**)

Fielding, however, was McPhee's forte. O.P. Caylor, who at the time was editing *The Sporting Times* in New York and also contributing columns to *Sporting Life*,[11] noted with approbation the view of McPhee expressed earlier in the Cincinnati *Enquirer*, quoting it as saying: "If Fred Dunlap is the kingpin second baseman of the League, then Biddy McPhee, of the Cincinnati team, is the best second baseman in the world. Cincinnati enthusiasts had an opportunity last week to draw comparisons between these two long-standing rivals for the honor, and one and all who saw the two men play are unanimous in pronouncing the Cincinnati captain in every way the superior to Dunlap. McPhee played all around him. It is true that Dunny was not in fix, but the contrast was so great that few will believe he can equal McPhee when at his best."

Then Caylor himself continued, "There has never been a question in the unbiased mind about McPhee's superiority as a player, and in disposition and worth to a team he can discount Dunny, yet he has never received by 25 per cent, as much salary as Dunlap. If McPhee is classed 'A,' Dunlap should certainly not be rated higher than 'B.'"[12]

A year later, *Sporting Life* noted: "McPhee has been doing wonderful playing of late, having an unusual number of chances game after game without error. Still one rarely hears any comments on 'Bid's' playing no matter how brilliant it may be. His work is so uniformly good that it never occasions any surprise with the patrons of base ball."[13]

McPhee led the American Association in fielding six times and the National League in fielding twice, in 1891 with a .954 average and the last time in 1896 when he posted a fine .978 mark.[14] Between those years, his fielding fell below the high standards he had set, but the nature of the game had been changing. All of his contemporaries were using gloves while McPhee still fielded bare-handed.

In an 1890 interview with a Cincinnati *Enquirer* reporter, McPhee explained his views on the use of a glove, saying, "No, I never use a glove on either hand in a game. I have never seen the necessity of wearing one; and, besides, I cannot hold a thrown ball if there is anything on my hands. The glove business has gone a little too far. It is all wrong to suppose that your hands will get battered out of shape if you don't use them. True, hot-hit balls do sting a little at the opening of the season, but after you get used to it there is no trouble on that score. Dunlap, Pfeiffer [sic] and Yank Robinson always play bare-handed."[15]

In 1893 McPhee was first persuaded to try a glove, but he opened 1896 with a sore finger and finally broke down and put on a glove for good. He proceeded to record the best fielding mark of his career. Indeed, *Sporting Life* called it "the greatest record ever made on the bag. In the last thirty-two games McPhee made but one misplay and in those games accepted 175 out of 176 chances."[16]

As McPhee went about quietly putting up his Hall of Fame credentials, quietness was a hallmark of his life, on and off the field. A.D. Sueshsdorf, writing in *Nineteenth Century Stars,* said of him, "In a rowdy era, Bid was one of the game's gentlemen. He performed spectacularly but was personally sober and sedate, always in prime physical condition and quietly proud of never having been ejected from a game." Indeed, he played almost seven full seasons in the American Association before he was even fined by an umpire for an insulting remark.[17]

Naturally, the single McPhee attracted the attention of available young ladies, and Joe Pritchard, Cincinnati correspondent for *Sporting Life,* in 1889 reported the attentions of one of McPhee's admirers, writing: "There is a lady in Cincinnati of uncertain age, who weighs 250 pounds, and who has become infatuated with John McPhee. 'Bid' never speaks about it himself, but it is well known that the fair damsel makes life a burden to the great second baseman by writing him notes, odes to his eyebrows, and all that sort of thing. Last Valentine Day, for instance, she sent him an 'epic,' as she called it, containing ninety-six verses. One of the boys got hold of it after the season opened and showed it to me the other day. I have room for only the first stanza. It reads like this:

> Oh, Bid McPhee,
> I've thought of thee
> With ecstasy
> Since '83.

"Think of ninety-five more verses just like that. Is it any wonder that 'Bid' was off in his work in the first part of the season?"[18]

McPhee had picked up the nickname "Biddy" or "Bid" as a young boy as he dabbled about in the kitchen of a hotel run by his uncle in Aledo, Illinois. The name, earned not on a ball field but in a family atmosphere, stuck. He was devoted to his widowed mother, a sister and two brothers, and made a home for all of them in Cincinnati. It was reported that his baseball salary went toward the comfort of the family.[19]

Then, in 1897, McPhee was in need of some comfort himself. He and Wilbert Robinson, the Baltimore catcher, were hospitalized after being injured in a home-plate collision. When he was out of the hospital, he became the recipient of a testimonial at the Cincinnati ball park. He rode to the park with the Cincinnati mayor in a street parade. There were two bands, police drills, singing by the Meckey Opera Company, acrobats, and a benefit game between the newspaper boys and merchants for which McPhee umpired. Initial reports were that the affair had raised $3,500, but when everything was accounted for McPhee received $1,800.[20]

The injury and the passing years took their toll, and although he was pressed to continue playing, he announced his retirement in March 1900 before the beginning of spring training. He did so in the style he had shown throughout his career, issuing an open letter. It read:

> To the public:
> After giving the matter much thought, I have concluded to end my career on the ball field, and have tendered my resignation to Manager Allen, of the Cincinnati Club. I take this step because I believe that my presence on the team would only handicap its chances during the coming season. I am surely in a better position than anyone else to know whether I am still capable of doing myself and the Cincinnati Club justice on the field, and I feel that I am not.
> My retirement is a step which I regret very much to take, for the reason that my associations, both with the Cincinnati Club, and with the members of my profession have been exceedingly pleasant to me during the 18 years that I have been wearing the uniform of the Cincinnati Reds. If I thought I was capable of aiding Manager Allen in the championship struggle which is soon to begin I would not retire from base ball, but I know I cannot aid him, but, to the contrary, would only be a detriment to the team.
> I have been assured that I can continue as a member of the Cincinnati team just as long as I see fit, even though I should not be able to play regularly. I appreciate this kind offer, but I must decline it for the reasons above stated. In leaving the team I think I am helping it. The Cincinnati Club wants a winning team, and the public longs for young, active players. I fear that I cannot fill the requirements. I have the utmost respect for the officials of the club and Manager Allen, whom I have known for many years, and whom I know to be a thorough gentleman, and every member of the team, which has my best wishes for this season, and for all seasons to come.
> Very respectfully yours,
> John A. McPhee

Sporting Life, in printing McPhee's letter, added: "The National League should arrange a grand testimonial for Biddy McPhee. This fine player has always been an honor to the game, and in his years of faithful service has never been the subject of discipline. He retires from the game carrying with him the respect of his fellow players as well as the confidence and admiration of the public. Base ball can ill afford to lose men of the McPhee calibre; they are few and far between."[21]

His retirement from baseball lasted just one season. In 1901, he was persuaded to return to the diamond as manager of the Reds. Unfortunately, he was unable to impart to his charges either his playing skill or his intelligence. By midseason of 1901, it was reported that "Manager McPhee, of the Reds, is a great admirer of thinking players. He has his scouts out now for new material for next season, and one of their principal injunctions is to keep their eyes open for players who have brains and can use them." Near the close of the season, *Sporting Life* noted, "John McPhee's first season's experience as a manager has caused many a gray hair to spring up under his hat."[22]

As manager, he labored not only under the burden of poor players but also under owner John T. Brush. A contemporary describing Brush wrote, "Chicanery is the ozone which keeps his old frame from snapping, and dark-lantern methods the food which vitalizes his bodily tissues." Certainly, he was a consummate conniver and inveterate schemer who was less interested in having a winning team than he was in manipulating himself into ownership of the New York Giants; a goal which he eventually achieved.[23]

In July 1902, when the end came for McPhee as a manager, columnist Ren Mulford Jr. reported: "King Bid's release has been hanging fire over a month, and in that time there have been numerous whispers that he would get it, followed by mild negatives. When the Reds were in the East 'King Bid' himself believed he was treading water. On that last tour he had very few conferences with John T. Brush, and observers then could divine the breach that was widening between them. The Red leader was released by written notice sent from New York."

Mulford continued: "Even New York, with its record of several years of fizzle has not been under so continual a fire from destructive critics as the Red club, and undoubtedly that has had much to do with the failure that led to John A. McPhee's release. It doesn't help a manager's cause any to continually tell him that he has a bunch of 'nuts' and that their poor work cannot be corrected by nice direction of a master hand. That is the handicap under which 'King Bid' has labored." McPhee moved to southern California, where he did some scouting for the team. He severed all connections with baseball in 1909.[24]

He resided in Ocean Beach, near San Diego, and a premature report of his death in *The Sporting News* in January 1932, prompted a letter from Corwin Sage of Los Angeles. In it he wrote: "John A. McPhee is an exceedingly lively corpse. We have been intimate friends for a great many years and exchange letters nearly every week. I wrote to him today (March 1, 1932). He is not as lively as in the days from '82 to 1900, but still is able to give some of them pointers on how to play second base and might be able to line one to the fence if he was served a cold one.... Bid cut out the article from *The Sporting News* and mailed it to me with the remark that it was not often a man had the pleasure of reading his own obituary. McPhee was one of the finest players and most perfect gentlemen the game was ever known."

He actually died on January 3, 1943, at his home. He was 83.[25]

6

The Matinee Idol

The 1881 playing season was fast approaching when the Akron Base Ball Association held a reorganization meeting on April 20. George W. Crouse again became president, and with the initial playing roster mostly set, Charlie Morton was named manager with Ed Swartwood as the field captain. The Cleveland *Leader*, which promoted the Akrons almost as much as the Akron newspapers, devoted an entire column to a preseason review of the club, headlining it "Akron's Annihilators."[1]

Along with the fluff, there were a few warnings of things to come. First, just three days before the opening game with the Clevelands of the National League, it was noted that Doc Mansell and McPhee had not yet arrived in Akron. Secondly, two key paragraphs read: "The management have, at their risk, expended a good amount of money. They have secured as fine grounds as can be found anywhere, and have now placed an excellent nine in the field, thus giving Akronites the pleasure of enjoying what few cities in the country can, and it now becomes the public to patronize this noble game.

"Certainly great interest has been and is now manifested by Akron people, but the expense of running the team is very great, and good patronage is the only thing which will support the game."[2]

On the morning of the opening April 28th game, it was noted that all of the players had arrived except Jimmy Green, but in the aftermath of the 25–1 Cleveland victory, additional explanation surfaced. With the late arrival of several players, only five members of the Akron club had practiced together before the game. Moreover, because the Akrons were short-handed for the game, Edward "The Only" Nolan and Jim McCormick not only pitched for the Clevelands, they also took turns playing center field for the Akrons. In fact, Nolan had one of the five Akron hits. Cleveland led 9–1 after the sixth inning, but scored eight runs in each of the seventh and eighth innings before the game was halted by darkness. When the game got out of hand, McCormick ran around the grounds with his tongue hanging out, mimicking a dog tired from chasing balls. On the other hand, a foul-bound catch made by Maskrey in the seventh inning was called "one of the brilliant and redeeming features of the game." Altogether, it was an ugly beginning, but under the circumstances, the lopsided outcome should not have been a surprise. Nevertheless, the dispatch to the *Leader* described the 700 fans who attended the contest as surprised and labeling the Akrons as "disastrously defeated."[3]

Besides the late arrival of Green, Tony Mullane also was a no-show for the opening fiasco, but at the time he was not a member of the club. Instead, he was negotiating with the club directors, and on April 30 he pitched for the White Sewing Machine team of Cleveland in a 15–2 loss to Detroit of the National League. The Whites lineup that day also included Dan Sullivan and Ed Andrews, who joined the Akrons later in the season. Mullane reached an agreement with Akron shortly after the April 30 game and pitched the Akrons to 2–1 and 10–3 victories over the Whites on May 6 and 7 in Akron. In the first game, before a crowd estimated at between 500 and 600, Mullane held the Whites to six hits, struck out ten, and a hit a double, the only extra-base hit of the contest. The Akrons pushed across the winning run in the top of the ninth inning. The next day he held the Whites to five hits while the Akrons scored seven in the top of the first inning and coasted to the win before an estimated 400 fans. Of the victories, the Akron *City Times* observed: "The Whites probably have the strongest non-league club in Ohio outside of Akron, and with the advantage of several weeks of steady practice with the Clevelands would have beaten our boys if the latter had not shown up unexpectedly strong."[4]

Mullane was a superb athlete who generally kept himself in good playing condition. Late in August 1881, he left the Akrons for a tryout with the Detroit club of the National League, but he refused to simply try out and insisted upon a regular contract for the balance of the season. Sometime during his brief stay in Detroit, he hurt his right arm and began pitching left-handed. When his right arm recovered, he rarely pitched left-handed, but he was skillful enough that he could pitch, field and throw with either hand. In this bare-handed era, it was said that his ambidexterity gave him a devastating pickoff move.[5]

Whether it was his sore arm, or the fact that he posted just one win and four losses with a 4.91 ERA in his five games with Detroit, or a combination of both, the team released him. That enabled him to sign with Louisville in the newly formed American Association for 1882 and marked the beginning of a seven-year period, running through the 1888 season, in which he was one of the dominant pitchers of the era. He won 30 games for Louisville in 1882, 35 for St. Louis in 1883, 36 for Toledo in 1884, and then 33, 31 and 26 successively for Cincinnati from 1886 through 1888. For his career he pitched in 555 games with a career record of 284 wins and 220 losses and a 3.05 ERA. In 1884 he made 65 starts for Toledo, pitched a career high 567 innings and struck out a career high 325 batters while posting a 2.52 ERA. During his major league career, he also played 154 games in the outfield and played all the infield positions. He was a career .243 hitter in 2,270 at-bats.[6]

In Toledo in 1884 he was reunited with Charlie Morton, the Akrons' 1881 manager, who was then managing Toledo. There he formed a battery with Moses Fleetwood Walker, the first black major leaguer.[7]

Mullane, however, was suspended for the entire 1885 season in what is sometimes described as a contract dispute. It was actually somewhat more complicated than that. Before the 1884 season he had jumped his contract with the St. Louis club to sign with the newly formed Union Association, a short-lived attempt at a third major league. Then he jumped from the Union Association back to the American Association to sign with Toledo for $2,500, a $1,100 raise over what he had received from St. Louis in 1883. Because St. Louis owner Chris Von der Ahe was unwilling to meet that salary, he reluctantly allowed Mullane to play in Toledo in 1884, but he did not surrender his interest in the star pitcher. What happened next was summarized in *Nineteenth Century Stars*: "After the season, with Toledo's franchise folding, the St. Louis Browns purchased his release and reached agreement on a $3,500 contract. But when the obligatory ten-day waiting period expired, Mullane signed with Cincinnati for $5,000 instead."[8]

The fight was long and bitter, and in the end Cincinnati

Tony Mullane (National Baseball Hall of Fame Library, Cooperstown, N.Y.

got to keep Mullane, but he had to pay a price. The contract was voided; Mullane had to return his $1,000 advance from Cincinnati; and he was suspended for 1885. Despite expectations to the contrary, Mullane stuck with Cincinnati, although his road was seldom smooth. After pitching 567 innings in 1884, the year-long suspension may have done his arm good, but he still managed to remain a black sheep by being a contract holdout for the 1886 season, seeking a $2,000 contract at a time when the major league owners were in a salary-cutting mode. In December 1885 *Sporting Life* offered Mullane its advice: "It behooves Tony to be very careful, as he is cordially detested by all the base ball magnates as well as many players and it may be that they are laying low to get another whack at him, and by putting him where the 'base ball dogs won't bite him,' make a 'shining example' of him. They would be only too glad to do it."[9]

Mullane signed and pitched well for the Reds. In fact, he even boasted about his physical condition, asserting at one time that he could pitch 24 hours without stopping. At 5-foot-10½ inches and 165 pounds, Mullane was a relatively big man for that era, and with dark curly hair, a carefully waxed handlebar mustache and a flair for showmanship, he generally attracted many female fans to the ballparks. This phenomenon was not lost on the owners, who began to schedule him to pitch on Mondays, normally a light crowd day, and designated them as "Ladies Day."[10]

Mullane liked to capitalize on his good looks by dressing off the field in loud ties, a frock coat and a high silk hat. Thus, he acquired the nickname "The Count," but like so much else in his life there was an inherent contradiction; his elegant attire was often trumped by a frugal nature. David Nemec wrote in *The Beer and Whisky League* that Mullane "undermined his matinee-idol looks by wearing his clothes until they rotted off him. *Sporting Life* flayed him for being a notorious tightwad."[11]

Morton, who rarely had a bad word to say about anyone, later told a story illustrating this aspect of Mullane's personality. In 1884, when both were in Toledo, Morton went into a cigar store operated by Mullane and asked to buy a nickel's worth of fine-cut chewing tobacco. Mullane wrapped the tobacco neatly in a paper, handed it to Morton, then came around from behind the counter and asked for a chew.[12]

The contradictions in Mullane's life inevitably carried over into his on-field performance, which showed a marked decline after 1888. He had always been volatile and was frequently fined by the umpires. It was known that the Cincinnati management paid his fines. Later, *Sporting Life* reported, "Mullane is a player of uncontrollable temper and a disposition that is anything but angelic. He is easily rattled, and every captain who faces the Cincinnatis knows that if he can get Mullane ugly he will almost certainly play poorly enough to lose the game. When the Cincinnatis are ahead and everything is moving along satisfactorily Mullane is a winning pitcher."[13]

The problems began to come to a head during the 1887 season when, believing he was underpaid for the amount that he was pitching, Mullane refused to pitch in a game unless he received extra pay for it. He was immediately fined and suspended and was ordered from the field by Cincinnati Club president Aaron Stern. This time *Sporting Life* opined that he "has gotten into a scrape out of which he will not be able to crawl without humiliation."[14]

Mullane, however, was unacquainted with the concept of humiliation. He filed a lawsuit against Stern and the police officer who had escorted him from the ballpark, alleging assault. Then he went off to Vermont for a vacation. Cincinnati won 81 games in 1887, and Mullane won 31 of them. Without Mullane taking his regular pitching turn, the club was in serious trouble. Stern was the first to cave in. He directed manager Gus Schmelz to telegraph Mullane in Vermont and ask him to report to the Reds when they played in New York. If Mullane did not reply, Schmelz was to go to Vermont to make a face-to-face appeal. Said *Sporting Life*, "Schmelz himself and nearly every member of the team is averse to Mullane's return under any consideration." The upshot was that Schmelz went to Rutland, Vermont, and returned with a reinstated Mullane, thanks mostly to the efforts of Mullane's wife to persuade him to "do the right thing."[15]

In 1888, Mullane spent three days in jail before he appealed to Henry Chadwick, who, typically, came to his defense. Chadwick, widely known as "the Father of Base Ball," was a baseball writer who had covered the game for a variety of New York and Brooklyn newspapers, and had served as the baseball writer for the weekly New York *Clipper* from 1857 through 1887. In 1888, he was writing a column for *Sporting Life* when Mullane contacted him at his Brooklyn office. Chadwick tells the story:

"This morning I was surprised by a message from pitcher Mullane of the Cincinnati Club, requesting to see me at the sheriff's office. Having no personal acquaintance with him I could not account for the request, especially as I had had occasion at times to severely criticize some of his doings in the base ball world. But I went to see him, as he was in trouble, and I did so on the principle on which I take sides with umpires, and that is that I am always ready to aid 'the under man in the fight.' Mullane was in great trouble over his arrest. It was a new and disagreeable experience for him to be incarcerated in a public jail. When he explained his difficulty to me I saw that it was, in the main, of trifling import; that is, it did not impugn his integrity, but was simply a case of improvidence in a business matter for one thing, and of ignorance of the routine of legal affairs in another. On Tuesday last Mullane was served with a summons to appear at court to answer a complaint for indebtedness on the part of a partner of his some years ago, and as the summons was directed to Thomas J. Mullane, instead of Anthony J. Mullane, Tony treated it with contempt and tore it up." Once Chadwick intervened to straighten things out, Mullane was found in contempt of court and fined $250 and costs. Added Chadwick, "Mullane was in custody three days, and he got thin under the operation."[16] It seems significant that after three days in jail, he sought help from a man he had never met rather than from someone on the Cincinnati team.

His next major on-the-field problem did not come until April 30, 1891, in a confrontation with umpire Phil Powers after a Chicago game at Cincinnati. There were two versions of the incident, which followed words over ball and strike calls. In Mullane's version, Powers crossed the field and confronted him. Mullane then attempted to kick Powers. The other version was that Mullane confronted Powers and punched him in the face. After almost a month of supposed investigation and consideration, National League President Nick Young announced that Mullane would not be suspended, and sent him a letter urging him to have gentlemanly conduct and to have no further problems with Powers.[17]

In behavior that mirrored that of his 1887 vacation in New England, Mullane again left the Cincinnati club in 1892 after his salary was slashed by $700 at midseason. This time he went to Butte, Montana, and pitched in the Montana State League. He was still pitching in exhibition games with Butte as late as November 1.[18]

As far as Cincinnati was concerned, the straw that broke the camel's back came early in the 1893 season in another controversy over salary. Mullane's salary had been cut, and he reportedly said he would pitch according to his pay. Subsequently, he was accused of losing deliberately to Pittsburgh. There was speculation that Mullane might not just be suspended, but that he might be blacklisted — permanently banned from organized ball. In a sequel to the on-field problems, Mullane went home and got into a physical fight with his wife which left both of them with visible injuries— him with a lump on the head and her with cuts on her head and right hand. His wife then filed for divorce. Mullane, the man who did not understand humiliation, filed an answer in the divorce case, denying all the allegations and seeking alimony from his wife.[19]

Unwilling to deal with him any longer, Cincinnati traded him to Baltimore. During this period, Mullane was generally alluded to in the Cincinnati papers as the "Count de Ipecac." The cap on all of this came in January when Mullane came to Cincinnati from Chicago for a hearing on the divorce case. In a sensational scene on the street, he threatened to kill his wife. She ran off and called the police. Once in court, Mullane's cross-petition for divorce was thrown out, and he was ordered to pay $140 in alimony then due his wife. *Sporting Life* reported that his domestic troubles had driven him to drink, and that his wife claimed that he was intoxicated when he attacked her.[20]

Mullane made 26 starts for Baltimore in 1893 and another 15 in 1894 before he was traded to Cleveland where he finished out his major league career. He began his 16th professional season in 1895 with St. Paul in the Western League and drew a few additional snide comments from *Sporting Life*, including the observation that "His arm has become as cranky as his disposition." About three months later, it added: "The Count de Ipacec [*sic*] Mullane will soon have lots of time to devote to his estates. His pitching arm is as dead as a smoked mackerel."[21]

In fact, Mullane pitched for St. Paul for four years and then went to Toronto of the Eastern League in 1899. During this period he also mounted a persistent campaign to secure an umpiring post. He met with Young, the National League president, at the league's annual meeting in Chicago in December 1896. Eighteen months later *Sporting Life*, reported: "Tony Mullane asks President Young twice a week by wire for a place on the National League's staff of umpires. Tony evidently likes the saying: 'If you don't at first succeed, try, try again'."[22]

Mullane started umpiring in the Western League in 1898 but continued his efforts to land a National League job. Whatever his drinking situation may have been in 1893–94, he apparently had cleaned up his act by 1901 when he was umpiring in the Western Association. At that point *Sporting Life* quoted him as saying, "There are two rules I follow strictly. I drink nothing stronger than coffee, and when possible sleep nine and ten hours every night."[23]

He was umpiring in the Pacific Northwest League in 1902 until mid-season when he took a brief and final fling as an active player with Spokane. He posted three wins in as many starts and appeared in 20 games with a .307 batting average.[24]

He retired to Chicago, where he had made substantial real estate investments, and became a police officer, working as a detective from 1904 until he also wrapped up his law enforcement career in 1924. He married several times and was survived by one daughter. He died of cancer in Chicago on April 25, 1944, at the age of 85.[25]

By then it had been long forgotten, but in 1881 he had been a key man for the Akrons, even when he did not play.

7

That Man Swartwood

On May 13, 1881, the Akrons lost to Boston 2–1, a showing that tended to encourage the Akron cranks, as the *Leader* noted: "The seven hundred people who turned out to see the contest were pleased with what they saw, and great were the complimentary remarks bestowed upon the heads of the local nine as the people left the grounds." While the score was very creditable against one of the strongest league clubs, the Akrons had suffered a loss on more than the scoreboard as Mullane came up with a lame arm and was removed from the pitching box in the sixth inning.[1]

Three days later they lost again to Boston, 5–1. Although Neagle pitched effectively for the Akrons, giving Boston just six hits, the club committed ten errors, two of them by the injured Mullane, who was playing centerfield. The Akrons' only run came in the eighth inning, when Kemmler was safe on an error and scored on a double by Wise. The match was played in a cold, stiff, wind, a condition that apparently held the crowd to a scant 300. The Akron *City Times*, edited by Clarence Knight, who had managed the club briefly in 1880, never missed a chance to promote the team. It observed: "The weather undoubtedly interfered with the attendance on Monday, but after the splendid game of Friday, it should have been larger in spite of unfavorable conditions. If Akron people wish to keep a good club here they should see the games are well patronized."[2]

The admonition of the *City Times* went unheeded. May 23 was hot and sultry, described by the *Leader* as "making it disagreeable to play." It was far more disagreeable for the Akrons in a 9–1 loss than it was for the visiting Troys. This time the Akrons committed eight errors, including two by Jack Neagle, who also gave the Troys 13 hits. Mullane went to the bench, and Charlie Morton played center field in his place. The following day Neagle was more effective against the visiting Whites, but the Akrons lost again 4–3 in 10 innings, because of seven more errors.

The losing streak reached five games on May 27 when the Akrons lost to the National League Worcesters 12–3. Mullane, having rested his arm for a game, started against the Worcesters, who were leading the league at the time. His sore arm, however, forced him back to center field after an inning, and Neagle was hit for seven runs by the Worcesters in the second. Bolicky Bill Taylor, then new with the Worcesters, started at catcher, and the Worcester paper called him very effective. "He had a hand in 10 retirements, including two double-plays, and was not charged with a fault," the paper reported. By July, Taylor had signed with the Akrons as a pitcher.[3]

Losing always discourages fans, but the Akron Base Ball Association directors also were discouraged. They had expected big crowds for the National League contests. A May 19th game with the Troys had been rained out, and the game that had been played had attracted only 300 fans. With the Mullane injury and the loose play of the Akrons, prospects and gate receipts had begun to look grim. On the morning of the Worcester game, the *Leader* published a dispatch from Akron warning that unless the attendance "materially increased" the club would be disbanded. Quoting an unidentified source, the dispatch said: "Our association has taken every step necessary to furnish lovers of the National pastime with good games, and it behooves our citizens to respond liberally if they wish Akron to have a first-class nine. We have a club of which we are proud, and we are not exceeded by an amateur nine in the State, and we hope with these facts before us that the association will receive the encouragement they truly deserve." Two administrative changes were contemplated. One was to start games an hour later, at 4 P.M. The other was to reduce admission for games against National League opponents from 50 to 25 cents.[4]

Then, with a respite from National League competition, the Akrons turned things around on the field. The Beaver Falls, Pennsylvania, club came to Akron for a Memorial Day contest, and the Akrons banged out a 23–4 win with Neagle in the pitching box. Because of an injury to the Beaver Falls shortstop, Sam Wise took over at short for the visitors and contributed a hit and scored a run in their cause. Then the Cleveland Malleables visited on June 4, and Akron whacked them 20–0, again with Neagle doing the pitching. Mullane had not been idle during this time, but had been playing first base for the Akrons while Swartwood moved to the outfield.. On June 11, Mullane again entered the pitching box and hurled the Akrons to a 13–3 win over the visiting Whites.[5]

But even with the return of Mullane to his pitching duties, things were far from bright for the Akrons. Difficulty was encountered in arranging local games. The *City Times* observed: "There seem to be very few good amateur nines in this section the present season. The Elyrias, Norwalks, Findlays and other strong teams of last year show no signs of reorganizing, and the Cleveland Whites are the only amateur club in Ohio at present that can furnish the Akrons with practice." An effort was made to organize a trip into western Pennsylvania, but it fell through. The Akrons were committed to a trip to Louisville, Ky., to play the strong Eclipse club beginning on June 21, but at a directors' meeting in mid–June it was announced that the club would be suspended for two or three weeks without reference to the trip. Somewhat ominously the announcement concluded, "Subsequent developments will decide the fate of the club."

It was not surprising that players began to look elsewhere. Neagle left the club to sign with the newly organized New York Metropolitans for a reported $100-a-month salary. The Mets, at that point, were an independent team. Doc Mansell had accepted an engagement to play for the Albany, N.Y., club. Daniel "Link" Sullivan, who had been playing with the Cleveland Whites, was added to the Akrons before the Louisville trip.[6]

On Saturday, June 18, the Akrons warmed up for the big trip by defeating a picked nine of Akron amateurs 28–11 in seven innings. It evened the club's record at 6–6, but the *Summit County Beacon* reported, "The professionals played as though they didn't care very much about it, and probably they didn't. Swartwood pitched for three innings and amused himself greatly by giving the visitors first on balls and various other ways."[7]

It was a bit hard to care when the word was out that the club would be disbanded when it returned from Louisville. Yet, the Akrons had more than a little professional pride in their baseball prowess, as the Louisville Eclipse was about to discover. The Eclipse was generally considered one of the strongest independent professional teams in the country. On June 18, while the Akrons were laughing their way through the 28–11 win over the picked amateurs in Akron, the Eclipse was meeting the St. Louis Reds in Louisville. It was a hotly contested game, and the Reds led until the ninth inning when the Eclipse was able to bunch two doubles and two singles good for three runs and a 6–4 victory. The following day the Eclipse entertained the largest crowd thus far in 1881, about 3,500 fans, by romping over the Reds 12–0. It meant that the Eclipse was still undefeated for the season.[8]

That was about to change. On June 21, before about 800 spectators at Eclipse Park, the Akrons beat the Eclipse 9–1 in what the Louisville *Courier-Journal* called "a disastrous defeat." Said the *Courier-Journal*: "The visitors [Akron] came backed by a hard-earned reputation, and they were known to be strong ball players, having on several occasions defeated league clubs. Notwithstanding this fact there were many home enthusiasts who wildly imagined that the Louisville boys were invincible in a contest with any but league clubs. They have been playing fine ball for two years, and up to yesterday had not lost a game this season. Their reputation has, of course, become more than local, and when in trim it requires an unusually strong team to beat them. Yesterday, however, they played like children. The visitors had a picnic and beat them at every corner. In the first inning they allowed themselves to become rattled and never afterward recovered."[9]

While focusing on how badly the Eclipse played in the loss, the *Courier-Journal* did conclude that the visiting team were "powerful batters and superb fielders. The game they played yesterday would have defeated almost any club in the country, let alone the Eclipse."[10]

Louis Rogers "Pete" Browning, then just 20 years old, had not yet attained his legendary status in Louisville and was still three years shy of becoming the owner of the first Louisville Slugger bat. Clearly the best athlete on the Eclipse and destined for a 13-year major league career, he regularly played third base or shortstop for the club.[11] Browning sat out the initial game with the Akrons but observed the hitting.

In the slang of the day, a hard-hit ball was said to have "hair on it." Browning reportedly turned pale when he heard the sound of Ed Swartwood's bat meeting the ball and saw the Eclipse center fielder gazing at a faint spec on the horizon. According to the *Courier-Journal*, when Browning grew sufficiently calm to speak he said, "That one had hair on it." Joe Sommers, playing shortstop for the Eclipse, also was reported to have remarked that one of the balls hit past him during the game was "wearing not only long, flowing hair, but a fine mustache and goatee."[12]

Cyrus Edward "Ed" Swartwood had been appointed captain of the club before the season began. In its preseason story the Cleveland *Leader* had identified Swartwood and manager Charlie Morton as gentlemen and first-class ball players. The *Leader* said of Swartwood, "The management in appointing him as captain of the nine have exhibited good judgment, as he is perfectly acquainted with the game and all its points." On that day in Louisville, he was not the only man in the Akrons lineup to hit the ball hard. Indeed, batting second and playing right field, he was credited with only one of the Akrons' eight hits. Nevertheless, four days and two games later, the *Courier-Journal* proclaimed, "That man Swartwood can hit anything."[13]

Swartwood, born in Rockford, Illinois, in 1859, was in his third season with the Akrons and had a nine-year major league career ahead of him. He was a big man for the time at 5-foot-11 and 198 pounds, and it was said that while in the field, he was like a bear with a sore head: "He is always growling." But like the much smaller Bid McPhee, Swartwood built a reputation as a reliable and gentlemanly player. Ten years after the games in Louisville, *Sporting Life* said, "Ed Swartwood, in the twelve years of his base ball career, was never fined but once, and that was remitted because it was unjustly imposed."[14]

Although he is credited with one game with Buffalo of the National League in 1881, he effectively began the major league portion of his career in 1882 with the Allegheny (Pittsburgh) club in the American Association. That season he hit .329, third highest in the association, led the league in runs scored with 86 and in total bases with 159. He also tied for the league lead with 18 doubles. The following season he led the American Association in hitting with a .357 batting average and 147 hits. Playing mostly for mediocre clubs he compiled a lifetime major league batting average of .310.[15]

After three years in Pittsburgh, where he subsequently made his home, Swartwood moved to the Brooklyn club, also in the American Association, for another three years. His offensive numbers fell off somewhat, but when the Brooklyn management signed him for the 1886 campaign in November 1885, it was rumored that he would again become team captain as he had been during the latter part of the 1885 season.[16]

Swartwood did serve as captain during the 1886 season, but at its close Brooklyn did not reserve him. That action left Swartwood free to sign with other teams, although the expectation was that he would again play with the Brooklyn club. During that off-season *Sporting Life* reported of him, "The genial captain has become quite economical, and is said to be the possessor of a bank account running into several thousands of dollars." He had become a respected member of the Pittsburgh community, and in March 1887, before the opening of the baseball season *Sporting Life* picked up a newspaper item from that city that "Ed Swartwood will be presented with the handsome Elk emblem offered to the member selling the largest number of tickets to the benefit. Swarty sold nearly 350 tickets. The emblem consists of an elk's head of gold. The eyes are diamonds. It is a magnificent piece."[17]

He did return to Brooklyn for a third season, but by midseason *Sporting Life* said, "It is hinted in Brooklyn circles that this will be Swartwood's last season upon the diamond." By the end of the season he was being criticized in the media for listless play, but apparently he had hopes of returning to Brooklyn for the 1888 season. He tended bar after the season and, to capitalize on his popularity, received a percentage of the sales, as well as a salary. Nevertheless by December it was clear that Brooklyn would not offer him a contract.[18]

In March 1888, Swartwood was released from reservation by Brooklyn, and there was a rumor that he would sign with the Des Moines Club of the Western Association. Morton, in one of his many managerial engagements around the country, had taken over management of the Des Moines team in August 1887.[19] Morton tended to seek out players he knew and respected, and many of those players tended to follow Morton from place to place. Swartwood was one of those players, but as it turned out, Morton and Swartwood would not be reunited until they were both back in the major leagues with Toledo of the American Association in 1890.

Instead, Swartwood agreed to play first base for Hamilton, Ontario, of the International Association in 1888. He served the Hamilton team as captain, and after the close of the 1888 season signed to play winter ball with a club in Los Angeles. Not only did he return to Hamilton for the 1889 season, but when he signed *Sporting Life* also reported he would be a playing manager for the club. *Sporting Life* also reported later that he gave up his position as team captain in the belief he could not handle both jobs. Actually, it appears that Swartwood did not become interim manager until June, and in July, Abner Powell was named as manager. This did not disappoint Swartwood, who had moved to a rooming house far from where the other players lived, apparently because he was uncomfortable imposing discipline on his teammates.[20]

Besides playing musical managers during the 1889 season, the Hamilton club ran into financial problems, which also led Swartwood into trouble with the National Association when he believed, justifiably, that Hamilton had granted him his release. First, he had made an oral agreement with the president of the Hamilton club to take a pay cut in return for his release at the end of the season. Later, Swartwood agreed that Hamilton could keep his name on the reserve list until December 1, so that it could sell his contract to another team, with Swartwood to get half of the sale price. Nevertheless, when he attempted to sign with Detroit of the International Association, Hamilton made a complaint of tampering against Detroit on the grounds that Swartwood was still reserved. Swartwood then had to take a complaint to the board of arbitration. The case wasn't decided in Swartwood's favor until February 1890, when the board ruled that: "The affidavits of President Dixon, of the Hamilton Club, corroborated the statement made by Swartwood."[21]

The arbitration case may have worked to Swartwood's advantage because he signed with Toledo for 1890, a move which brought him back to a major league and reunited him with Morton, then the Toledo skipper. Swartwood responded to his return to the American Association with a .327 batting average while playing in 126 of the team's 134 games. He drew 80 walks, third most in the league, and posted an .887 on-base plus slugging mark, fifth in the league.[22]

While he hit only three home runs for the season (the league leader hit nine), Swartwood became the first player to knock a fair ball over Toledo's right field fence, an act which made him "lion of the day." *Sporting Life* reported, "On Saturday he touched [Jack] Easton [of the Columbus club] up for a clean home run, which went over [the] right field fence at a height of twenty feet. The right field fence is so far from the plate that a homer can be made on a ball batted inside the grounds, so the length of Swarty's hit can be estimated. The hit was worth $75 to him, as he gets a suit of clothes from Joe Huber, a silk hat and numerous other little necessaries along with it, including the season's tonsorial work."[23]

Haircut and all, Swartwood found himself swinging his bat for Sioux City in the Western Association in 1891. He hit .286 in 109 games for a very competitive club. In postseason exhibition play, Sioux City won four of six games from the National League Chicago club and five straight from the St. Louis Browns. *Sporting Life* noted, "Ed played good ball in Sioux City and is very well thought of in the Western Association."[24]

In the off-season, he became a traveling salesman in the cigar trade, and when the National League absorbed the American Association, creating a single 12-team major league, Swartwood found his way back to the "big league" with his home-town Pittsburgh club. He played only 13 games in 1892 before Pittsburgh released him, and he hooked on with Rochester, New York, in the Eastern League. There he hit .307 in 100 games. In Rochester he was reunited with former Akron teammate Sam Wise, but both men were released before the end of the season. Swartwood went to Providence, R.I., and Wise to Binghamton, N.Y., where they played against each other for the Eastern League title.[25]

Swartwood wrapped up his playing career by hitting .317 in 40 games with Providence in 1893. He was appointed a National League umpire in 1894 and an Eastern League umpire in 1895. He also umpired in the Eastern League in 1896 and in the National League again from 1898 through 1900.[26]

In the winter of 1896, however, Swartwood apparently had a brief dream of big-time riches. According to *Sporting Life*, he was said to have struck it rich in the Cripple Creek, Colorado, diggings. Said *Sporting Life*: "He holds two-sixths of a claim, which lays directly alongside of the immense Stratton mine. The latter was once a resident of the First ward, Allegheny, where Swarty lived for many years. When Swart gave up his position as a cigar salesman and went West he told Elmer Smith and other players that when he came back he felt sure he would have enough cash to keep him from umpiring or wanting the balance of his existence." Two weeks later, he was back and ready to resume his Eastern League umpiring position.[27]

When Swartwood returned to National League umpiring, he proved to be something of an innovator. He used a shield buckled to his left arm so that when he held his arm across his chest, the shield protected him from foul tips. About a year later he lost the shield, and *Sporting Life* took a swipe at his umpiring skills, reporting: "Umpire Swartwood is mourning the loss of that peculiar chest protector that so often distracted attention from poor decisions. Some gentleman of Chicago is supposed to have purloined it."[28]

He lived out his life in Pittsburgh, where he operated several small businesses and also served as an Allegheny County deputy sheriff, a post in which he had a hand in another innovation. Swartwood, the man who didn't like to discipline his teammates as manager, was called on to assist in an execution in 1907.

In those days county sheriffs frequently had the duty of executing prisoners convicted and sentenced in their counties. Addison C. Gumpert, a former National League pitcher, then sheriff of Allegheny County, hanged his first man, wife murderer Dowling Green, on July 23, 1907. Swartwood assisted Gumpert, and because neither liked the duty a contrivance was arranged by which Green practically hanged himself. The trap was set so that when Green stepped on it the weight of his body sprung it. According to the report, "the contrivance worked well and will be used in the future hangings in the county."[29]

Swartwood died in Pittsburgh on May 15, 1924. He was 65 years old.[30]

8

The Most Remarkable Game

Swartwood and the other Akron players had opened a lot of eyes in Louisville with their 9–1 victory on June 21. Now they had to face an Eclipse team that had revenge on its mind and pride to defend in the June 22 afternoon game before the largest crowd any of them had ever seen.

Louisville was hosting the Midsummer Encampment of Masonic Lodges in honor of St. John's Day. An estimated 12,000 people had flocked into the city with drill teams, bands, and even artillery units. The game between the Eclipse and the Akrons had been scheduled not at the Eclipse Park but at Central Park to follow a program of horse racing. When the game started there were 7,000 fans in the stands. The *Courier-Journal* reported, "a game of base ball was never witnessed before in Louisville by such a vast concourse of spectators."[1]

Moreover, there wasn't any grass on the field, and a ball that went over an outfielder's head was expected to be good for three bases. In an era when there was little uniformity in the quality of balls, the ball was exceptionally lively and the batting was correspondingly strong. Yet, the *Courier-Journal* noted that at the start of the game the betting, "which was lively on the quiet," was two to one in favor of the Akrons. Later, it said, "more even bets were made."[2]

One reason for the change in the odds was that Akron's starting pitcher wasn't Tony Mullane, who had pitched the 9–1 Tuesday victory, but James F. Green. While the score was 1–1 after two innings, "the home boys got on to Green, and they just batted him all over the field," the *Courier-Journal* said.[3]

Jimmy Green had first come to the Akrons in the fall of 1879 and had stuck with the team in 1880 and 1881 mostly as an extra player. Green had been born in Connecticut and apparently was living in Cleveland at the time he first joined the Akrons. He had a brief brush with a major league when he played ten games with the Washington, D.C., team in the Union Association in 1884, but mostly he was always a minor leaguer. In 1883 he was playing left field with the Anthracites of Pottsville, Pennsylvania, and in 1884, he played with the Riversides of Portsmouth, Ohio, before his brief trial with Washington. Subsequently he played on a number of other minor league clubs including the Canton, Columbus, and Dayton, Ohio, teams, and Wheeling, West Virginia, of the Tri-State League. While playing with Wheeling in 1889, Green married Annie Engert of Akron. When his baseball days ended, he worked as a laborer in Cleveland, where he died Dec. 13, 1912, at the age of 58.[4]

Before the big crowd in Louisville, Green pitched through the fifth inning and left trailing 7–3. Green, however, did not leave the game, but as was common in those days went from pitcher to another position — in this case, first base. Mullane, the regular starting pitcher, took over the hurling in the sixth inning and surrendered four more runs to the Eclipse in the eventual 11–6 loss.

The pitching change is related in the game story but is not reflected in the box score, which shows Green only at first and Mullane only at pitcher. The rules varied somewhat from place to place, but most teams followed National League rules. Typically, a substitution could be made for a starting player only when the starter was unable to continue because of injury or illness. As a result, the "change," or substitute pitcher usually started in the outfield, so that if called upon, the players only changed positions. Likely, that is what happened in this case, probably with Swartwood starting at first and going to the outfield when Mullane came in to pitch and Green went to first.[5]

The game story also reports that "Mansell played especially well in the right field, making one wonderful running catch of a foul bound." Until 1884 the National League rules included a provision that a foul ball caught on the first bounce (bound) was an out. It is likely that the Eclipse and the Akrons also were using the foul bound rule.[6]

But, Mansell doesn't appear in the box score, which shows Dan Sullivan in center, Leech Maskrey in left and Ed Swartwood in right for the Akrons. Since players wore no identifying marks on their uniforms, it is possible that the reporter, being unfamiliar with the Akrons, mistook one player for another. Sullivan and Swartwood are listed at about the same size, both 5-feet-11 with Sullivan at 194 pounds and Swartwood at 198. John "Doc" Mansell was listed at 5-feet-10 and 168 pounds, while Leech Maskrey was 5-feet-8 and 150 pounds.[7]

Regardless of the game account, there is reason to believe that Mansell did not go to Louisville with the club, even though the *Summit County Beacon*, in reporting that he had accepted an engagement to play for the Albany, New York, club, added, "He has asked for a week's absence, in order to accompany the boys to Louisville." On June 22, the day of the game in Louisville, the Akron *City Times* reported, "Mansell has gone to Albany, where he has an engagement." It also noted, "Mansell's place is filled by Sullivan of the Whites." Moreover, the *Summit County Beacon* did not report the departure of either Green or Mansell from the Akrons until almost a month later.[8]

Mansell had been a popular player with the fans and a solid contributor to the Akrons in 1880 and 1881. During the 1880 season he was described by the *Sunday Gazette* as "the man who doesn't do anything but smile; none of your half-way smiles either." When he joined Albany, reuniting with his two older ball-playing brothers, it was believed to be the first time that three brothers had played professionally for the same club. He then finished the 1881 season with the Atlantics of Brooklyn, and with the organization of the American Association in 1882, made the major leagues on the Athletic Club of Philadelphia. He played in just 31 games before suffering an injury and ended up playing the balance of his career in the minors.

His brief tenure with the Athletics was marked by an exceptional throw in a game against the Eclipse that was described in the New York *Clipper* as being "from extreme centre-field to the home-plate in time to put a base-runner out was claimed to equal any previous record." The *Clipper* also said of him: "His quiet, unassuming deportment has made him a great favorite in every city he has played in during his brief but brilliant professional career."[9]

Brief appears to be the operative word, as he was out of baseball by 1890. He died in Romulus, New York, on February 20, 1925, at the age of 63.[10]

After the Eclipse had pounded out its 11–6 win before the large Wednesday crowd, Akron still had two more games scheduled on its Louisville trip. With Thursday and Friday off, the two clubs should have been on their mettle for the Saturday game, but it appeared only the Akrons had come to play. A crowd of about 1,000 turned out for the Saturday game at the Eclipse Park, and the Louisville club took a 4–2 lead in the second inning before the Akrons started to hit the ball and the Eclipse started to throw it around. The *Courier-Journal* reported that "errors piled up alarmingly," and the Eclipse ended up charged with 13 errors as the Akrons won easily, 10–5. Said the *Courier-Journal*, "The last of the series of games will be played this afternoon at Eclipse Park when it is to be hoped a sure-enough game of ball may be played."[11]

That hope was realized and then some. Before that Sunday was over a report of the game between the Eclipse and the Akrons had been flashed

8. The Most Remarkable Game

around the country by The Associated Press, which hailed it as "one of the most remarkable games of base ball on record."[12]

The teams had played a 2–2 19-inning tie that was halted only by darkness. In the second inning Fred Pfeffer tripled and scored to give the Eclipse a 1–0 lead, which held up until the bottom of the seventh inning, when Sullivan singled and came around to score the tying run on two Eclipse errors. The Eclipse took the lead in the top of the eighth on a run-scoring double by Pete Browning, but the Akrons tied it again at 2–2 in the bottom of the inning. The Akrons had a chance to win it in the 18th inning when Swartwood attempted to score from second base on a hard hit by Tony Mullane only to be thrown out at the plate on a relay from Pfeffer. Mullane and John Reccius each pitched the entire 19 innings.[13]

Dan "Link" Sullivan (*New York Clipper*)

Just as the Akrons' 4–3 win over Cap Anson's Chicagos in 1880 had done much to establish the club's reputation, the 2–2 19-inning game with the Eclipse helped to burnish it. For some of the players, the memory of the contest followed them to the grave.

An obituary of Ike Van Burkalow, who played center field for the Eclipse, reported his participation "in the memorable nineteen inning game." Similar language had appeared in the earlier obituary of Sullivan, who had been the Akrons' center fielder in the game. In part, that obituary read, "While catching for the latter team [Akron] he took part in the memorable contest with the Eclipse Club, June 26, 1881, at Louisville, when darkness caused a cessation of play with the score tied after nineteen innings had been completed, he having made one of the two runs credited to the Akron team."[14]

Sullivan, who joined the Akrons in 1881 just before to the Louisville trip, was one of several players recruited by Morton from the White Sewing Machine team of Cleveland. While Sullivan's major league career was mostly as a catcher, and despite what his obituary said, he did not catch for the Akrons.[15]

He was a native of Providence, Rhode Island, where he died of consumption in 1893 at the age of 36. He had played ball for semiprofessional clubs in Providence, Rhode Island, Stoneham, Massachusetts, and Holyoke, Massachusetts, before coming to Cleveland and Akron, where he effectively began his professional career.[16]

His time with the Akrons was relatively brief. Before the end of July 1881, he had been engaged by Detroit for the remainder of the season to be given a trial as change-catcher. His initial time in the major leagues also was brief. A week later the New York *Clipper* reported, "Sullivan did not come up to the expectations of the Detroit management in regard to his ability as a catcher, and he was released July 30." Sullivan then joined the Metropolitan Club of New York and finished the 1881 season with that team. According to the *Clipper*, he filled the catcher's position acceptably, catching among others, the pitching of another former Akron player, Jack Neagle. When the American Association was formed as the second major league in 1882, Sullivan went to the Eclipse Club of Louisville. That season he caught 53 games.[17]

In all, Sullivan played five years in the major leagues: with Louisville from 1882 through 1885; also with St. Louis in 1885; and with Pittsburgh in 1886. During this time he played in 198 games and had a total of 788 at bats with a .232 career batting average. In 1886 Sullivan played with Savannah and Memphis of the Southern League, and a year later was appointed an umpire in the Northwestern League before returning to Providence for the balance of his life.[18]

Clearly, the apex of Sullivan's career was during the Akrons' series with the Louisville Eclipse. He batted lead-off for Akron and in the first four of the five games, he had nine hits in 23 at bats, with a double and a triple. In the memorable 19-inning game, he had three hits in eight at bats, besides scoring the first of the two Akron runs.[19]

9

The Home Town Boy

When the 19-inning Sunday game was halted by darkness, the Akrons agreed to remain in Louisville an extra day to "play off" the tie with a fifth game. About 800 spectators were at the Eclipse Park on Monday, June 27, and, according to the *Courier-Journal*, "It was generally expected that the contest would be spirited throughout. Those who had expected this, however, were sadly disappointed."[1]

Reccius of the Eclipse and Mullane of the Akrons each had pitched the entire 19 innings on Sunday, but both started again on Monday. Said the *Courier-Journal*, "Reccius went in to pitch with a sad lack of energy, and his delivery was way off in effectiveness. The strong-armed boys from Ohio got on to him right in the first inning, and knocked him all over the field, making, thanks to Burkalow's assistance in the way of several inexcusable errors, five runs before the home boys went to the bat."[2]

The Akrons led 9–2 after the first two innings and went on to a 14–5 victory. The *Courier-Journal* reporter took a stab at explaining the one-sided loss, writing: "Though the result was wholly unexpected, it would not be fair to criticize our boys too severely. The wonderfully lengthy game on Sunday had about exhausted them, and when they went into the field yesterday none of them were fit to play ball. It is highly creditable to the Akrons, however, that they stood the rub so much better than their opponents and captured yesterday's game as handily as they did."[3]

Burkalow came in from center field to relieve Reccius as pitcher for the Eclipse in the fourth inning, and Sam Wise greeted him with a home run. Home runs were relatively rare in this era, and most of them were inside-the-park blows. In this case, Wise's homer carried over the outfield fence and out of the park. It was, said the *Courier-Journal*, "a severe blow to Burkalow's pride."[4]

Wise was born at Johnson's Corners, now a part of Barberton, Ohio, on August 18, 1857. He grew up in Akron, and began playing baseball early in life. He was an accomplished hitter by the time he became the hometown boy around whom the Akrons had been first organized in 1879.⁵

In the first three Akron games in Louisville in 1881, Wise had just two hits, both doubles. Then he went three for eight in the 19-inning game with a double and a triple and wrapped up the series with a four-for-five afternoon on Monday with another double and the home run. Throughout his subsequent professional career, he always had a potent bat and had great range in the field while playing shortstop and second base. However, he also had a scattershot throwing arm and eight times during his career committed more than 70 errors, including leading the National League with 88 errors at shortstop for the pennant-winning Boston club in 1883.⁶

His major league career covered 12 years, beginning with a single game with Detroit of the National League in 1881 and concluding with Washington of the National League in 1893. He played for Boston of the National League for seven seasons, from 1882 through 1888, before playing with Washington of the National League in 1889, Buffalo of the Players League in 1890, and Baltimore of the American Association in 1891. He played 1,175 major league games with 4,715 at bats, amassing 1,281 hits, 221 doubles, 112 triples, and 49 home runs. He also stole 203 bases with stolen base totals unavailable before 1886. His lifetime major league average was .277.⁷

Excluding his years with the Akrons, Wise also played seven years in various minor leagues, six of them following his final major league season in 1893 with the Washington Nationals. He hit more than .300 in five of those six seasons and had a lifetime minor league batting average of .319 and slugging of .462 on 910 hits in 2,849 at bats. His minor league totals included 166 doubles, 87 triples, and 22 home runs.⁸

Always popular with fans and his fellow players, Wise's penchant for the long ball fueled many stories. One of them, dating to 1886 when he was with the Bostons, is that he had hit the longest ball ever seen on the Kansas City grounds. The story is also a testimonial to the Kansas City left fielder Jim "Grasshopper" Lilly as well as a vivid example of nineteenth century playing conditions.

Kansas City played in the National League in 1886 and its field, Association Park, was nick-named "The Pit." It was in an excavation that remained when dirt had been removed to create a roadbed for Independence Avenue. The playing surface was 25 feet or more below street level, and the bordering embankment sloped upward at a steep angle.

Wise came to bat in the eighth inning with two men on base, two men out, and Boston trailing by a run. He launched the ball high in the air to left and Lilly took off after it, running up the steep slope. He was about half-way up when a warning shout alerted him that he had outrun the ball. He turned and leaped after it, snared it with his left hand, and tumbled headlong down the embankment. At the bottom, he banged his head against a boulder and was knocked unconscious. But, he held onto the ball, and Wise was the third out of the inning.[9]

Mark Sternman, writing in *Baseball's First Stars*, noted that Wise had a "unique combination of skills and deficiencies."[10] While Wise was never a troublemaker on the order of self-absorbed Tony Mullane, he was an outspoken critic of the reserve clause, repeatedly held out for higher salaries, was an early and vocal supporter of the Players League, and had the misfortune to be the principal in the first court case in professional baseball history. From

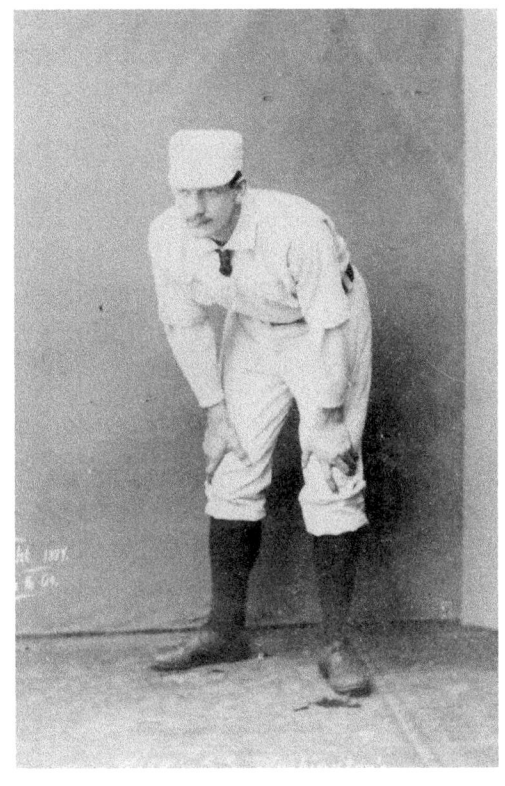

Sam Wise (National Baseball Hall of Fame Library, Cooperstown, N.Y.)

the standpoint of club owners, all of these things were deficiencies as troubling as his tendency to throw the ball into the stands.

Oliver Perry "O.P." Caylor, sometimes credited with being the first newspaper baseball columnist, not only worked for the Cincinnati *Commercial Gazette* in 1881 but took a direct hand in organizing the American Association as a second major league and the Cincinnati Reds team in that league. One of Caylor's moves late in 1881 was to send Charley Jones, a blacklisted National League player, off with three blank contracts. He came back with the signatures of three of the Akrons: second baseman Bid McPhee, catcher Rudy Kemmler and third baseman Sam Wise. By November 1881, the New York *Clipper*, reporting on the nucleus of the Cincinnati Club for 1882, said that McPhee, Kemmler and Wise had made "enviable reputations" with the Akron Club.[11]

In the end, only McPhee stayed with Cincinnati, and Wise, while not the only player to end up with his signature on multiple contracts during the inevitable bidding war between the American Association and the National League for players, became an early target in the war between the upstart association and the established league. Writing of Wise in January 1882, the New York *Clipper* said, "He recently received offers from the Boston and Providence Clubs, and, as the terms of the former were the most satisfactory, he accepted them, paying no attention whatever to the contract he had made with the Cincinnatis. This is the second player the League has stolen from the American Association. At a meeting of the directors of the Cincinnati Club on January 18 it was decided to compel the performance of all contracts with players at whatever cost. President Thorner was authorized to at once employ an attorney in each League city, as well as in New York and Philadelphia, to enjoin Wise, or any other 'revolver' in every city where he may attempt to play ball next season, except with the Cincinnati Club."[12]

Caylor tried unsuccessfully to coax Wise back to Cincinnati with a letter "in which taffy, entreaty, and bull-dozing were very beautifully blended," according to Harold Seymour in *Baseball: The Early Years*. Marking the first time professional baseball went into the civil courts to settle a dispute, the Cincinnati club applied for an injunction in Massachusetts to restrain Wise from playing with Boston and compelling him to return to the Reds. The judge refused to grant the injunction, and Wise remained with Boston for seven successful seasons.[13]

While popular with the Boston fans, Wise's tenure there was not always smooth. After Boston won the National League pennant in 1883, Wise, who had inked his contract for the coming season, granted an interview in Cleveland on his way home to Akron. Among other things Wise noted that every member of the Boston Club had received "a handsome increase" in salary, but he went on to add, "I should like to play in Cleveland, but the reserve rule holds me solid. There is lots of kicking against the rule ... because it protects associations and not players. This is not fair, and the kicking will go on until a change comes."[14]

Criticism of the reserve rule was seldom overlooked by management, and before the end of the winter *Sporting Life* published an unattributed report that "Wise is getting too big and fat to play short, and he and [John] Morrill will probably change places in the Boston nine, the latter going to short and the former to first base." The unusual aspect of this report is that Wise hadn't been sitting at home but had joined a barnstorming group of professionals organized by outfielder George Gore of the Chicagos to play in the South. Wise made a home run in each of the first two games, and *Sporting Life* reported that the New Orleans' natives "think him a perfect wonder in both batting and fielding." Wise also won a medal as the best player for the Crescent City, the name adopted by the professionals, in four games with the Eclipse Club of Louisville.[15]

Despite the item that he was too fat, Wise returned to shortstop for Boston in 1884 and had his best professional season in 1887 when he hit .382 with 192 hits in 503 at bats with 27 doubles, 17 triples and nine home runs. He also stole 43 bases.[16]

For his efforts Wise was awarded a solid silver bat by the Boston *Globe* for the best batting on the Boston team. It was more respect than he received from the Boston management, and he soon found himself in a contract dispute when the baseball owners launched an effort to cap salaries. Wise wanted $2,500 for the coming season. Management offered $2,000, and *Sporting Life* reported: "Sam is boiling mad. As the leading batter in the team, according to the scoring of actual hits, and as one of the leading short stops in the League, he believed himself entitled to more money. He said he was one of the lowest paid men in the business, and that he wanted more than the limit."[17]

Whatever the cause, Wise batted only .240 for the 1888 season and was benched. Upset again over his treatment by Boston, he sought his release and *Sporting Life* reported on Oct. 31 that Wise said he had an offer from "one of the strongest clubs in the League" if he could get away from Boston. A week later it reported, "Sam Wise is in great demand. Almost every club in the League is dickering for his release. Sam is a wise child if he can name the diamond on which he will frisk next spring. Von der Ahe [owner of the St. Louis Browns of the American Association] also would like to have him, but he won't be able to get out of the League."[18]

After another winter-long standoff between Wise and Boston management, he reported to Boston at the end of March but returned his contract unsigned. Shortly afterward he found himself part of a multiplayer trade that sent him to the woeful Washington Nationals. Whatever his feelings about the deal, he made an immediate positive impression in the nation's capital when he showed up at an exhibition game between A.G. Spalding's Chicagos and the All-American team, which had just completed its world tour. Said the *Sporting News*, "Big Sam Wise strolled into Capital Park last Monday before the Chicago-All-American game commenced, looking like a howling Boston swell. He wore a silk hat, a light-brown overcoat, a pair of nobby trousers, and in his hand he carried a silver-headed walking stick. He received quite an ovation from the crowd that entered the gate, and Sam remarked to me [reporter R.M. Larner] at the time that it was extremely gratifying to be greeted so cordially by his new-found friends. He further endeared himself to the Washington public by his magnificent display of stick work Thursday. He was third on the batting list, and when he stepped to the plate he was greeted with applause and cheers. He raised his hat gracefully and then directed his attention to Pitcher Bishop, Jack Chapman's prize twirler. Wilmot was on first base, having reached there on four bad balls. Sam sized up the pitcher and then let drive. Away went the ball far over the centre fielder's head for two bases, sending Wilmot home. This was a pretty good opening for Boston's discarded shortstop. The second time he went to the bat he lined out a beautiful single to right field. Later in the game he planted another two-bagger against the centre field fence. In spite of the mud he stole two bases and fielded his position for all it was worth. He seems to be somewhat shoulder bound, but he manages to get the ball to first base ahead of the runner just the same. He throws his whole soul into the game, and all things considered, Washington is very well pleased with the Boston contingent."[19]

A month later in another dispatch to *Sporting Life*, Larner wrote, "It would have made Sam Wise's Boston friends happy could they have seen big Sam's work last Monday. Such a game as he put up at short will not be excelled this season. He chopped off base hits behind third and second base, and threw the runners out at first in a style that made Jack Glasscock turn green with envy. On four separate occasions the crowd stood up and shouted "Wise! Wise! Wise!" He also had on his batting clothes, and he appears to have kept them on ever since, for today he found Getzels for a single and a three-bagger. At the present writing, Wise is worth more to Washington than two Johnny Wards, and I make this statement without intending to detract one iota from Ward's ability as a ball player."[20]

While the 1889 season with last place Washington proved to be ordinary for Wise, he had one more special moment when the Nationals visited Boston in August. *Sporting Life* reported, "When Sam Wise came to the bat in the first inning at Boston Friday, Umpire Knight called for a halt in the hostilities and handed the ex–Bostonian an elegant bouquet of flowers, to which there was attached a little bag containing $150 in $5 gold pieces. The whole was a gift of Boston friends."[21]

At the close of the 1889 season, Wise, the longtime critic of the reserve clause, joined with former Akron teammate Ed Andrews as an early and vocal supporter of the Players' League revolt against the major leagues. By November, Wise had signed with the Buffalo club of the Players' League. While he had exchanged one last-place team for another, his 1890 season in Buffalo was a fine one as he hit .293 with career highs of 29 doubles and 102 RBIs.[22]

There is no direct evidence that Wise and other Players' League men were blacklisted, but most of them had relatively short major league careers after the collapse of the players' revolt. Wise signed for the 1891 season with Baltimore of the American Association, where he also served as team captain — effectively the on-field manager. Snippets in *Sporting Life* commented on his work. One reported, "Sam Wise has handled the Baltimores very cleverly so far." Another said, "Sam Wise has the Baltimores working under one of the most complete code of signals in the Association or League."[23]

Always an easy talker, Wise granted a lengthy interview to a Boston reporter when the Baltimore team made its first visit north. In it, he reflected on his baseball travels since being traded by Boston and also touched on the fact that he was now a second baseman rather than a shortstop. When asked if he liked to play second, Wise replied, "No, I'd rather be at short, my old position, and it comes more natural." He praised the other men playing the position on the Baltimore club but sounded a bit wistful about returning to Boston.

"I like to come up here and play — it seems like home. But still, it's a good idea for a player to change about — I found that out," Wise said. "Oh, yes, Baltimore is a good ball town. For that matter I find they are all alike, so long as you are playing winning ball. Let a fellow slip up for a week, and they haven't any use for you anywhere, I don't care what city it is." [24]

After a rather lackluster season in Baltimore, Wise returned to Utica, New York, where he was then making his home. There he found himself as part of a picked nine representing Utica in a Labor Day game against a picked nine from Syracuse. The contest, won by Syracuse, reunited Wise with two other players from the Akrons of 1879 and 1880 as Mike Mansell played left field for Syracuse, and Charlie Osterhout, who hadn't played in two years, did the Syracuse catching. Subsequently, there was speculation that Wise, released by Baltimore, would play for Utica in 1892.[25]

Instead, out of the major leagues for the first time since 1882, Wise began the 1892 season as second baseman and captain of the Rochester club in the Eastern League. By August *Sporting Life* reported, "Samuel Washington Wise has taken good care of himself, has batted hard, and fielded finely, and has so finely captained the Rochesters that they stand a good chance of winning Eastern League championship No. 2."[26]

But less than a month later Wise and Billy Hoover were released by Rochester as a cost-cutting measure. Said the Rochester *Democrat and Chronicle*, "In Hoover and Wise the team loses its most valuable players. As hitters and fielders they were without question the strongest men that Rochester has had this season, or any season for that matter." The team president was quoted as saying, "We had arrived at a point where we had to decide whether to let the team go up altogether or reduce expenses, and we decided to make the cut and finish the season in order that we might retain our franchise."[27]

Wise was immediately signed by Binghamton, which, according to *Sporting Life*, "is leaving nothing undone to win the Eastern League pennant." With Rochester, Wise had been playing with another former Akron teammate in Ed Swartwood, but Swartwood also was released and went to Providence. The two played against each other for the title. In the end, *Sporting Life*, concluded, "Sam Wise proved a most useful man to the Binghamtons, and his batting and fielding after he joined the team helped them greatly in winning the Eastern League pennant."[28]

Collectively, between Rochester and Binghamton, Wise had put together one of his best seasons, hitting .329 with 33 doubles and 21 triples for the Eastern League clubs, and stealing 36 bases.[29]

Wise had been hampered with a sore arm from time to time, and he also had suffered from sore feet, chiefly bunions and corns. Now, with the good 1892 campaign on his resume, he set his sights on returning to the majors and quickly signed once more with the Washington Nationals. *Sporting Life* reported that he had written a letter to a friend in Washington "in which he said he was glad to get back into the major League, that he was never better in his life, and he would play a regular old-time game for the Washingtons next year. When Wise is in proper trim he is a star player."[30]

Early in the 1893 season *Sporting Life* noted, "Sam Wise is knocking out the hits in a manner that will keep him near the top of the heap." Playing second and third for the Nationals, Wise had his finest major league season since 1887 in Boston when he won the silver bat. He hit .311 for the season with 27 doubles and 17 triples, scored 102 runs and knocked in 77. Nonetheless, Washington offered Wise a pay cut, and another salary wrangle ensued. He returned his contract to Washington without a signature in February but reported for spring training in March. He was not to play another major league game. Before the season started Washington released him because he "expressed dissatisfaction with his surroundings."[31]

Wise landed with Allentown in the Pennsylvania State League in 1894 and ended the season with Yonkers in the Eastern League. Then old friend and fellow Akronite Charlie Morton intervened in his life. Morton, who had been managing Erie in the Eastern League, was hired to manage the Buffalo club in the same league. Before Christmas, Wise and Morton traveled together from Akron to Buffalo, where Wise became the first player signed by Buffalo for the 1895 season.[32]

He played for four seasons in Buffalo, and as a veteran, inevitably became known as "Pop" in the Eastern League. In 1896 he was voted a cup as being the most popular player on the Buffalo team. After suffering a split finger in 1897, Wise missed ten days but came back with his hand bandaged. *Sporting Life* correspondent C.F. Holcomb wrote, "I know that he must have suffered terribly in handling the stick with his split finger, and in attempting to pick up hot ones at second, but he would keep at it. Although the bleachers have sometimes jeered the veteran for fumbling while in this condition, the fact is that his [fielding] average is about .925 even now, a good deal better than some Eastern League second basemen, I fancy." He hit .317 in 1895, .347 in 1896, and .337 in 1897 before tailing off to .290 for 1898. He finished his playing career in 1899 with 140 at bats for Newark in the Atlantic League and a .314 average.[33]

During this period, Wise made his home in Buffalo, worked for the Buffalo Street Railway Company and subsequently went into the saloon business. As early as 1890, after his season in Buffalo with the Players' League, *Sporting Life* had reported that Wise was contemplating opening a saloon. Wise denied the report at that time but turned to the business when his playing days ended. Billy Nash and Wise had played together for four seasons in Boston, and Nash came to Buffalo in 1899 when Wise was wrapping up his playing career in Newark. They opened a saloon in Buffalo that winter, and by the spring of 1900 it was reported that the business was doing so well both had abandoned all idea of returning to baseball. It didn't last. Nash sold out his interest in the fall of 1900 and returned to the diamond as a manager. Wise displayed the same tenacity he had on the field, but to no avail. By November 1900 the sheriff had seized the saloon's entire stock of liquor for debt. Likely part of the problem was Wise's garrulous good nature. Years later, when he had returned to Akron and was asked about the saloon, he replied, "It's poor business anyway."[34]

Wise, who once worked at the Buckeye Mower & Reaper Works, returned to Akron to work for the Diamond Tire & Rubber company, reflecting in part the changes that had occurred in the city during the intervening 25 years. Wise also umpired around the Akron area, and in 1906 Morton once more found a baseball job for Wise, appointing him an umpire in the Ohio-Pennsylvania League.[35]

The same garrulous good nature that may have contributed to his failure as a barkeeper also was a bad trait for umpires. The Ohio-Pennsylvania League, like most professional leagues of the era, used only one umpire per game. Inevitably, the umpire missed some calls, had his back turned at times, and then had to cope with arguments about what he hadn't seen. One example of how Wise was abused occurred in a game in which the Mansfield team was playing in Akron. Walter East, then player-manager of the Akron club, was coming to bat. East told Dick Nallin, the following batter, to watch him if he got on base and attempted to steal second. Nallin was to shove the Mansfield catcher so he couldn't throw to second.

East was hit by a pitch and the plan was put into execution. East took a big lead and started for second just as the Mansfield pitcher delivered the ball. As he started to run, East shouted, "Sam! Sam!" Wise, who was umpiring from behind the pitcher, turned to look. Nallin did his part and shoved the catcher so hard he almost knocked him over. Wise turned back to see the catcher standing there with the ball in his hand. Of course, the catcher rushed out to Wise shouting, "He shoved me, Sam. He shoved me."

"What if he did," responded Wise. "I didn't see him do it." The *Beacon Journal* reported "No end of argument could persuade Wise to change his decision. Wise, however, stopped the game long enough to bawl out East and wound up by telling him he'd call [him] out every time he came to bat if he tried anything like that again."[36]

Moreover, on May 20, when the Mansfield, Ohio, and Sharon, Pennsylvania, teams attempted to play a game at Shelby, northwest of Mansfield, a riot broke out when constables armed with warrants from a local magistrate attempted to enforce the Sabbath law. Wise, caught in the midst of the melee, called the game. Six weeks later he resigned from the umpiring staff. Subsequently, Wise declared he would never umpire another game, saying, "They abuse the umpire too much. I don't have to take it from them."[37]

In addition to the Mansfield riot, Wise had had an earlier experience with the Sunday baseball controversy during his final season with Buffalo. It was not unusual for one player from a team to be tried for violating a Sunday playing law rather than trying the entire team. Wise, as the Buffalo captain, went to trial in August 1898 on a Sunday playing charge and was acquitted by a jury. *Sporting Life* opined that Wise's acquittal meant that the Buffalo team could play Sunday ball unmolested for the balance of the season.[38]

In January 1910, Wise was stricken with appendicitis. Apparently he attempted to keep his illness secret from his family, and as he would have on the ball field, tried to play through the pain. By the time he was taken to the hospital for an operation on January 19 it was too late. He died of peritonitis. It is unclear from the death certificate whether it resulted from a burst appendix or as a result of the operation.[39]

As the end approached on the morning of January 22, Wise turned to his wife and said, "Tell the boys I have fought hard; I have tried to be brave." He was 52 years old.

While Wise was lingering in the hospital, Billy Sunday, the ballplayer turned evangelist, was holding a revival campaign in Youngstown, Ohio. Sunday and Wise had played in the National League at the same time; Sunday with Chicago and Pittsburgh, while Wise was with Boston and Washington. When Sunday heard of Wise's illness, he called him on the telephone to pray for him, and later sent the family a magnificent floral wreath. At the same time, John L. Sullivan, the former heavyweight boxing champion, was in Akron on a vaudeville tour. Sullivan was a great baseball fan and had been friendly with Wise in Boston. He not only expressed his regrets, but visited the Wise home.[40]

10

From Louisville to Limbo

With the lopsided win over the Eclipse on June 27, the Akrons returned home in what the *Courier-Journal* called "high feather." Whatever elation the players may have felt from their Louisville success had to be tempered by the knowledge that the team was to be disbanded when it reached Akron. This was not an unusual situation for independent clubs of that era, as directors attempted to keep team finances from tumbling into vats of red ink. Indeed, the Akrons went 15 days without a game, and then emerged from limbo in a reorganized form.[1]

The club got back to Akron on the evening of June 28 and were released from their contracts. Mullane had accepted an offer from the Louisville Eclipse. Morton and Maskrey were to play with the Cleveland Whites. Green had reportedly gone to work for the New York, Chicago and St. Louis railroad. McPhee and Swartwood were remaining in Akron temporarily. Two days later the reorganization effort was under way in the form of a stock company to buy out the old association and to purchase the uniforms and the right to the grounds.[2]

Said the Cleveland *Leader,* "As soon as matters can be adjusted a club will be organized, as many of the Akrons being retained as possible." The stockholders of the new association met on the evening of July 5 to elect officers and directors. A *Leader* dispatch reported: "Morton returned last night; Maskrey is coming tonight." The relative speed of the reorganization was likely due in part to the fact that the association had received what the *Leader* called "a very flattering offer from St. Louis." The success of the club against the Eclipse in Louisville had earned it an invitation for a series of matches with the Browns in St. Louis. Suddenly, the Akrons, who had been the victim of excessive expectations against major league opposition, were recognized for what they were: a very talented club to be proud of.[3]

This was reflected as the Akron *Daily Beacon* began beating the promotional drum, writing: "Akron's base ball matters are rapidly assuming a tangible and permanent shape. Prominent business men and others have taken hold of the question and are determined that Akron shall have a nine. Their object is not so much to make money, as it is to pay off the debts of the old association and place the reorganized club on a sound financial basis. This can only be successfully accomplished by the hearty co-operation of our citizens. No one will undertake to deny that Akron has not possessed a strong nine, and that the games here are as good as anywhere else. Many citizens and business men will want to see occasionally a game of ball, and they do not want to go to Cleveland to see it, either. The fact is, we have not fully appreciated the excellence of our former club, and finally when our eyes were opened it was too late. Under proper management the Akrons might have cleared several hundred dollars at Louisville, just as well as not. Merely to show that our nine was a good one, the St. Louis Association wrote for games saying that the base ball folks were all agog over the results of the Louisville games and want dates, offering very flattering inducements. Solicitors are now out and we urge upon all to do what they can for Akron's reputation as a base ball town."[4]

While the Akrons were emerging from limbo, reliable catcher Rudy Kemmler was mulling over an offer from the Louisville Eclipse. In the meantime, both the Cleveland catchers were injured, and Kemmler got a brief promotion to the National League for a Cleveland game against visiting Worcester on June 30. Sans contract, Kemmler was "loaned" to Cleveland for the game, but was charged with six errors and three passed balls. Cleveland had eight errors for the game, which Worchester won 6–1.[5]

Born in Chicago in 1860, Kemmler had earlier played two games with Providence of the National League in 1879. After his time with Akron, he first signed with Cincinnati before going to Pittsburgh of the American Association for the 1882 season. In all, he played parts of eight seasons in the majors, a total of 236 games with a lifetime batting average of just 195.[6]

Obviously, his strength was not at the bat, but behind the plate. Despite his showing in the Cleveland-Worcester game, he was a good defensive catcher and had the important characteristic of being extremely durable during a career that began before the introduction of the face mask, chest protector or catcher's mitt. Kemmler had come to the Akrons late in the 1880 season, when the Kansas City club disbanded. Judging from the available box scores, he played in every Akrons game in 1881. It is a testimony to his perceived value as a catcher that when the Cincinnati Reds were being organized for the 1882 season, Kemmler was one of three men signed by Charley Jones when O.P. Caylor sent him out with three blank contracts. The other two men signed were Akron players Bid McPhee

Rudy Kemmler (*New York Clipper*)

and Sam Wise, and the New York *Clipper* noted that all had "made enviable reputations" during the past season.[7]

Kemmler further proved his durability in 1883 with Columbus of the American Association when he caught more games than any other player in the country. Later he signed with the St. Louis Browns for the 1886 season as a backup catcher and was able to share in a championship season.[8]

He spent the 1887 and 1888 seasons in the minors with Duluth and Davenport and spent at least a part of the 1889 season with an amateur team in Chicago before returning to the majors briefly with Columbus. The supposed amateur team was the Butler Bros. Club, which won the amateur championship of Illinois and a purse of $100 against a team from Aurora, Illinois. Nat Hudson pitched and Kemmler caught. Asked the *Sporting Life:* "By the way, what sort of an 'amateur' contest could that have been with such noted professionals as Kemmler and Hudson among the contestants?"[9]

Columbus released him again before the end of the 1889 season, and he apparently spent the rest of his life in Chicago, where he died in June 1909 of heart disease. His death certificate listed him as a laborer and noted the severely gnarled and arthritic condition of his hands.[10]

By July 12, the reorganized Akrons, including "Blondie" Purcell, were ready to make their debut against the White Sewing Machine team on the Akron grounds. Paid admission amounted to $69.90, which meant that about 300 watched the game from inside the park, although attendance was reported as 500. The *Summit County Beacon*, however, noted that the east fence, bordering Union Street, was decorated with crowds of interested spectators. It opined, "There is no use in kicking against fate trying to prevent it. It would take the full force of the Akron police half a day to make an impression."[11]

It did not take nearly that long for the Whites to make an unfavorable impression. At 4:40 P.M., with the score 6–6 after the eighth inning, the Whites picked up their bats and made a quick exit. Said the *Summit County Beacon,* "The crowd didn't realize the maneuver until the retreat had been safely effected or the Whites would certainly have had difficulty in getting out of the gate. It was most assuredly a shabby trick, for more than enough time remained to play the ninth inning at least, and allow the brave Clevelanders opportunity to catch their train. But no; that might involve their losing the game, and so it was out of the question. It is to be hoped that the Whites will never be brought here again. They would certainly meet with a chilly reception and a thin audience." Following the game, Dan Sullivan again signed with the Akrons. He had batted leadoff for the Whites and had collected two hits including a double, the only extra-base hit of the game.[12]

Three days after the tie with the Whites, the Akrons entertained the Detroits in a tight, well-played game. The Akrons got only three hits off Frank Mountain, but bunched them in the top of the seventh inning to cut the Detroit lead to 3–1. Detroit won 6–1. Another three days later, on July 18, the Detroits were back, and this time it took a ninth-inning rally for them to defeat the Akrons 8–7. Mountain again pitched for Detroit, and Purcell, rather than Mullane, was in the box for the Akrons. Mullane, who always fancied himself a shortstop, took that position, and the *Daily Beacon* reported that he played "an immense game at short." Morton, who was sick, moved from short to center. Said the *Beacon,* "Morton's health was almost too low to permit his playing ball, but he played a good game in the field for all that." Purcell, Maskrey and Mullane all doubled, Sam Wise tripled, and Ed Swartwood added a home run. The *Beacon* concluded: "Purcell's pitching was effective but rather wild. This defect will disappear when he is in better practice."[13]

William Aloysius Purcell had a varied major league career that spanned 12 years, beginning as a pitcher with Syracuse and Cincinnati of the National League in 1879 and ending as an outfielder with Philadelphia of the American Association in 1890. At various times he also played first base, third base, shortstop and catcher. As a major league pitcher he appeared in 79 games with a record of 15 wins and 43 losses and a 3.73 ERA. In total he appeared in 1,097 major league games and had 4,563 at bats, 1,217 hits, and lifetime batting average of .267.[14]

Purcell also managed briefly with Philadelphia of the National League in 1883 and in 1886 in Atlanta of the Southern League, where admirers presented him with a gold-headed cane for his efforts. Out of baseball after the 1890 season, he became a professional bookmaker, which pretty much precluded any return to the professional baseball ranks. Still later he became a boxing manager.[15]

Before joining the Akrons, he had played in 20 games in the outfield for Cleveland's National League team and had umpired the Akron's opening game against Cleveland. He was with the Akron team for only about a month before signing to pitch with Buffalo, also of the National League. It was evident that Purcell was not going to stay in Akron long as Detroit of the National League telegraphed him for terms shortly after he joined the Akrons. Purcell answered but got no reply. Then he left Akron on the morning of Aug. 13 without notice. Said the *Summit County Beacon*, "He had promised the management here that he would play with them for the balance of the season, but he silently stole away and signed with the Buffalos. The action of [Orator Jim] O'Rourke of the Buffalos has called out much condemnation, in engaging Purcell without saying anything to the Akron management."[16]

Purcell, however, still had some playing to do for the Akrons, and the revitalized club lost its third straight to a National League team on July 21 when the Clevelands rang up a 4–0 victory. It was the shortest game of the season, just an hour and 14 minutes before a crowd of about 800, as both Mullane of Akron and The Only Nolan of Cleveland pitched well. It was 2–0 in the eighth inning before Nolan doubled home two insurance runs. The Akrons could manage only five singles.[17]

But it was time for a turnaround, and the Keystones of Meadville, Pennsylvania, were just the ticket. The Keystones billed themselves as the champions of Western Pennsylvania and were undefeated when they arrived in Akron on July 22. They confronted an Akron lineup that was in flux. Sullivan had departed for his tryout in Detroit, Kemmler was unable to catch and moved to right field, and an Akron amateur named Weeks was recruited to play center and bat ninth. Wise went to catcher, Morton to third, and Purcell to short with Mullane pitching. No matter. Akron coasted to a 10–0 win, and the *Daily Beacon* declared: "The Akrons, it was evident, had the game in their hands from the first and didn't choose to exert themselves unnecessarily, or the score would have been run up much higher." Attendance for the game wasn't given, but the *Beacon* said it was witnessed by a "larger crowd than an amateur nine can usually bring out." In contrast, the Cleveland *Leader* said, "The attendance, because of the rainy forenoon, was small."[18]

It was the start of a ten-game winning streak for the Akrons, and the second of the victories came on July 23 with a visit to the Whites in Cleveland. The Whites had taken umbrage at being accused of a "shabby trick" in leaving Akron on July 12 with the score tied. In a letter to the *Leader*, later picked up by the *Daily Beacon*, the Whites protested that they had agreed to play if the game started at 2:30 P.M., but that it hadn't started until after 3, and that they had played until 5:05, when the last train to Cleveland on the Valley Railroad was scheduled to leave Akron at 5:16. As it was, they claimed the "gentlemanly conductor" had held the train for them for ten minutes. The Akrons, of course, had claimed that the Whites had walked off at 4:40. Regardless of where the truth rested, the Akrons took no chances, or prisoners, in Cleveland. They pounded out 27 hits in a 29–1 victory as Purcell held the Whites to just two hits.[19]

The Akrons also had a controversy with the Keystones in the wake of their win over the Pennsylvanians. They had an agreement in which the Keystones got a $50 guarantee in Akron, and the Akrons were to get a similar guarantee for a return game in Meadville. Two days after the game the Keystones' captain wrote to Akron that they would not play. Telegrams flew back and forth, but the bottom line was a flat refusal to play a return match. The Cleveland *Leader* reported: "It is understood that $50 was raised in Meadville for the Akrons, but was appropriated by the local club."[20]

Blondie Purcell (National Baseball Hall of Fame Library, Cooperstown, N.Y.)

11

Art, Music, Literature and Left Field

The Akrons had been hoping to arrange a series of games with Pennsylvania teams, but the unwillingness or inability of the Keystones to play sabotaged that plan. Nevertheless, the Akrons traveled to Mercer, Pennsylvania, on July 27 and chalked up a 13–2 win. A wild pitch by Purcell with two outs in the ninth inning allowed the Mercers to tally their two runs. Appropriately, Maskrey's fine fielding in left was cited as a noteworthy feature of the contest.[1]

Samuel Leech Maskrey was playing before his hometown fans. Born in Mercer in 1854, he also died there in 1922 at the age of 68. His major league career was relatively brief, less than five full seasons, as he played with Louisville of the American Association from 1882 through 1885, and with Louisville and Cincinnati in 1886. He appeared in 418 games with 1,601 at bats and a career .225 major league batting average.[2]

Maskrey, however, was in many ways the most interesting of all the Akrons. He had a long and successful minor league career, including managing several teams, and for a season even played, coached and managed in England when A.G. Spalding hired him to teach baseball to one of the teams in an English league Spalding was attempting to start. Moreover, Maskrey had rather universal interests. Quoting from the Louisville *Commercial*, *Sporting Life* reported him to be "a man of more than ordinary literary attainment. He is also a finished artist at the easel, and a musician of no mean ability. He reads Dickens, Thackeray and Bulwer almost constantly during the week."[3]

Indeed, Maskrey apparently took on some literary aspirations of his own, as it was reported in August 1885, and again in January 1886, that he had publishing intentions. Once again quoting from the Louisville *Commercial*, *Sporting Life* reported in the first instance that Maskrey had written a number of "really pretty poems" which were to be published by

Darlinghouse of Boston. At the same time, it reported that he was turning his attention to a novel called "The Ball Players' Board Bill or, The Mystery of a Missing Trunk." Publication was to be within a month. In the second instance, *Sporting Life*, reported that Maskrey would soon publish a book titled "Trips of the Louisvilles," apparently a narrative or memoir of the first four seasons of the Louisville team. His intention to complete that work may have waned when Louisville released him in May 1886. He signed on with Cincinnati but was released again by the end of July when injured Cincinnati players were available to return to the lineup. Said *The Sporting News*, "No better fielder can be found than Maskrey, but he is not heavy enough at the bat."[4]

Whatever may have happened to Maskrey's "Trips of the Louisvilles," at least one version of what happened to his "The Ball Players' Board Bill" can be found in a column written by O.P. Caylor in December 1887. Al Spink, founder of *The Sporting News*, once referred to Oliver Perry Caylor as being "in his day the most famous baseball writer in America." He was also referred to as the "baseball Boswell of the Midwest." He had a distinctive, forceful writing style that included humor, a biting wit, satire and sometimes merciless criticism. When O.P. Caylor unloaded on someone, the victim knew he'd been unloaded upon, and he gave Maskrey's unpublished novel his full satirical treatment.[5]

After relating how Maskrey had worked on the manuscript during the baseball season, carrying a suitcase full of the manuscript and blank paper with him from city to city, and had confided to his teammates that the novel was finished and ready for publication, Caylor wrote that Maskrey had taken the work to a Cincinnati publisher rather than to one in Louisville. Caylor gave his imagination full rein in a story of Maskrey entering the office of the Cincinnati publisher and being invited to read his manuscript while the publisher opened his mail. In his inimitable style Caylor wrote:

> Leach untied his package, picked up three or four hundred pages, cleared his throat and began:
> "Chapter I
> The Death of the Erratic Fielder.
> Imperious Caesar, dead and turned to clay,
> Might stop a hole to keep the wind away."
>
> As Leach's voice died away on the "away," he partially raised his eyes and glanced at the publisher. That worthy had dropped his paper-knife and the letter he had been opening on the floor and wheeled half around in his chair, staring at the youthful author with both eyes popping out of his head. "Ah, ha," thought Leach, "I have already impressed him favorably." Then he continued his reading:

"It was midnight. Not a sound broke the almost Ethiopian stillness of the ball ground, save the mewing of a still-born kitten, which—"

That was all the further Maskrey ever got. The publisher sprang from his chair as though thrown by a catapult and flew through the back door.

By twenty-first century standards the balance of the account was somewhat crude and certainly politically incorrect. Suffice it to say the publisher was painted as being in the back room throwing up, and a black office boy who spoke in dialect appeared to tell Maskrey that the publisher had directed him to weigh Maskrey's paper and give him a quarter of a cent more a pound for it than they generally paid because he had carried it into the office himself.

Concluded Caylor: "Then it was the catapult's turn to work on Leach, only it impelled him toward the front door, and the office boy heard him go down stairs two steps at a time. A vigorous 'blankety-blank-blank' kept time to each jump, while the precious manuscript was knocked all over the office by the vigorous kick which Leach gave it just as he leaped from his chair."[6]

With his major league career behind him, Maskrey played with Milwaukee in the Northwestern League in 1887 and was credited with being "one of the best batsmen" in the league. By 1889, when he was playing with Des Moines in the Western Association, he was called as good a hitter as the club had, and that he gathered in flies "with no apparent trouble."[7]

Maskrey's outfielding skill became a key factor when A.G. Spalding hired him as one of the instructors for the four English baseball clubs which Spalding was sponsoring to popularize the game in England in 1890. In fact, all four of the English clubs—Stoke, Derby, Aston Villa of Birmingham, and Preston North End—were made up of the players of four professional football [soccer] clubs. Football was a winter sport, and the professional teams tried the baseball experiment as a possible source of summer income. Maskrey went to Preston, home of the football champions for the 1889–90 season. According to *Sporting Life*, the president of the Preston North End club took a "great interest in base ball and he is doing all in his power to make his team a good one, and as he is one of those men whom we Americans call a hustler, he will certainly accomplish his object."[8]

In addition to teaching and coaching the Preston players, Maskrey also played 35 games in the outfield for the club, posted a .347 batting average, which was tenth in the English league, and scored 74 runs. His skill as an outfielder particularly impressed the people of Preston, and the players themselves showed their appreciation at the close of the season when they presented him with what *Sporting Life* termed "a costly watch-chain and charm." Maskrey and Jim Hart, another of Spalding's instructors, made a brief tour of Ireland and then sailed home in September 1890.[9]

After his return from England, Maskrey signed to manage the Tacoma team of the Pacific Northwest League and also played for the club, although he did not serve as team captain. Having participated in the Akrons' 19-inning 2–2 tie with the Louisville Eclipse in 1881, he now participated in a 22-inning 6–5 Tacoma victory over Seattle which the *Spalding Guide* called the second longest in baseball history at that time. Maskrey played right field, had three putouts and two assists and hit a double in the game. For the season, however, he hit only .200.[10]

Maskrey returned from the West Coast to his native Mercer, Pennsylvania, and on February 1, 1892 married Olive Goff, another Mercer native who, according to a dispatch to *Sporting Life,* was "one of the fairest, most popular and talented of the many lovely young ladies of this city." Both Maskrey and his bride came from prominent families of the small western Pennsylvania town. His father, William Maskrey, a stonecutter, had come to the community in that capacity and supervised construction of the Mercer County courthouse. He also was credited with planting a large cypress tree that stood on the west side of the courthouse park well into the twentieth century.[11]

Despite his marriage, Maskrey signed to manage the Atlanta club in 1892, but lasted only until June. His experience was not unusual for "damned Yankees" going south in the latter half of the nineteenth century. Although the Atlanta team sustained a number of injuries, leading to a series of losses on the field, *Sporting Life* provided an additional insight, calling him the victim of a cabal. It wrote: "From the first there has been a crowd of fans working against him, and they had the two evening papers working with them. The result was that he has been blamed for everything. To-day, while he was coaching, a runner was caught napping. Then the crowd of fanatics in one corner of the grand stand, who have been howling for Mobile throughout, jeered and hissed Atlanta's manager. After the game, Maskrey went to the directors, and saying that he believed his presence was proving detrimental to the club, asked for his release. There was opposition, but he insisted, and his resignation was accepted."[12]

In subsequent years Maskrey attempted to organize a team at Meadville, Pennsylvania, to enter a proposed Iron and Oil League, and as late as 1901 he was managing an independent team in Warren, Pennsylvania. Most of his time, however, was spent in business with his younger brother, Harry, mostly in the management of hotels. As early as 1896 it was reported that Leech had leased the Revere House in Kent, Pennsylvania.

He was associated with his brother in conducting what was called the St. Cloud hotel and later took over successively the management of the Spier House and the Arlington hotel in Greenville, Pennsylvania. He was confined to his home for about a month before his death, likely suffering from congestive heart failure, and died of a heart attack on April 1, 1922. The local newspaper called him "a man of fine character and ability — a true gentleman. His integrity was unquestioned and he possessed an unfailing courtesy and genial manners that won for him the respect and admiration of all with whom he came in contact."[13]

12

The Streak Continues

The Akrons returned from Mercer to play the Cleveland Red Stockings on July 29 on the Akron grounds, rolling up an easy 15–0 victory behind Mullane's three-hit pitching. The club followed that up on August 2 with a 24–0 win against the visiting Cantons when Mullane hurled a no-hitter. That game also marked the first appearance of William Henry "Bolicky Bill" Taylor with the Akrons. Said the Cleveland *Leader*, "He strengthens that nine very materially."[1]

Like Purcell, Taylor was a baseball nomad. He had first played in Akron in May as a catcher with the Worcesters of the National League. Also like Purcell, "Bolicky Bill" stayed with the Akrons for only about a month before returning to the National League with Cleveland. By the end of the season, he had also migrated to Detroit. His baseball career began in 1876 as a pitcher with the Cass Club of Detroit and continued in 1878 with the Peoria Reds, a well-known semiprofessional team which included six other professionals, including "Old Hoss" Radbourn. There Taylor played left field. Then he played a portion of the 1879 season with Dubuque, the championship club of the Northwest League. Next, after playing a few games with a Denver team, he went to San Francisco where he finished the 1880 season. Between playing with Worcester and the Akrons in 1881, he also had a brief stint with the Bradford, Pennsylvania, club. With the organization of the American Association, he was one of the first players engaged by the Allegheny Club (Pittsburgh) in 1882. Despite all the moving around, Taylor played parts of seven seasons in the major leagues, compiling a lifetime batting average of .277 with 1,164 at bats. He also pitched in 100 major league games, including 84 starts, with a record of 50 wins and 36 losses and a lifetime 3.17 ERA.[2]

A native of Washington, D.C., Taylor tried his hand in the advertising business after his baseball career, but when he died of Bright's disease in Jacksonville, Florida, in 1900, *Sporting Life* reported that he was penniless. He was 45 years old.[3]

With the victory over Canton, the Akrons' streak had reached five victories, during which the club had outscored its opponents 91–3. But it was time for another trip to Louisville, where the going would be tougher. Accordingly, in addition to Purcell and Taylor, the club was strengthened with the signing of Andrew J. Piercy.

He had played for the Cleveland Whites in the Akrons' 29–1 win on July 23, but was already with the Akrons by July 29 when he played shortstop against the Cleveland Red Stockings and contributed two hits in the 15–0 victory. His major league career, such as it was, was behind him when he came to the Akrons. A California native who had come east to play ball, Piercy had a total of two games and eight at bats with Chicago of the National League. After his time with the Akrons in 1881, he returned to the Pacific Coast to play ball, and in 1886 retired from playing to become a manager. He died in San Jose, California, in 1932, at the age of 76.[4]

Purcell, Taylor and Piercy played key roles when the Akrons returned to Louisville for games with the Eclipse on August 4, 6 and 7. After the Akrons' 6–4 win over the Eclipse on August 4 before a crowd of about 1,200, the *Courier-Journal*, noting the new players, reported that the Akron club had been "materially strengthened." In its game summary, it said, "Taylor covered first base almost faultlessly. Purcell made a fine running catch of a red-hot line ball from Pfeffer's bat in center field, and then dropped his laurels by muffing a bum fly." The writer was less impressed with Piercy, but Taylor and Piercy each had one of the Akrons' four doubles, and Piercy played errorless ball at shortstop as manager Morton benched himself.[5]

The Akrons recorded two more wins over the Eclipse by scores of 8–4 and 5–3, the latter before a crowd of about 2,000 on August 7. It was a 1–1 game until the bottom of the seventh inning, when two Eclipse errors opened the door for the Akrons to take a 4–1 lead. Piercy had only two hits in 11 at bats for the three games, had a putout and 11 assists and did not commit an error. Taylor, playing first base and center field, also had only two hits in 12 at bats, but one was a key double. Purcell, who played first base, center field, and pitched, had four hits in 12 at-bats, including a double and a triple. On August 8, the Akrons played a game with the amateur Louisvilles at the Fourth-street Park in that city. The *Courier-Journal* called the Akrons 20–5 victory a fair game, noting that Mullane had played center with Purcell pitching and that Kemmler and Swartwood did the catching. Fred Pfeffer of the Eclipse did the umpiring. The box score, clearly incomplete in terms of various substitutions and position changes, reflects that Taylor also did some of the pitching and that Charlie Morton entered the game at some point because he is credited with hitting a double. Sam

12. The Streak Continues

Wise also had a double for the Akrons, and Swartwood, Wise and McPhee were credited with triples.[6]

Thus the winning streak had reached nine games as the club returned home for an August 10 game with the National League Buffalos. Before a crowd of 600 the Akrons chalked up their tenth straight win, and their first over a league team in 1881. Said the *Daily Beacon*, "It was evident to the far-seeing, from the ferocious appearance of the Akrons, that something would happen before the close of the game and the sagacious immediately put up their quarters on the home team, with great effect."[7]

William H. "Bolicky Bill" Taylor (*New York Clipper*)

Swartwood led off the game with a single and came around to score on three passed balls to put the Akrons on top. In the second inning, they knocked Pud Galvin out of the box when they seized a 3–1 lead. Buffalo scored two runs in the seventh inning to cut the lead to 5–4, but when it was over the Akrons had added a 9–4 win to their streak. Mullane was in the pitching box for the victory, and Taylor led in batting, with four hits, including a home run and a double. Taylor's homer was over the left-field fence, where Galvin was playing after being relieved of his pitching duties. According to the *Daily Beacon*, Galvin mounted the fence and spotted the ball in the hands of an urchin. "Throw it over, Johnny, quick," yelled Galvin, in the *Daily Beacon* report.

"Is he in yet?" yelled back the urchin.

"Just over the home plate," said Galvin.

"Well," said the youth, "I'll hold it awhile and make sure."[8]

The day following the tenth straight win, Swartwood had a tryout with the Buffalos in Cleveland, and on August 12 the Buffalos were back in Akron with revenge on their minds. They scored in the first five innings and coasted to a 17–4 victory, pounding Mullane, Purcell and Taylor in the rout. After the game, Purcell walked away to join the Buffalos.[9]

After the loss that ended the winning streak, the Akrons rebounded with a 26–4 win over the neighboring Kents on August 13, and then met the Detroits again on the Akron grounds on August 15. Mullane held the Detroits to just five hits but was sabotaged by six errors, three of them by Piercy, and lost 4–0. None of the Detroit runs were earned. Taylor had two of the Akrons' six hits.[10]

Then the club rebounded again with a 29–6 victory in East Liverpool, Ohio, over the Crockery City club. The game had been scheduled earlier in the season but had been delayed because it was during the period when the Akrons were being reorganized. When the game was played on August 17, it was a major event in East Liverpool, with many of the trappings of the amateur matches of earlier base ball. The East Liverpool *Tribune* reported:

"The visiting club was met at the train and escorted to the hotel by the 'Old Band,' they having kindly volunteered their services. After dinner the Akrons were taken down to the ball grounds in carriages. The game was called [started] about 3:30, with the Crockerys at the bat, which resulted in a 'goose egg.' As this was the first time our boys had ever met professionals on the diamond, they were naturally nervous, and at no part of the contest did they play anything like the game there were capable of. The Akrons furnished the ball, which was a very lively one, and they being noted as remarkable heavy batters, pounded it for two and three bases. They seemed to be able to send the ball sky skinting away over the fielders' heads, or hot grounders out of the infielders' reach. Fully five hundred people assembled to see how our boys could hold up against the crack club of Ohio, who do nothing but play ball. Mullane, their terrific pitcher, who puzzles the league players, put them in for eight innings with such a mysterious curve that the Crockerys did not earn a run. In the last inning the Akrons put in Swartwood, a straight but very swift pitcher, when the Crockerys fell on the ball for five runs. The score makes us blush to mention."[11]

The Crockery Citys earlier had run into shabby treatment in both Canton and Kent and the *Tribune* subsequently made special mention of a report in the Akron *Daily Beacon* that "Our boys [the Akrons] report a very pleasant time and say that they have not enjoyed such courtesies anywhere this season as was shown them during their stay in East Liverpool. They are very grateful to their fellow ball-players and will reciprocate at their earliest opportunity."[12]

Back home, the Akrons chalked up their second and final victory against a National League club with an 8–6 decision over the Detroits before what had to be a disappointing crowd estimated at between 400 and 500. Mullane appeared to have the game well in hand when it was halted after the seventh inning so the Detroits could catch the train to Chicago. While all of this was happening, Morton was advertising through the New York *Clipper* to arrange a trip for the "strengthened" team through New York, New Jersey and Pennsylvania. Apparently, no Eastern clubs wanted a piece of the Akrons, and it was just as well. Before long Taylor walked away to join the Clevelands and Mullane's last appearance with the Akrons was in the box for the win over Detroit on August 19. On August 27, he made his National League debut with the Detroits.[13]

13

A College Boy

From early July when the club was being reorganized until the middle of August 1881, while Morton and the club directors were always searching for men to fill the vacancies, one of the players they wanted was Ed Andrews. In fact, on July 7, the Cleveland *Leader* reported, "The association would like to know the whereabouts of Andrews of last year's Elyrias." Eventually, the search was successful as Andrews made his first appearance in an Akrons' box score as the center fielder in the 4–0 loss to Detroit on August 15. On August 17, the *Summit County Beacon* reported that "Andrews, of last year's Elyrias, has been engaged by the Akrons." This is the Andrews who had played for Western Reserve College against the Akrons in their final game of the 1880 season. Although he did not join the 1881 club until mid–August, it is significant that in his 1885 interview Charlie Morton included Andrews as one of the nine players who made up "the celebrated team that represented Akron, Ohio."[1]

George Edward "Ed" Andrews was born in Painesville, Ohio, in 1859, and, as a college graduate, looked forward to a business career. After playing for the Akrons in 1881, he left baseball and in 1883 he was a stenographer for the Jackson Iron Company of Cleveland. In his own words he was "well liked, well paid and contented. No one could possibly be better situated." Nevertheless, he wasn't forgotten and was recruited once again by Morton, this time to play third for the Toledo team in the Northwestern League. He took a month's leave from his job and went to Toledo to help Morton win the league pennant.[2]

It was at Toledo that Andrews came to the attention of Harry Wright. Wright not only played for but managed the first purely professional team, the Cincinnati Red Stockings of 1869 and '70. Later he was a player-manager for the Boston club of the National Association, and managed Boston in the National League before moving to Providence of the National League, and finally to Philadelphia, also of the National League, in 1884. His integrity was unquestioned.[3]

13. A College Boy

Andrews recalled that Wright had learned of him in Toledo and "made advances to me after I had resumed my position in Cleveland and kept at me until I was dissatisfied with my place. Finally I was worked on so that I threw up my position and signed for $2,000." That was the beginning of Andrews' major league career as he played with Philadelphia of the National League from 1884 through 1888, and with Philadelphia and Indianapolis in 1889, before jumping to become an outspoken advocate of the Players League, where he played for the Brooklyn club in 1890. With the demise of the Players League, he played with Cincinnati in 1891 and then walked away from the game, largely due to his intense dissatisfaction with the team owners. In eight seasons he had 3,233 at bats with a lifetime average of .257. His chief tool was speed, and he stole 205 bases in six seasons, from 1886 until the end of his career. Stolen bases were not tallied in 1884 and 1885.[4]

Ed Andrews (National Baseball Hall of Fame Library, Cooperstown, N.Y.)

Embroiled in a bitter contract dispute in 1888, Andrews ostensibly wrote a letter to a friend, and the friend ostensibly passed the letter along to the *Sporting Life* for publication. In it he characterized his initial contract with Philadelphia as "going straight into a trap." He had made a belated discovery of the reserve clause and complained, "Imagine my astonishment when after a season's work they cruelly informed me I had been cut $300." In fact, his initial major league season was mediocre at best with just a .221 batting average. Nevertheless, in 1886 he led the National League in stolen bases with 56, and in 1887 he had hit a career high .355 with 57 steals, so he had plenty of ammunition for the 1888 salary dispute.[5]

While seeking top dollar for his baseball talents, Andrews kept his contacts in the business world, and in 1886 spent part of the off-season working in the office of an Akron rubber company. By the winter of 1887–88, he was working for a Detroit company and was in Philadelphia on business when he had an interview with team owner Al Reach. Andrews' purpose was to find out the terms on which he might purchase his release. According to *Sporting Life*, "He was informed that the Philadelphia Club would not part with him on any terms. Ed has nothing against the club or the city, and is willing to play for a substantial increase in salary, but thinks he could make much better terms elsewhere if he could purchase his release. He informed Mr. Reach that seven League clubs wanted him. Al's reply was that eight clubs wanted him, and that as soon as Ed would make his terms the Philadelphia Club would do business with him. Andrews left town, however, without indicating his desires as to salary, but Reach anticipated no trouble in both sides coming to a satisfactory understanding with Andrews as soon as he realized that the Philadelphia Club will not let him go to any other club."[6]

Andrews' attitude toward Reach was reflected in the letter published in *Sporting Life* later that month. "All the country knows how I stand and have always stood as a batter, fielder, and base-runner for three years. Yet they have not done me justice and I have forgotten how to respect them," Andrews wrote. "They might give me $5,000. Still my heart would not be in the work. When one man gets it into his head another is unjust, and has learned to heartily dislike him and his methods, it is time to part. And that is how I feel toward Mr. Reach," Andrews continued. "I wish Mr. Reach would accept one of the many offers for me and have foresight enough to see that I cannot possibly be of any use to him. Money can not make one man respect another."[7]

While Andrews had a hearty dislike for Reach, his unhappiness did not extend to Harry Wright, the man who had first persuaded him to go to Philadelphia. When Wright died in 1895, Andrews told a story that reflected upon the character of both men. According to Andrews' recollection: "I can recall two instances in which angered by continued defeat, I had opportunities to win the games by cutting third base. The first was in Detroit. Gaffney was umpiring, and, not expecting such a thing from me, turned his back and I cut the base 20 feet, and was thus enabled to score the winning run. As I walked up to the bench, where Harry was sitting, he looked at me with his face as white as a sheet, saying: 'Ed, don't ever let me see you do that again. I don't want any games won in that way.' To tell the truth, I felt like a chicken thief, and particularly so when Gaffney asked at dinner if I cut the base and I said I did. He looked at me reproachfully says, [sic] 'Well, Andy, I didn't think you were that kind of a player.' The second instance referred to was in Chicago the next day, and it is safe to say that I didn't cut the bag, and I lost the game by not doing it."[8]

The year after his 1888 contract dispute he became a stalwart of the Players' League. Twenty-four years later, when another players' revolt was looming and the Federal League was on the horizon, Andrews authored a series of articles for *Sporting Life*, warning both sides to learn from the lessons of history. Andrews wrote, "I can well remember the amount of ginger I threw into the old players' movement, having the big end of the newspaper work for our side during those strenuous times, but I now say my big mistake was my connection with that revolt."[9]

On November 10, 1913, David Fultz, president of the Base Ball Players' Fraternity, had sent to the National Commission and the National Board certified copies of the players' demands. Commenting on this, Andrews advised, "I wish to say to the magnates also do not mess up the whole matter by a bull-headed refusal to hear patiently what the players have to say. It was just such a fool management that caused the break with us 24 years ago, and this last remark is caused by an interview reported to have been given by Mr. Herrmann of the Cincinnati Club, in which he is made to say that Mr. Fultz would not be heard. There is absolutely no used in having nearly murdered the game once without learning something beneficial from the near crime. So then, to the magnates I say if you have any idea of refusing to hear the players' side of it just take a walk around the block and change your mind." Referring to the players' demands, he added there was "not one of them that cannot be settled with several ounces of brains on each side being used sensibly in a calm discussion." Finally, reflecting on the situation as it existed in 1890, he wrote, "The irony of the whole mess simply makes me sick."[10]

In delving more deeply into his personal history of the 1890 revolt, Andrews continued, "We now know that just three players from our Brotherhood were the ones for which we all suffered, and without one exception they all handed us the biggest, yellowist, lemon when it came to a show down. I well remember the shock when I learned that the very men for whom we were supposed to be bleeding and dying for jumped from our Brotherhood and went over to the enemy, and I am sorry to say that of the full team that John Ward had signed, with my assistance, for Brooklyn, only three reported. I sincerely hope that no more of that rottenness will crop out now."[11]

Picking up the story in his next article, he wrote, "Three of the star players of the Indianapolis team never visited another city that they did not make it a point to drop into the home club's dressing quarters a few minutes before each game, and continuously yap about their hard luck in having to play ball in such a rotten town as Indianapolis. ... The horrible injustice of the reserve rule was so continuously harped on that the majority of the different players finally worked themselves up to the point where they really thought they were the worst used lot of men alive; myself included."[12]

Andrews, who had been trying for years to get out of Philadelphia, was dealt to Indianapolis, then owned by John T. Brush, late in the 1889 season. At the time of the move he knew he was headed to Brooklyn with John Montgomery Ward in 1890. In his recollections, Andrews then gives an insight into his own lack of guile and Brush's shrewdness. "Mr. Brush I always liked well," Andrews wrote. "We usually sat together on our trips, as at that time he nearly always went with us, and as the season drew to a close the Brotherhood was mentioned between us. We discussed it pro and con, the contracts, the reserve rule, and a hundred little things connected with the game, from club owners' and players' viewpoints." Andrews recalled, "One day Mr. Brush asked me point blank if I had taken any side in the then impending fight. I said 'yes, but was pledged to absolute silence.' It was only a few days before the close of the season and little did I know that Mr. Brush, who had asked me the above question, knew far more about our Brotherhood plans than I did myself."[13]

Andrews summed up the 1890 Players League experience in these words: "Everything was chaos, no people to see us play, salaries long overdue along the last of the season and personally I had foreseen the result. I had never said a word about my salary. In fact, I was so sore and disgusted that had it not been for payments coming due on my Florida farm, I doubt if I would have said a word. All this time the truth was gradually leaking out as to what Glasscock and others had really gotten out of their betrayal of us."[14]

When his personal financial condition forced Andrews to go to see Wendell Goodwin, backer of the Brooklyn team, Goodwin told him that the team was broke. Goodwin, however, gave him a personal check for what was due him. At that point Andrews believed he was done with baseball for good. He took a job as private secretary to the president of the Seventh National Bank in Philadelphia. Then, on the day before the 1891 season opened, he got a telegram from Mike Kelly, manager of the Cincinnati Club in the American Association. As Andrews tells the story, the telegram read: "'What will you play with the old sport for. King Kell.' I thought this over, with a decided smile, and wired terms. Back came an answer closing the deal — reading thus: 'You are mine. Report at once. If you have no carfare walk. Kell.'"[15]

13. A College Boy

Andrews characterized his 1891 season as a nightmare and walked away from the game as a player at its close. His experience led him to include a treatise on baseball finances in the third of his 1913 columns, writing: "Every business has its positive limits of burden it can carry in expenses. Base ball is no exception and the limit of expense has been reached. If the game is to continue attractive to capital and is to continue the clubs must have a margin of safety, and any league, whether it be the Federal or any other who, in order to secure the stars of the game, says to them: 'You are getting $3,000; we'll give you $5,000,' are simply spiking down their own coffin for an early burial."[16]

Ever the businessman at heart, Andrews had not been neglecting his future. He had first visited Florida in 1884 and thereafter cruised Florida waters each winter with his father, a former Great Lakes captain. He invested in property, which he referred to as his Florida farm. In 1888 he had married a Philadelphia woman, and in 1891 he moved the entire family to what *Sporting Life* referred to as his "pineapple plantation" on the Indian River near Fort Pierce in Florida.[17]

Andrews, however, was not finished with baseball. In 1895 he umpired in the National League for a time until he suffered a broken leg. Then he wrote baseball spring training reports for several newspapers in 1896. In 1898 he joined former Akron teammate Ed Swartwood as a National League umpire and returned to the league again in 1899 for about half a season before he resigned, apparently in disgust. *Sporting Life* said he particularly blamed three managers—Buck Ewing, Ned Hanlon, and Patsy Tebeau for the umpires' troubles "as they continually insist upon and bully for everything close or not close. These three men, says Andrews further, are the largest factors in the manifest decline of popular interest in the game."[18]

In 1899 he moved his family to West Palm Beach and became associated in business with Henry M. Flagler, managing the casino and yacht basin in Palm Beach. After leaving the service of the Florida East Coast Hotel company, he took up real estate development in West Palm Beach and nearby locations. Later he organized the Pinewood Deep Springs Water Company.[19]

Andrews even tried to combine baseball with his Florida real estate development efforts. In 1913, at the same time he was recalling the Players' League revolt of 1890, he also was promoting what he called a "national training camp" for baseball teams. "Do not confound this great enterprise with smaller movements of any small town or company fixing up grounds for any one team," he wrote. "Our plan calls for perfection of equipment from our own hotel to everything years of experiments have taught me to understand, namely perfect playing fields as good as any in the world, running track for straight away work, hand ball, tennis, squash, and after a workout the finest salt and freshwater showers, plunges, rubbing tables and steam facilities, recreation in the evening, billiards, bowling, etc., and then the ocean bathing."[20]

He identified himself as an old, successful league player. "I know the game and what is needed to get in shape," he wrote in a pitch directly to other ball players. "I have started our stock subscription list with $50,000. I want every prosperous ball player in America to take as much stock as he can afford to take. I have four hundred thousand dollars worth of real estate to sell to carry this plan. One hundred thousand dollars worth now ready and the rest to be developed." He made a similar pitch to club owners, with investments to be sent to the Pioneer Bank in West Palm Beach. Investments in the National Resort and Training Park Company were to pay 33 percent for three years and then ten percent a year afterward.[21]

Farsighted as it may have been, Andrews' plan was, at best, premature. In 1914 just four of the 16 major league baseball clubs went to Florida for spring training.[22]

While he promoted baseball and other athletic endeavors in the Palm Beach area, his most abiding interest was in waterway development, particularly the establishment of a port and improvement of the East Coast canal, leading eventually to the Intracoastal Waterway. In 1933, he attended a celebration of the golden anniversary of the organization of the Phillies, and was the oldest former player to appear on the field. He was a frequent contributor to outdoor and yachting publications, and had just returned home to West Palm Beach from a trip to the Florida Keys, where he had gone for magazine material, when he suffered a heart attack. Hailed by the local newspaper as a "pioneer developer and sportsman," Andrews was 75 when he died in 1934.[23]

14

Some Country Hardball

Despite the additions of Andy Piercy and Ed Andrews to the Akrons' roster, the departures of Purcell, Taylor, and finally Mullane after the August 19 win over Detroit left the club short-handed. In particular, the Akrons needed another pitcher before they left on the long-anticipated trip to meet the Brown Stockings in St. Louis. The first place Charlie Morton looked for help was the Cleveland Whites. He came away with two players—Len Stockwell and Daniel Albion "Jumping Jack" Jones. When the Akrons took the field at the Grand Avenue grounds in St. Louis on the sultry afternoon of August 27, Piercy, Andrews, Stockwell and Jones were all in the lineup with Jones in the pitching box.[1]

The Akrons came to St. Louis with a hard-earned reputation. They had earned the invitation on the basis of their first visit to Louisville, including the 19-inning tie with the Eclipse. Since then they had also managed to defeat two National League teams and to sweep another series with the Eclipse. When their first St. Louis game was halted by darkness after seven innings that Saturday the Akrons had earned a 10–5 victory over the Browns before what the St. Louis *Globe-Democrat* called a large audience.[2]

With its first victory, the Akron club added the grudging respect of the discerning St. Louis cranks to the reputation that had preceded it. The reporter for the Missouri *Republican* wrote, "The Akrons played a magnificent game, their base running being simply superb, and their batting a perfect wonder." The writer for the *Globe Democrat* said, "The Akrons play a strong game, their fielding and base running being very good. They are as fine a looking lot of ball tossers as are likely to be seen."[3]

Among the newcomers in the Akron lineup, Stockwell was well acquainted with many of his teammates, not only because he had played against them with the Whites, but because of an earlier connection with the Davenport, Iowa, club of the late 1870s. Stockwell played with Davenport for parts of the 1877, '78 and '79 seasons. Those clubs also included

Bid McPhee and Leech Maskrey of the Akrons, and Rudy Kemmler joined them on the 1878 and '79 clubs.[4]

Stockwell, who was born in Cordova, Illinois, in 1859, and died in Niles, California, at the age of 45, played in six major league games spread over twelve years with a total of 23 at-bats and a lifetime batting average of .136. He played in two games with Cleveland of the National League in 1879, two with Louisville of the American Association in 1884, and two more with Cleveland of the National League in 1890.[5]

Nevertheless, in a profile published in December 1882, the New York *Clipper* called him a "promising young professional" who had begun his baseball career with amateur teams in Davenport. Said the *Clipper*, "In 1877 he was engaged by the Davenport Club, and creditably filled the positions of centre-field and change-catcher, showing remarkable skill behind the bat and proving himself to be a heavy batter. After the Davenports disbanded, he was engaged by the Forest City Club of Fort Madison, Iowa, for the remainder of the season. His hard hitting enabled the Forest Citys to win first prize in a tournament of Illinois clubs, he making a home-run after two men were out in the last inning and bringing in three runs. In 1878 he was again engaged by the Davenport Club, alternating as centre-field and catcher. At the close of the season he went to Texas, having accepted an engagement with the Stars of Dallas to catch for and captain their newly organized nine. He remained South until the season of 1879 opened, when he rejoined the Davenports, but not to remain, as he was soon engaged by the new professional club of Council Bluffs, Iowa, where he played as catcher and captained the nine until the end of a very successful season. In 1880 he was engaged by the Westerns of Topeka, Kansas, and again filled the catcher's position, where he won himself a name, as well as one for his club, who found him to be a very valuable acquisition to their playing strength. He also showed himself to be an unusually hard hitter, by making four successive safe hits, including two home runs, in one game off Rowe's pitching. During the last two seasons he caught for the representative organization of his native place. He stands 5 ft. 11 in. in height, weighs 165 lb., and is very active and graceful in his movements behind the bat, being a sure catch and a swift and accurate thrower. He has also ranked high as a batsman each season, and may be commended as an honest, hard-working young player, who always strives for the best interests of his club."[6]

In 1885 he played for Milwaukee, and in 1886 with the Savannah, Ga., club as a catcher. He requested and received his release from Savannah about midseason, and ended up with Eau Clair of the Northwestern League. During the 1887 season he caught for St. Paul. Later he served as an umpire in the Illinois-Iowa League and as manager of the Galesburg team in the Iowa League.[7]

Jones, a native of Litchfield, Connecticut, would have been 21 years old in 1881, and was a student at Yale. He subsequently made 12 pitching starts with Detroit of the National League in 1883 and another seven starts that same season with Philadelphia of the American Association, posting a total major league record of 11–7 with a 3.14 ERA in 157 innings. His "Jumping Jack" appellation stemmed from an exaggerated pitching delivery in which he jumped into the air with both arms extended over his head before hurling the ball to the plate. In his later managerial travels, Morton frequently attracted players from his earlier teams, and in 1883, in addition to his 19 major league starts, Jones also pitched with Toledo of the Northwestern League. That championship club won its league title under Morton's management.[8]

Lenny Stockwell (*New York Clipper*)

The Akrons' St. Louis debut was about as rough and tumble a baseball game as it is possible to play. It was shortened to seven innings because of darkness, but the game had been slowly played because of repeatedly injuries to the players. George "Jumbo" McGinnis, chief pitcher for the Browns, was the first to bite the dust. In the third inning Ed Swartwood hit a line drive off McGinnis' pitching hand, which was described by the Missouri *Republican* as "taking the top nearly off the index finger." Substitutions were not allowed, so McGinnis went to the outfield where he put a "plaster" on his finger and wrapped a spool of thread around it. But on the first ball pitched by the Browns' "change" pitcher, the catcher took a foul tip just below the breastbone, and the game was delayed again while the catcher regained his breath. He then also went to the outfield and the Browns shuffled positions again.[9]

After Akron had scored six runs, McGinnis and the starting catcher came back out of the outfield to resume their original positions. The Akrons also suffered injuries in the game. McPhee and Stockwell both took foul balls off their own bats that glanced up and hit them in the head, and Ed Swartwood suffered an unspecified injury that was sufficient to keep him out of the game the next day. While the Akrons won 10–5, the *Republican* reported, "At times it looked as though one nine was trying to kill all the members of the other."[10]

The Missouri *Republican* headlined its account of the game of August 28 with the word "Sluggers," and called the contest an "old-time game of ball." The St. Louis *Globe-Democrat,* headed its story, "The Leather Larrupers," and said the game was a "regular old-fashioned hard-hitting, 'bum'-fielding and run-getting contest." The two papers also agreed that the crowd at the Grand Avenue grounds was the largest in years. Said the *Republican,* "Over seven thousand persons, by actual count, passed the gates. Although new seats had been erected, the seating capacity was not sufficient to accommodate the crowd and the results was a great ring of persons around the players." The *Globe-Democrat* had a smaller estimate, reporting, "There were at least 5,000 spectators in attendance, all the stands and the extra seats erected during the week being thronged. In addition to this the grounds were encircled by a crowd six deep in some places. The diamond, owing to the drought, was as hard as adamant, and the two balls used—one was lost—were of the liveliest description."[11]

The result was an 18–14 Browns victory with the teams combining for 35 hits and 16 errors. And, like the Saturday contest, it was a game marked by injuries. Ed Swartwood, hurt on Saturday, sat out the Sunday game for the Akrons. Jumbo McGinnis had his finger sewn up overnight and wore a glove on his pitching hand. The *Globe-Democrat* called McGinnis "practically disabled," explaining, "His injured finger was so sore that his pitching was not to be compared to what it usually is." Notwithstanding, McGinnis pitched the entire game for the Browns. Jones, who again started for the Akrons, was not so fortunate. He strained his arm, and Ed Andrews served as the Akron "change pitcher." Jones' injury, however, was not the only one for the Akrons as Andrews "bucked his head against the home plate," Rudy Kemmler hit Magner, the Browns' leftfielder, in the pit of the stomach, apparently in a play at the plate, and Andy Piercy, playing shortstop for Akron, was hit in the face by a ball and suffered a black eye. The *Republican* reported that a boy in the crowd said, "If this keeps on, the Akrons will all be dead men before they leave St. Louis."[12]

The *Globe-Democrat* singled out Wise, Stockwell and Jones of the Akrons for particular mention because of their hitting, each had three hits in the game. The *Republican* made special note of another player, reporting, "Maskrey, for the visitors, played a splendid game at left, going clear into the crowd twice and taking the ball on the run." It could also have noticed that Maskrey had a double and a triple.[13]

After the slugfest, the Akrons and the Browns met again on the Grand Avenue grounds August 29, and the Akrons came away with an easy 14–4 win. The St. Louis papers made much of the injured condition of the Browns. The *Globe-Democrat* reported, "The Browns appeared in a terribly crippled condition. In their strait Dan Morgan, of the Reds [another St. Louis team], was called on to do the pitching; Seward was sent behind the bat; Baker went to right, and McGinnis to center field, while McCaffrey was called in to play second base. In those positions the Browns made a very poor showing against the fine fielding and hard hitting of the Akrons, who played a quiet earnest game throughout."[14]

The St. Louis papers did not mention, however, that the Akrons had also sustained injuries during the first two games, and that Jumping Jack Jones, their starting pitcher in those games, was, like McGinnis of the Browns, unavailable to do the hurling in the third contest. In fact, Morton, who had benched himself in the latter part of the season and turned over shortstop to Piercy, took the field that Monday as the Akrons' starting pitcher. At some point, likely the fourth inning when the Browns scored three runs, Morton and Piercy switched positions for the balance of the game. The Akrons were to leave St. Louis bound for Louisville on a Tuesday morning train. The *Republican* concluded, "They were very well pleased with their reception here. A good crowd was out yesterday to bid them good-by." With a bit more edge, the *Globe-Democrat* opined, "They will be here again, perhaps, later in the season, when the Browns will show them what they can do when their men are in anything like shape."[15]

The Akrons were well rested by the time they played the Louisville Eclipse again on September 3, coasting to an easy 14–2 win as the Eclipse committed 14 errors and Akron only two. Piercy pitched, Morton played short and Jumping Jack Jones served as umpire. Said the Louisville *Courier-Journal*, "Piercy pitched effectively yesterday, but he is far easier to hit than Mullane, and the boys will get on to him hard enough to-day if they try."[16]

The Eclipse tried, but Piercy again held them to just two runs in a 3–2 Akrons' victory on September 4. After this game the *Courier-Journal* headline called them the "Invincible Akrons," and the game story said, "The Akrons after a hard fight captured the contest and once more convinced the public of the fact that they are ball players and unquestionably the strongest non–League team in the country." The game was not decided until the ninth inning when the Eclipse had the bases loaded with none out and the heart of their batting order coming up, but were unable to score.[17]

The triumphant Akrons returned home and defeated the Oberlin College team 14–0 on September 7. Piercy and Swartwood pitched for the Akrons and held the college boys, who were called "a little rusty from want of practice," to just four hits. The Walker brothers, Moses Fleetwood at catcher and Welday at short, were unavailable for the Oberlins, but it probably would have made little difference in the outcome as the Akrons pounded out 20 hits and played errorless ball. The same day it was reported that the club had cleared $400 on its western trip. Apparently satisfied with the results, the club directors officially disbanded the team on September 9.[18]

But the end was not yet. There was money to be made in St. Louis, and the bulk of the team stayed together under Morton's leadership for one last trip as a co-operative club. Ed Andrews and Jumping Jack Jones did not make the trip, and Morton had to find replacements. They were Harry Arundel and Frank Mountain. Both were pitchers.

Arundel in some respects was the more local of the two, and was definitely the least significant of the two. He had been born in Philadelphia, Pennsylvania, in 1855 and apparently came to Cleveland sometime in 1879 with another ball player named Joe Ardner as a battery. Pitchers and catchers often moved together from team to team in those days. Arundel had some success because he was an early practitioner of the curve ball. His major league career was brief as he pitched for Pittsburgh of the American Association in 1882, and one game for Providence of the National League in 1884. His lifetime record was five wins, ten losses and a 4.40 ERA in 129 innings. In 1881, he had been playing for Findlay, Ohio, when Morton recruited him for the final St. Louis trip. Eventually, he returned to Cleveland, where he settled down as an insurance agent and died in March 1904 of Bright's disease, leaving a widow and 6-year-old son.[19]

Frank H. Mountain (*New York Clipper*)

Mountain, on the other

hand, came to the vagabond former Akrons with a more impressive resume and higher expectations. Born in Fort Edward, New York, in 1860, he first took an interest in baseball while attending the Union Classical Institute in Schenectady, New York. It was said that as a high school student he would dash from school to the college campus and join in the games with the college boys. When he finally entered college, he soon captured the position of second base on the varsity nine. His reputation, however, came as a pitcher when he helped the club win the state college championship in 1880. That summer he made his professional debut with Troy of the National League and hurled the club to a five-hit victory over Chicago.[20]

According to his obituary, "Just before he graduated in 1881, Mountain received a message from Detroit to report for a tryout in New York where the team was playing at the time. Mountain packed a clean collar, told his family he would be back next day and was off to the big city." His "tryout" involved pitching two successive games, apparently one in the afternoon of his arrival and the other the next morning. He was effective each day, giving up just one run and five hits in each appearance. Mountain then remained with the Detroits until the latter part of August that year when he was released and apparently joined Haverly's Mastadon Minstrels. That was not as unusual as it may sound, because in that era a number of traveling theatrical companies also had baseball teams as an added attraction.[21]

In any event, Mountain was free to join the barnstorming Akrons in September 1881 for the final trip to St. Louis, and he was exactly what Morton was looking for: a man with a fastball, an effective curve, and good control.[22]

In 1882 he pitched for Worcester in the National League and Philadelphia in the American Association. Then he spent two years with the Columbus, Ohio, club in the American Association and finished up his major league career with Pittsburgh, also in the Association in 1885–86. He had a lifetime major league record of 58–83 in 142 starts covering 1,215 innings with a 3.47 ERA. He also played another 51 games as an outfielder, first baseman and shortstop with 717 at-bats and a lifetime .220 batting average.[23]

For Mountain, who later claimed that "modern" pitchers didn't pitch enough, his career was defined by his two seasons in Columbus. In 1883 he started 59 games, had 57 complete games, posted a 26–33 record and had a 3.60 ERA. He followed that up in 1884 with 42 appearances including 41 starts with 40 complete games, a 23–17 record and a 2.45 ERA. Thus, in two seasons he had pitched in 101 games, made 100 starts, had 97 complete games, and pitched 863 innings. It was small wonder that his arm went dead before the end of the 1884 season. In his two subsequent seasons with Pittsburgh he pitched in only seven games.[24]

The quiet and unassuming Mountain was mentioned early in 1887 as a probable manager if a Columbus team was organized for the proposed Ohio State League, but within a month he had declined the job because he intended to go into business in Schenectady. Then in October he notified the Columbus club that he would like to pitch and manage the team in 1888. Instead, he was appointed manager of the Toledo team for 1888, and by August of that year he was umpiring in the Tri-State League.[25]

After the 1888 season, Mountain took a job as a railway postal clerk on the Syracuse to New York City route. Later he went to work for General Electric in Schenectady and was assistant fire chief for nearly 40 years, retiring in 1930. In 1937, the National and American Leagues sent Mountain a silver lifetime pass as a Christmas present "in appreciation of his long and meritorious service." He died at his Schenectady home in 1939 at the age of 79.[26]

15

Into the Mist

The first of the three final games was played in St. Louis on September 17, with the Browns determined to show the upstart Akrons something about ball playing. Jumbo McGinnis, injured on the Akrons' first trip to St. Louis, was primed and ready, but so was Frank Mountain. The Browns managed just three singles off Mountain, but the Akrons, in turn, got only three hits off McGinnis, although two of them were doubles by Kemmler and Wise. Aided by errors and five passed balls by Kemmler, who had as much trouble with Mountain's curve as did the Browns' hitters, the Browns scored a single run in the third and three more in the fourth. The Akrons responded with a single run in the sixth and two in the seventh on three errors and a two-run single to center by Morton to pull within 4–3. It was as close as they got. In the end, the Missouri *Republican* called Mountain "by all odds the best man in the position that has visited St. Louis this year." He was, however, undermined by nine Akron errors and Kemmler's passed balls in the 5–3 loss.[1]

Mountain and McGinnis faced each other again the next day before a large Sunday crowd. The *Republican* called it "the largest crowd of the year," and said it numbered 6,500 "by actual count." It added: "Every seat in the park had an occupant, and there was a great crowd around the players, but, thanks to the park's officers, all were kept in bounds, and the field kept clear throughout the contest." The *Globe-Democrat* was just a bit more conservative, reporting: "A more delightful day could not have been desired, and the weather clerk, who has been extremely kind throughout the season, has the thanks of the fraternity. There never was a larger crowd at the Grand Avenue Park, every inch of seating capacity being occupied, and the grounds bordering the enclosure being thronged. The number present, as shown by the gate receipts, was between 5,000 and 6,000."[2]

However big the crowd, they were treated to another tight game which was in doubt until the final out as the Browns came from behind to hand the Akrons their second straight loss, 10–8. McGinnis and Mountain again were more effective than the score would indicate as the Browns were charged with 12 errors and the Akrons with eight. The Akrons held a 7–5 lead after five innings, but the Browns rallied for three in the sixth inning and two more in the ninth. It was getting quite dark by the time the Akrons came to bat in the bottom of the ninth, trailing 10–7. With two outs in the bottom of the ninth, Kemmler was safe on an error, stole third and scored on a wild throw. Maskrey also was safe on the third Browns' error, bringing Bid McPhee to the plate representing the tying run. McPhee lofted a high foul pop-up and George Seward, then catching for the Browns, dropped the ball but grabbed it again on the first bounce. McPhee was out under the foul bound rule, a foul ball caught on the first bounce being an out.[3]

Between these two evenly matched teams, it may have been inevitable that the final game, a 13–11 win by the Akrons, ended in discord with the Browns' claiming that they had been robbed by the umpire, and the newspapers offering the excuse that the home team had been crippled by injuries. Yet, Andy Piercy, who had relieved Mountain in the second game, started the game in the pitching box for the Akrons, and Harry Arundel started in center field.[4]

From the Browns' perspective, as detailed in the St. Louis newspapers, the problem was with umpire John Peters, a veteran major league ballplayer who had been with Buffalo of the National League during the 1881 season. It started in the bottom of the sixth inning after the Browns had rallied to take a 6–5 lead in the game. Arundel led off with a single to right, and Swartwood followed with a grounder through short. Arundel went to third and Swartwood attempted to go to second while the ball was being retrieved. The Browns believed Swartwood was thrown out at second, but Peters called him safe. Sam Wise then pounded another ball to short and Arundel attempted to score. Again the umpire called him safe, and the Akrons went on to score eight runs and take a 13–6 lead.[5]

While the St. Louis fans hooted and howled at these decisions, the real controversy came in the ninth inning. The Browns had rallied for four runs in the seventh and went to the top of the ninth trailing 13–10. After an out, Seward and Cuthbert hit safely for the Browns with Seward advancing to third. Leech Maskrey, attempting to make a play on Seward at third, threw the ball past Wise and into foul territory. Seward attempted to score, but Wise threw to Kemmler at the plate and Peters called the runner out. The St. Louis papers believed that this was the decisive play, but the fact is that McGinnis followed the play with a single and then was picked off first and tagged out in a run-down between McPhee and Len Stockwell. While the rundown was going on Cuthbert scored the final run for the

Browns, but the fact is that if McGinnis had not been picked off the Browns would still have had a chance to tie or win the game.⁶

While blaming the umpire for the loss, the Missouri *Republican* offered him a word of consolation, such as it was. It said, "This does not mean that Peters meant to be anything but impartial, but that he erred in judgment and was assisted in so doing by the shouts of disapproval which were leveled at him at so many points of the game."⁷

It was the last game for the Akrons. The team's brief moment of splendor was about to fade into the mists of baseball history. But the players undoubtedly were happy to split up the proceeds from the big St. Louis crowds before they went their separate ways, and Morton must have had a smile on his face when he headed back to Akron that night on the train with cash in his pocket and the satisfaction of a job well done. Morton had been the key man, if not on the diamond, then certainly in keeping the club together, stocked with top-notch talent capable of playing against the best opposition.

Like so many independent town teams, the Akrons were never far from the edge of collapse. The end could easily have come after the first trip to Louisville. But, as much as the investments of Akron businessmen were essential, so, too were Morton's leadership and personal qualities that kept the team together. It was Morton who brought the players back into the fold after the June reorganization when many had offers from other teams. With his eye for talent and his memory for any opposing player who caught his eye, he managed to replace departing Akrons with capable players on short notice. Even after the team had officially disbanded in September, he had kept the bulk of the players together for the final trip to St. Louis.

And he had many more years of baseball ahead of him during which he established a reputation as a successful minor league manager who was generally liked by his players and the team owners. At various times he was called clever and level-headed, universally popular, and a sober, industrious worker who commanded the respect of his men.⁸

But, despite his successes he was haunted by illness, injury, near disaster, and finally by a mental breakdown.

He was born in the hamlet of Kingsville in Ashtabula County, Ohio, in 1854, and spent part of his early life on the shores of Lake Erie. He was the son of the Rev. Aaron D. Morton, who at one time was presiding elder of the Akron District of the Methodist Episcopal Church. The entire branch of the family was supposed to be descended from John F. Morton, a signer of the Declaration of Independence. After completing his education, Charlie Morton apparently entered the grocery business until he was warned that he should seek more of an outdoor employment because of his fragile health. He had been interested in baseball, and his ability soon opened a career door for him.[9]

With his Akron success behind him by the fall of 1881, he joined the exodus from that club to the major leagues in 1882. His major league playing was limited to time with Allegheny (Pittsburgh) and St. Louis in the American Association in 1882, with Toledo, also in the American Association in 1884, and with Detroit in the National League in 1885. In all it totaled just 88 games, 325 at-bats, and a .194 lifetime batting average, plus a 1–0 record and a 3.09 ERA in 23 innings as a pitcher.[10]

While he made his home in Akron, and married Margaret Faber, a native of Germany, on December 1, 1883, Morton could almost have claimed a second home in Toledo because of his popularity in that northwestern Ohio city, particularly after piloting the Toledo Club to the championship of the Northwestern League in 1883. Hoping to catch lightning in a bottle, the backers of Toledo baseball teams kept inviting Morton back, but the success of 1883 was elusive.[11]

The Toledo Blue Stockings of 1884 were one of four new teams in the major league American Association which had expanded to 12 teams for that season. The club, mostly a carryover from the '83 Northwestern League champs, finished eighth with a 46–58 record. Tony Mullane, Morton's ace from the '81 Akrons, recorded 37 of the victories. It was also during this season that Morton became the first major league manager with an integrated team, as Moses Fleetwood Walker did most of the catching. Although there were four worse teams than Toledo on the field, it was the smallest city in the league, and when the American Association contracted to eight teams again for the 1885 season, Toledo was left out. Morton, however, moved to Detroit of the National League as manager. It was another poor second division team, and he lasted 38 games.[12]

By the fall of 1885, however, Morton had signed to manage the Savannah, Ga., team which was to take the place of Birmingham in the Southern League for the 1886 season, and in January of that year *Sporting Life* reported, "Morton is a clever and level-headed fellow, and is securing a team that will do Savannah proud." In fact, although he was a newcomer to the Southern League and a Northerner to boot, he was appointed to the league's scheduling committee and reportedly did "the lion's share" of the work on the league's schedule.[13]

Once the season started it was said that the Savannah team that Morton assembled was the best behaved of any Southern League club on the road. It was not long, however, before he ran into a pair of problems. The first was an experience that arose with many Northerners who took on the responsibility for Southern teams. He had released the team's third baseman, a native of Savannah, and replaced him with another player. That raised the ire of some of the fans and soon after produced an anonymous letter threatening Morton with violence.[14]

The second problem was Morton's health, possibly compounded by family problems. His wife had given birth to their first child, Freddie, in the spring, and the boy was not well. According to a story from Savannah, "Mr. Morton had been unable to become acclimated to the South, and his health had been miserable since he first came here; in fact he had been under a physician's care almost constantly since he came here. When the Association umpireship was offered him he urged acceptance of his resignation, which had been handed in two weeks previous to the receipt of the cowardly letter already alluded to, in order that he might get back into the bracing air of the North, and the directors granted his request with reluctance, which was sincere and unfeigned. Morton was universally popular with all who knew him, including every member of the club, and if he ever returns to Savannah he will be warmly welcomed by all those whose friendship is worth having."[15]

Whether Morton had actively solicited appointment as an American Association umpire, or whether the offer came to him unsolicited, his umpiring did not last long. He had resigned the post before the end of June, causing *Sporting Life* to first opine, "He is of too fine a mould for such a position" and then to report that he had quit "because he wouldn't stand the abuse and his voice gave out."[16]

Two months later Morton, writing from Akron, gave his own version of events in a letter to the editor of *Sporting Life*: "I have not dropped out of baseball permanently, as your item in last issue would imply. My health failed me while managing the Savannahs and I was compelled to resign all work for a time. I had several offers to manage and play, but knowing that I could not stand the strain, refused all. My health, which has been poor for the past three years, has improved so that now I am better than at any time during that period, and expect to be soon managing or playing again." Morton continued in the letter to praise the operation of the Southern League in general and the conduct of the directors of the Savannah team in particular.[17]

By October 1886, he was being mentioned as manager of Milwaukee in the Northwestern League, but he was soon felled again by illness. Then, in January 1887, about the time *Sporting Life* was again suggesting that he was out of baseball, the Savannah club reorganized and offered him the manager's post. He accepted and *Sporting Life* reported: "Savannah has never been so enthusiastic over base ball or in such good condition as now."[18]

Despite the apparent mutual admiration between the Savannah club directors and Morton, the team was in better shape than he was. In February, Freddie died at the age of 11 months. Morton still went South to begin the season, but he resigned again by early May and returned to Akron. Once more *Sporting Life* reported: "His health is none of the best and it was partly on that account that he left Savannah."[19]

Morton, however, did not desert the diamond for long. He quickly came full circle when he signed to manage and play shortstop on an Akron team. And by August, he was on the road again "reaching out in all directions to strengthen Des Moines, where there is no lack of cash for good material."[20]

He returned to Des Moines in the Western Association in 1888, and his trouble followed. While umpiring a spring practice game between Davenport and St. Paul, he was struck in the face by a foul tip. Even serious injuries were sometimes treated lightly in that era, when players were expected to continue in the game unless physically incapacitated. The seriousness of Morton's injury may perhaps be judged by the report that he was "confined to his room for a day or two." Whatever the seriousness of the injury, it did not prevent him from piloting Des Moines to the league title. His charges managed to beat out Kansas City for the pennant on the last day of the season. The accomplishment was recognized by *Sporting Life* in an editorial that said, "It was a close, hot battle, with remarkable features from start to finish, and Des Moines won through superior steadiness and skillful management. We congratulate Manager Chas. Morton and his plucky men upon their well-deserved success."[21]

Exultation over winning the Western Association crown had hardly worn off when Morton was back in Toledo. Said a Toledo dispatch of November 13 to the *Sporting Life*: "He arrived here this morning in response to a telegram to look the situation over. Mr. Morton and Frank Cooke, of the [Toledo] *Bee*, were out but half an hour this morning, and in that time they secured nearly $2,500 stock." The effort was launched to place a Toledo team in the International Association for 1889. Morton was to go to a league meeting in Syracuse, New York, the following week with $1,000 in his pocket as a guarantee of Toledo's good faith. The Toledo dispatch concluded: "You know what Charley Morton says he does."[22]

Throughout his career Morton apparently was well-liked by players as well as club directors, and he appeared to be extremely loyal to men who had performed well for him in the past. As a result, he was able to lure men from one team to another, including pitcher Ed Cushman from Des Moines to Toledo. Part of the attraction for the players may have been Morton's mode of operation. His Savannah team had been called the best behaved in the Southern League. In Toledo it was said that he prided himself upon the gentlemanly team he has gotten together for the city, and that he didn't "believe in having rowdies even if they can play ball." He put his trust in the honor of his players, and his rules for the team were few, simple, and only severe in regard to drunkenness.[23]

His success was sufficient enough that he managed Toledo again in 1890, this time back in the American Association when the city had a major league team for the second time. The club, which included former Morton players Ed Cushman of the Des Moines and Ed Swartwood of the Akrons, who also was making a return to the majors, was good enough to finish fourth in the Association with a 68–64 record.[24]

Toledo was out of the American Association again in 1891, and an effort was made to organize a Toledo club for the Northwestern League with Morton as manager. By April of that year, the Toledo effort had collapsed and Morton was in the job market. By May, he had taken on the management of a team in Jamestown, New York, and a month later resigned, obviously looking for a greener pasture. The *Sporting Life* speculated that he had offers from the major league clubs in Pittsburgh and Washington. In fact, he signed with Rochester. Subsequently *Sporting Life* reported: "Charley Morton is getting out of the Rochester team some of the work it is capable of. The changes, though few, have been judicious and the team is now able to cope with any of its Eastern Association competitors."[25]

In 1892, Morton moved to Minneapolis in the Western Association where he took the playing field again when "Jiggs" Parrott, the regular third baseman, was spiked and could not play. Already lauded as sober and industrious, and commanding the respect of his men, Morton collected the additional adjectives of nerve and pluck when he got a hit, stole a base, and accepted seven fielding chances without an error.[26]

He had even greater success with the Erie Club in the Eastern League in 1893, piloting the team to the championship. For Morton, however, the season was marked by another frightening personal experience during a trip to Buffalo, where his team was staying at the Mansion House hotel. He boarded the elevator to go to his room, but at the fifth floor the elevator went out of control and raced to the top of the shaft. Then it started down again at what was described as a "Nancy Hanks gait." Nancy Hanks was a fast and well-known race horse of the time. According to the report in *Sporting Life*, "It happened to be a safety elevator, and on each landing was a mechanical arrangement which broke the force of the rapid descent. As each landing was reached in the mad plunge Mr. Morton and the operator, its only occupants, were thrown in the air, striking the floor for a violent rebound when the next landing was reached. This was continued without variation until the ground floor was reached and the runaway machine stopped." It continued, "Mr. Morton thought his base ball days were over and has developed a decided aversion to hotel elevators. He will carry painful bruises for some time as a result of this experience. The elevator was an almost total wreck."[27]

Despite the falling elevator, and besides the league title, the 1893 Erie season ended on a high note for Morton. Before the September 12 game with Binghamton was started, he was presented with a $275 buggy by his Erie players.[28]

He returned to Erie for the 1894 season but was unable to repeat the championship. Moreover, near the close of the '94 campaign, he was involved in another life-threatening episode out of which he was hailed as a hero. On August 25 at Erie's Union Depot, Morton engaged in a conversation with a gentleman named W.C. Shaw. For some reason the two of them were standing on the track a short distance east of the station platform and were so intent upon their talk that neither of them noticed an approaching train until the shouts of bystanders finally got their attention. According to the report, "Mr. Morton seemed to have his head with him, and quickly jumped to the south side of the track. Mr. Shaw, on the other hand, seemed to lose his head and became bewildered, for, instead of imitating his friend's example he stood still like one dazed. Manager Morton saw the danger and in a twinkling made a spring to Mr. Shaw's side, grasped him firmly around the waist with his right arm and lifting him bodily from the ties, cleared the rail with his burden at one bound, landing on his face with the body of Mr. Shaw across his body. Those who imagine it was not a close call can form their own conclusions when they read that one of Mr. Shaw's shoe heels on his further protruding leg was clipped off by the wheel of the locomotive."[29]

By December 1894, Morton had been lured away from Erie to the apparently greener financial pastures of Buffalo. His standing in the Eastern League is reflected in the fact that he was appointed to the committee to revise the league constitution as well as to the scheduling committee. And, when he made a pre–Christmas trip from Akron to Buffalo he was accompanied by his old friend and teammate Sam Wise, who became the first player signed by Buffalo for the 1895 season. Wise remained in Buffalo for four seasons and was a fan favorite. Morton barely lasted through the 1895 campaign.[30]

By June 1896, when Morton was back home in Akron with a broken arm suffered in a fall, a *Sporting Life* dispatch from Buffalo purported to give the "inside facts" of Morton's Buffalo managerial demise at the hand of James Franklin, a Buffalo alderman and team president. "It is given on the authority of a Buffalonian very close to Franklin to the effect that Franklin got 'sore' on Morton last year because the Buffalo scribes laid all the blame for the poor work of the Bisons to Franklin's interference with the management of the team instead of blaming Morton." Within a month of the report Morton was appointed an Eastern League umpire.[31]

During the fall of 1897, there was speculation that he would become manager of the Indianapolis team in the Western League. Instead, Morton, referred to as "the popular veteran manager," was appointed that December to manage Rochester in the Eastern League for the 1898 campaign.[32]

His tenure was short and not sweet. Not only was the United States engaged in war with Spain, but the nation also experienced a recession, and the economic downturn put pressure on baseball teams and leagues across the country. The Eastern League was not an exception, and a decision was made to shorten the season. That produced a conflict between the league's players and management. Another cost-cutting measure was to reduce each team to 12 players. Morton and Billy Brady, one of the Rochester team directors, represented Rochester at a league meeting in Syracuse on May 20. There formal action was taken to reduce the rosters, and the players were rebuffed in a request to extend the season, although the directors held out a slim and withered olive branch with a promise that "if the summer's business warrants it, the request will be granted."[33]

Besides the generally unsettled conditions, Morton also was under pressure because of the team's lack of success on the field. At the time of the Syracuse meeting, Rochester was in last place with a 3–11 record. After the meeting he was quoted as saying that the Rochester team would be "made over considerably" before June 1 when the new roster limit was to be effective. From newspaper reports the following day it was clear that Morton was no longer in charge. Team directors had apparently been on the telephone attempting to round up replacements, and the *Democrat and Chronicle* said, "When it is all over and the dust has settled, about four of the present aggregation will remain." It may be that Morton's tendency to surround himself with veteran players whom he had managed in the past had finally caught up to him. Brady, the primary source on the plans of the owners, was quoted as saying: "I agree with the remarks in the Democrat and Chronicle the other day, which said that the team is composed greatly of has beens. It won't be, you can bet."[34]

It is not entirely clear exactly when Morton was either fired or resigned. A dispatch to the *Sporting Life* dated May 24 reported: "The record up-to-date made by the Rochester Club has not been a credit to anyone. The team did not put up a winning game, and in consequence Manager Morton resigned last week." On May 25, a Rochester paper said, in part, "The changes in the make up of the Rochester baseball team have taken place in part, and other changes will be made within a short time, as the owners of the club are determined to spare neither money nor effort to place a winning team in this city.... Manager Charles H. Morton has resigned and Billy Clymer has been appointed in his place."[35]

16

And Into the Darkness

Morton returned to Akron, his long career as a manager effectively over, and *Sporting Life* reported, "Ex-Manager Charley Morton is thoroughly disgusted with base ball, and says he is done with the game." Of course, he wasn't done with the game, although he was relegated to hanging around the edges of lower level professional ball in Akron. He was briefly mentioned as a potential manager for a Youngstown team at the end of 1899, but it was not until the spring of 1905 that he returned full-time to the baseball scene, not as a manager, but as a league president.[1]

Morton was the moving force behind the organization of what was initially called either the Independent Association of Base Ball Clubs, or the Protective Association of Independent Clubs. Nine independent clubs were represented at a meeting in Akron in March 1905 to form a league, and as many as 20 teams were expected to join the association. Independent clubs were teams that were operated much as the 1881 Akrons had operated, outside the structure of any league, arranging games when and how they could. That alone was enough to keep the league, such as it was, outside of the National Association, the governing body of the minor leagues. In addition, some of the teams had signed blacklisted or reserved players. Thus, it was considered an "outlaw" league at the outset. The initial nine teams were Homestead, Pennsylvania, and from Ohio, Canton, Massillon, Zanesville, Akron, Mount Vernon, Newark, Youngstown and Lancaster. Morton was elected president.

Under his guidance, the initial group soon was reorganized into the Ohio and Pennsylvania League, and before the close of the 1905 season Morton had been able to persuade Secretary J.H. Farrell of the National Association that the Ohio and Pennsylvania League qualified for membership, thus erasing the "outlaw" designation and allowing the member teams to reserve players. Even at that the league membership varied from time to time, sometimes listed with ten, sometimes with 13 clubs, and with as many as 21 members at one time or another. It is not surprising that

Sporting Life reported that Farrell would assist Morton with reorganization of the league in the off-season.[2]

The off-season brought Morton other opportunities as the Akron club of the Ohio and Pennsylvania League offered him management of the team after Walter East, a player-manager, announced that he had give up the manager's reins. Morton turned it down, apparently because some of the teams in the Central League were urging him to seek the presidency of that circuit. As it turned out, the conversion of the O&P of 1905 into a stable, eight-club league occupied Morton's efforts. A league meeting held in Akron on October 26 resulted in Morton being appointed a committee of one to investigate the cities which had applied for admission to the league for 1906 in regard to population, mileage, and Sunday ball. Morton was to report at the annual meeting of the league, which was to held in Zanesville in January 1906.[3]

Although there was a rumor that Morton would have opposition in being reelected president of the league, the January meeting resulted in the formation of an eight-club league with Morton as president, secretary and treasurer at a salary of $1,000 for the season. The cities represented were Akron, Lancaster, Mansfield, Newark, Youngstown and Zanesville in Ohio and New Castle and Braddock in Pennsylvania. Although all was cheerfulness when the schedule meeting was held in Akron in March and the delegates were feted at a banquet at that city's Empire House hotel, there were some inherent problems. The most serious was that the four southern and western clubs—Lancaster, Mansfield, Newark and Zanesville—were in substantially smaller cities and depended upon the revenue from Sunday ball games to stay afloat.

Charlie Morton (National Baseball Hall of Fame Library, Cooperstown, N.Y.)

16. And Into the Darkness

Such games were illegal, but enforcement of the Sunday law in Ohio had always depended upon the attitude of local authorities. Increased and more strict enforcement had been promised, leading Morton, the son of a minister, to assert: "There is no doubt but that the clubs will suffer a great loss in revenue if they are compelled to stop playing on Sunday, but no one need think that with the thousands of dollars that they have invested they will stop without a hard fight. I'm sure they will contest every step taken to prevent Sunday ball, and if they are defeated it will be a hard blow."[4]

In fact, Sunday ball continued unabated in many locations, and it was a common practice, not only in Ohio but throughout the country, for clubs to move their Sunday games to locations where they would be unmolested. Mansfield players had been arrested and fined for Sunday playing, and on May 20, 1906, the club tried to avoid a repetition when it moved its game with Sharon to Shelby, another community northwest of Mansfield. Constables, armed with warrants issued on behalf of the Law and Order League, again arrested the players but sparked a riot in the process and, according to one report, the justice of the peace who had issued the warrants was left sitting on the field when the crowd surrounded his buggy and removed the wheels. Morton's old friend, Sam Wise, who was umpiring the game, called it. Morton eventually ruled that the game, which had been interrupted in the fifth inning, had to be replayed.[5]

The Sunday playing problems were not unusual, and Morton's management of the O&P as a league had been generally regarded as efficient. While he did not actively solicit re-election for a third term, he clearly looked forward to the job, and *Sporting Life* observed, "President Morton has combined business principles and economy, as the prosperous condition of the league shows." But the underlying problems in the league were quickly revealed at its annual meeting in Cleveland on January 15, 1907. Morton had two rivals for the league presidency, but was re-elected on the ninth ballot by a 6–2 vote. In the end the Sharon, Pennsylvania, and Youngstown, Ohio, delegates held fast for Sam Wright, city editor of the Youngstown *Vindicator*, to run the league. Morton's salary was increased to $1,500, but the split between the eastern and western portions of the league was evident. It came to a head after the close of the 1907 season in a stormy meeting when the representatives of the four eastern clubs—Youngstown, Akron, Sharon and New Castle—announced that they would not continue in the league as it was then constituted because the drawing power of the four western clubs—Newark, Lancaster, Marion and Mansfield—was not commensurate with the long railway jumps necessary to reach them.[6]

Morton then set out to save the league that he had been instrumental in organizing. He took the problems to J.H. Farrell of the National

Association and asked for an investigation of conditions in the league. As a result, the National Association considered "redistricting" the O&P at the association's meeting on January 7, 1908, in Cincinnati, and agreed to meet with the league representatives at Cleveland. A week later the National Board of the National Association met with the O&P representatives and worked out a settlement. Akron, Youngstown, Sharon and New Castle each contributed to a pool of $1,000 to be paid to Mansfield, Marion, Lancaster and Newark for the purpose of forming a new league. The territory for the new league was reserved for them by the National Board, and they were granted ten days in which to form the new circuit. Then the remnant of the O&P was to receive Canton from the Central League, Erie from the Interstate League, and McKeesport and East Liverpool from the P.O.M. (Pennsylvania, Ohio, Maryland) League. But there were contingencies. Erie would have to pay for the losses of other Interstate League teams from 1907, and the liberty of McKeesport and East Liverpool to withdraw from the P.O.M. depended upon whether other clubs in that league could pay delinquent league assessments.[7]

Against all odds, the pieces came together and the O&P was reorganized once more at a February 3, 1908, meeting in Sharon, Pennsylvania, with Erie, Canton, Akron, Youngstown, Sharon and New Castle represented. Morton was unanimously re-elected president. Although not represented at the meeting, East Liverpool and McKeesport also were members. Whatever plaudits Morton might have earned for engineering the reorganization quickly disappeared in the reality of the 1908 season. The extra expenditures in paying off the four former league clubs and in getting the four new clubs clear of their financial entanglements with their former leagues left the new O&P in a weakened financial condition at the beginning. Then the national economy went sour. By summer the steel mills in Youngstown, Sharon, New Castle and McKeesport and the potteries in East Liverpool had shut down. At first, Morton insisted on playing out the season schedule, but the club directors prevailed and the season was closed on Labor Day. Morton, feeling beset by events and mounting criticism, wrote a rather optimistic letter to Francis Richter, editor of *Sporting Life*, setting forth the situation in the O&P. To the letter, Richter appended: "The league was also exceptionally well managed by President Morton, whose energy and resourcefulness several times averted collapse at various points."[8]

Those were practically the last kind words Morton was to read as events quickly spiraled out of control. When the season was shortened, the Akron and Canton teams paid their players in full to the original September 30 closing date. Then, on October 26, the Akron club filed a lawsuit against the league in Akron, alleging that it had suffered a $3,000 loss by the premature close of the season. It secured a temporary injunction preventing Morton from paying out any league money until the hearing on the suit. In its complaint, the Akron club charged the other seven teams of conspiring to break up the league. Then the Erie club filed suit in Pittsburgh to compel Morton to return its $500 guarantee which had been posted before the season. Morton was between a rock and a hard place. When the league met in Pittsburgh on October 27, Morton informed them that he could not preside, and that no legal business could be transacted because of the Akron injunction.[9]

Under fire from all directions, Morton granted an interview in which he charged that the Youngstown club had never paid its $500 guarantee; that Erie had not paid a single assessment during the season; that Canton had paid only one; that Youngstown, Sharon and New Castle had paid only when they felt like it; that all the teams had violated the salary-limit rules; and that his hands had been tied because the offending clubs controlled the league's board of directors. Morton, it was said, did not wish to remain president of the league for another year "under the existing conditions."[10]

The wrangling, legal and otherwise, continued through the balance of 1908 and into January 1909. Morton called a league meeting for January 12 in Cleveland, but Ed Clepper, president of the Sharon club, circulated a petition calling for a meeting on January 4 in Pittsburgh. Morton told the Akron *Beacon Journal*, "you can just pass the word along to Mr. Clepper that he isn't president of the league yet. I am still president of the league and the meeting is going to be held at the place and time I named." The four eastern clubs—Youngstown, Sharon, New Castle, and East Liverpool—held a meeting in Youngstown on January 5 and decided to support Sam Wright of Youngstown for league president. The *Beacon Journal*, quoting a dispatch from Youngstown, reported, "The four club owners are also believed to have talked over the admission of another club to take the place of Akron, should Akron keep up its fight against the league."[11]

On the morning of January 12, Morton boarded the B&O train at Akron's Howard Street Station and rode to Cleveland in the company of league directors John T. Windsor of Akron and Adam Shorb of Canton. Two Akron newspaper reporters rode in the seat behind Morton and the others.

Said the *Beacon Journal*: "Mr. Morton was in a very nervous condition during the ride to Cleveland. The Akron and Canton representatives had been trying to have him again run for president although he had given his word that he would not do so.

"Leaning over the back of the seat, Mr. Morton said to the reporters,

'They want me to be president again. God knows I don't want the job. But I don't want to go back on my friends. I don't know what to do.' As he talked his fingers worked nervously along the back of the seat."[12]

At Cleveland, Morton walked with the party to Public Square, where he reportedly told the others, "I'm not going to the hotel right away. I'll be there at 12 o'clock." The meeting had been called for 11 A.M., and the club owners believed that Morton would appear after the Pennsylvania teams had been served with the legal notices of Akron's lawsuit against the league. The papers were served, but Morton did not appear. One o'clock passed. The Akron representatives denied any knowledge of Morton's whereabouts. He had been carrying what was described as a "grip" containing all the league papers, and some fears surfaced that he might have become the victim of a robbery. Cleveland hospitals were called, but Morton could not be located. At 2:15 P.M. the league directors began a meeting without him, electing Sam Wright as president and making some other tentative arrangements, but without Morton and the league records, not much could be done.[13]

Morton was gone. Disappeared. Rumors abounded. Harry U. Morton, vice president of the General Railway Supply Co. in Chicago and brother of the missing Charlie Morton, came to Akron. Harry Morton made a personal request to Cleveland police to search for his brother. The search was unsuccessful. He also went to Canton to talk to Shorb, who had been the last to converse with Charlie Morton. He talked to Windsor and then went to Pittsburgh to carry on his investigation there.

Bits and pieces of information popped up. Nate Tuholsky, secretary to Charlie Morton during the baseball season, revealed that he had completed the annual O&P League report for *Spalding's Base Ball Guide* and that the day before Morton had disappeared he had told Tuholsky he had directed that the check for the Spalding report be sent to Tuholsky in care of the Hamilton Cigar Store.

Harry Morton revealed that Mrs. Morton had received a letter from her missing husband. When asked if the letter had been peculiarly worded, as Harry Morton had indicated, Mrs. Morton first replied "No," and then asked, "What if it was?"

Ralph Read, an owner of the New Castle club, said the Charlie Morton had told him that newspapers stories critical of him made his children cry, and that they had asked him to resign. In contrast, Mrs. Morton said that her husband did not seem much worried about league affairs at home. She said she and the children often asked him about abusive newspaper stories, and that he always passed them off.

Finally, it was learned that Charlie Morton, who was bald, had purchased a wig before attending the National Association meetings several months earlier. Taken alone, that might not have been unusual, but he had also purchased a false mustache in a Cleveland store.

On January 21, Harry U. Morton wrote to Windsor, officially giving up the search for his brother. Six days later, when the O&P directors met at the Buchtel Hotel in Akron, nothing more had been learned of Morton's whereabouts, but the first hour of the league's meeting was devoted to discussion of the affair. The letter received from him by his wife, although never made public, was read to the league meeting. It was described as "a confusion of words, incoherent, unmeaning." The letter, combined with Windsor's description of Morton's actions on the train the day he disappeared, persuaded the league directors to conclude, in the words of the *Beacon Journal*, that Morton's "reason had been temporarily dethroned."[14]

In retrospect, it is interesting to note that A.R. Cratty, a correspondent for *Sporting Life*, had filed a story datelined November 9, 1908, about a Pittsburgh meeting between Charlie Morton and Richard Guy, former president of the P.O.M. League. Cratty wrote that Guy called their conversation a "commiseration meeting." Guy is quoted as saying, "Charley and myself swapped experiences. Morton, without joking, is almost a mental wreck as a result of his strenuous year." Continued Guy, "The general public hasn't the slightest idea of the wear and tear on the mind of a boss canvas man of a minor league. Club owners will make it hot for a president in every old way. Beneath the surface you are trimmed and harpooned right and left. He will work his head off in order to keep a league from blowing up. All he ever secures as a reward is the worst of it. Morton vows that, old stager that he is, the past season broke all records for annoyances. He wanted to keep the union afloat. Instead of getting aid from certain clubs they set out to give him the conge, etc. Many men buy stock in the small ball teams who are far from sportsmen. They will show the meanest tactics possible under the slightest provocation."[15]

As usual in such cases, Morton's disappearance quickly faded from public notice. Except for his family, and the men involved in running the Ohio and Pennsylvania League, few people cared. Then Morton suddenly reappeared in Chicago on March 11 in a manner as mysterious as his original disappearance. According to the account in the *Beacon Journal*, which may have been lifted in large part from a Chicago paper, Harry Morton was called to the telephone in his Chicago office.

"Is that you Harry: is this 'Chick Chuck' Charlie Morton?" said the voice.

"What," responded Harry, "My brother Charles?"

"Never mind. I'll call you again," was the answer, and the end of the call.

Harry Morton immediately contacted the police, who determined that the call to Morton had come from downtown Chicago. A search was launched, and late that night Harry Morton came face to face with his brother on Wabash Avenue near Van Buren. At first Charlie failed to recognize Harry, but eventually he was induced to accompany his brother home where he was placed under care of a physician. He was diagnosed with acute dementia.

Harry Morton immediately wired Charlie's wife in Akron, and she left for Chicago the next morning. A letter from Harry Morton to John Windsor in Akron was cited by the *Beacon Journal* as authoritative private confirmation that Charlie had been found. Windsor told the newspaper, "Mr. Morton states that he has found his brother, Charles. He does not say where or under what conditions. He adds that his mind is gone. That he has no memory of any events that have occurred in the past few months. He expresses his delight at finding his brother and also regret at his condition."

Windsor added, "He [Harry Morton] states that he has come into possession of a number of papers and documents relating to the business of the O&P league."

The documents were to be sent immediately to Akron, and Windsor said, "As soon as the papers arrive we will be in a position to close up the affairs of the old Akron club and to ascertain just where the league stands in a financial and business way. This has heretofore been impossible on account of the absence of papers and statements in the possession of Mr. Morton."

Akron attorney Fred R. Ormsby, appointed by the league to investigate Morton's affairs, indicated that he would begin his work immediately. His first appointment was with Harry Williams, cashier at the National City Bank, where the league funds had been deposited in Charley Morton's name.[16]

On a more personal basis, Fred Morton, Charlie's son,[17] received a letter in Akron from his mother in which she told him that his father still did not recognize her, but that he was "somewhat improved" over his condition when first found.[18]

Shortly afterward, Harry Morton expressed confidence that the league would lose nothing due to his brother's management, and that when everything was accounted for it was likely that the league would owe Charlie some money. In the end, when the tangled finances were finally straight, it was found that the league guarantee fund was short about $1,500. While Charlie was still under care in a Chicago hospital, Harry Morton made good the amount.[19]

16. And Into the Darkness

On August 10, 1909, Charlie Morton returned to Akron, apparently in good health, physically and mentally. According to the *Beacon Journal*, his voice sounded to his friends as familiar and as pleasant as ever. He also told reporters he did not wish to make any statement about the past. He was quoted as saying, "There is nothing that I think ought to be said at present about O&P affairs, as it is not necessary to enter into these matters, especially as satisfactory arrangements have already been made to settle them."[20]

It was his last public statement. When his old friend Sam Wise died in January 1910, Morton was mentioned in the obituary, but was not quoted. By the time Morton died on December 10, 1921, he had been virtually forgotten. Nevertheless, the *Beacon Journal* gave him a front page obituary, although it consisted only of an old photograph and two brief and inaccurate paragraphs. It reported that he had died at his home. The *Sporting News* picked up the same inaccurate information. In fact, he had died at the Massillon, Ohio, State Hospital for the Insane. His death certificate showed that he had died of general paralysis and that he had been under the care of the hospital doctor since July 1921.[21]

With the explosive expansion of the rubber industry the quiet canal town of 16,000 in 1881 had mushroomed into a bustling boomtown of 200,000 in 1921. Few residents remembered the once famous Akrons of 40 years earlier, or Morton's contribution to their fleeting glory in the brief era of independent town teams during baseball's infancy.

Of course, there had been no 1882 for the Akrons. The American Association began play that season, and with six more major league teams seeking quality players, it was inevitable that the Akrons would be raided out of existence. And, in addition to the two major leagues, there were five minor leagues in 1882, and the minor loops had swelled to 13 by 1885. Town teams could not compete with those professional teams for players. The era of strong, independent town teams was over.

Morton knew none of that as he rode the train back to Akron from St. Louis in September 1881. Then he had the glow of victory and the warmth of success to keep away the darkness.

17

Toward the Light

With the advent of the American Association in 1882, the Akrons as an independent, professional town team had disappeared. That era had ended forever, but a new era was dawning; an era of many professional leagues in which cities, large and small, competed for clearly defined, though limited championships. Often leagues and teams were created with great enthusiasm, but frequently that enthusiasm was blunted by poor teams and by teams and leagues that were consistently underfunded and badly managed.

Enthusiasts and promoters were always trying to get new teams and new combinations organized. For example, a convention of base ball clubs in Ohio and Pennsylvania was called to meet in Youngstown, Ohio, in November 1883, for the purpose of forming an interstate league of eight clubs for the 1884 season. Early indications were that the American Association rules would probably be adopted with but little change. It was proposed to make the headquarters of the new league in Youngstown, and clubs from Dayton, East Liverpool, Akron, Youngstown, and Cleveland in Ohio, and New Castle, Pittsburgh, Johnstown, Altoona and Harrisburg in Pennsylvania were to be represented. The early report said no club will be admitted to the league except on satisfactory financial basis. The guarantee would be fixed at $60. Just two weeks later another movement was reported under way to organize a Northern Ohio Base Ball League that would include Alliance, Canton, Akron, Oberlin, Elyria and Cleveland. Said *Sporting Life*, "A convention will be called at an early date."[1]

What actually happened in Akron in 1884 was part of a wider fiasco that emerged from the determination of the American Association and the National League, briefly at peace, to unite in opposition to the Union Association as a third major league. Not only were the reserve clause and team territorial rights at stake, but the magnates of the established leagues were searching for some mechanism to hold down salaries. What they came up with was reserve teams as auxiliaries of the major league clubs. Similar in a way to the first nine and second nine designations of the old social baseball clubs, each major league team was to have a reserve team, complete in itself, which would play the other reserve teams for a reserve championship. Ideally, this would double the number of players under contract with the existing major league teams and in theory would keep as many players as possible out of the control of the Union Association. It was merely a secondary idea that reserve teams would give first nine major league clubs a ready and cheap source of players during the season when they needed to replace a player either because of injury or poor performance. Harold Seymour, in *Baseball: The Early Years,* observed that the reserve teams melted away as the season progressed. He wrote, "Temporary expedients of war though they were, the reserve teams bore the closest resemblance to modern baseball's farm system yet discernable." But the rationale for true farm teams was not in place, and the reality of the reserve teams was more a nightmare than a dream.[2]

Akron was, in part, held hostage by the indecisiveness of the Cleveland National League club's management. In February 1884, things looked relatively good as *Sporting Life* quoted the Cleveland *Herald* as saying: "The chances look bright for the location of the Cleveland reserve club at Akron. The ground has been looked over, and the old spirit that made Akron so good a base ball town in the past still exists, and though the old grounds have gone others can easily be secured. By this arrangement with the Cleveland Club Akron can get a far better team than she could gather at this time. Akron is too well situated, close to the League city of Cleveland, to be without a team. With proper management one should pay handsomely. It is a convenient calling place for League teams, all of which would be glad to go to Akron if it was in the Ohio League and a member of the National group."[3]

A week later it was reported that the Cleveland reserve team would be located in either Akron or Youngstown, with the probabilities in favoring the latter. While the location and makeup of the reserves had not been determined, three games had been scheduled in Cincinnati with the "colt" team there for mid–April. Others were projected with the Toledo, Indianapolis and Columbus "Colts," as well as with Springfield, Dayton and other Ohio League teams. In 1884 Cincinnati, Toledo, Indianapolis and Columbus were all American Association major league clubs. Said *Sporting Life*, of the Cleveland reserve team, "If located in Youngstown the team will play in the Interstate League; if in Akron with the Ohio League. Either city will gain a team of which it can be proud, and will be able to witness the playing of the best League teams, with whom Cleveland will arrange to play the 'colts'."[4]

After all the vacillating, the Cleveland directors finally decided to keep their reserve team in Cleveland. The immediate result was that Akron ended up with a co-operative club under the management of Clevelander W.H. Voltz. He was to furnish and pay the players, and the proprietors of the Akron baseball grounds would provide the field and the uniforms.[5]

The initial 12-man roster for the now-independent co-op Akron club was published on April 9, along with the facts that Voltz had now taken up residence in Akron, that three more players were on the way, and that season tickets, good for 25 games, were to go on sale for $5. Nevertheless, the relative standing of the team is reflected in the fact that the *Summit County Beacon* devoted most of its sports column to a report that the Akron Bicycle Club, with a membership of 20, wanted to build a bicycle race track around the ballpark, then located in South Akron and called Recreation Park. Said the *Beacon*, "It was, however, reported that the baseball park managers would not construct the track, but would give the club the privilege of doing so. In view of this the plan of having a bicycle track has been abandoned."[6]

At that point, Akron had applied for admission to the Oil and Iron League but was turned down, and launched an effort to form an independent league including Johnstown, Meadville and Warren, Pennsylvania, along with Akron. *Sporting Life* said, "Other towns will probably be taken into the combination."[7]

By the end of April, it was announced that Cleveland's reserve team would be disbanded, and that the Cleveland reserve games would be transferred to Akron. When that happened, three of the Cleveland players were transferred to the Akron squad, and the Akron club, although it apparently remained a co-op team, was treated as if it were the Cleveland reserve team. It was, however, simply overmatched against the other reserve teams. On the Akron grounds, in the second week of May, the club lost successively to the Alleghanys, the Pittsburgh reserves, 10–0, to the Cincinnati reserves 3–0, and to the St. Louis reserves 17–3.[8]

Problems persisted off the field as well as on it. William Bohn, a pitcher who had pitched for the Cleveland Whites in 1881 and other Cleveland clubs and had been on the initial 1884 Akron roster, was expelled for drunkenness. According to *Sporting Life*, the story was that Bohn was induced to drink heavily by the manager of the Springfield team in the hope that he would get his release from Akron. Bohn's expulsion, however, blocked him from signing elsewhere. By the end of May the Akron Club had been reorganized with only eight of the original 15 players remaining. Inevitably, rumors that the club was on the point of being disbanded circulated and were denied. Strangely enough, when the end finally did come in the middle of June, Akron had outlasted all of the other reserve clubs. *Sporting Life* took a bit of a cheap shot at Akron for allowing the club to dissolve for lack of $80, but the fact is that it truly never was an Akron team. Indeed, all of the reserve teams operated pretty much as orphans deserted by their major league parents. In a more charitable tone *Sporting Life* observed, "What a hard time the reserve teams must have had. Voltz, the manager of the late Akron Club, had to borrow his railroad fare from Mr. Von der Ahe, of the St. Louis Club."[9]

In March 1885, Akron, still looking for a baseball home to call its own, was reported to be among the clubs to be in a new Inter-State League, but once more ended up on the outside looking in. According to a synopsis of Akron's baseball history published in the *Beacon Journal* in 1935, Akron fielded a team in the Ohio League in 1887 and won the league pennant in 1889. The accuracy of that report is questionable as *Sporting Life*, which identified the league as the Ohio State League, reported that it did not operate in 1888 and that it folded in 1889 when the Akron, Tiffin and Newark franchises ceased operations and Youngstown was awarded the pennant by default.[10]

Such midseason collapses were not unusual, but there were always promoters ready to try again. Akron teams played in the Tri-State League in 1890, and in the Ohio-Michigan League in 1893. In 1895, when the Inter-State League became known as the "Interchangeable League" because of its multitude of franchise shifts, Akron fielded a team for a total of five games. Albeit briefly, it was enough for another future Hall of Famer to follow Bid McPhee in wearing an Akron uniform.

Honus Wagner, in his rookie year of professional ball, played seven games for Steubenville before the team was moved to Akron. The last of the five Akron games was tied 5–5 in the seventh inning when an argument erupted over a player called out at third. The Canton manager demanded to have an "abusive" Akron player ejected. When the Akron manager refused to remove the player, the umpire ordered the game forfeited. Following the game, "Akron went to pieces," and the franchise was awarded to Lima just eight days after it had been moved from Steubenville. Honus Wagner promptly signed with Mansfield.[11]

Then, more than 20 years after Akron had boasted of "the strongest non-league club in the country," the city found a nitch, if not a legacy, from the 1881 Akrons, when Charlie Morton directed the creation of the Ohio and Pennsylvania League. Despite its problems, and Morton's personal collapse, the league itself proved quite durable for the era, lasting through seven seasons. In those seven years, the Akron team finished second twice, third once, and then won four straight flags from 1908 through 1911.[12]

The *Beacon Journal* synopsis of 1935 speculated that Akron's streak of pennants helped kill the league after the 1911 season. In fact, the East Liverpool and Steubenville teams had disbanded on August 20, 1911, and the Akron, Canton, Erie and Youngstown teams all moved up to the Class B Central League in 1912. The same four teams moved to the Class D Interstate League in 1913, and Akron and Canton joined the Buckeye League in 1915. Both of the latter leagues folded during the seasons that Akron joined.[13]

While Akron was experiencing success on the diamonds of the Ohio and Pennsylvania League, the city also was producing its own future Hall of Fame baseball player. George Harold Sisler was born in the rural Manchester area of Summit County in 1893 and moved to the Akron home of Joseph D. Thomas Sr., chairman of the Akron Recreation Commission, to attend Akron High School. He was a relief pitcher for the high school team in 1909, and then a fire-balling starting pitcher for the 1910 and 1911 teams. In the latter two seasons the team posted an 11–2 record against high school competition, plus a 13–3 loss in 1911 to Akron's championship O&P League team.

Sisler was clearly the best local player since Sam Wise had emerged from the Buckeye Mower & Reaper Works in 1879. In 1911, Sisler struck out 20 in a 3–2 victory over Massillon, 21 in a 16–0 win over Cleveland's University School, and another 20 in an 8–3 win over Massillon. He finished the season with a 2–0 no-hitter over Canton.[14]

Besides his interest in the recreation commission, Thomas also sponsored a sandlot team known as the Collegians. Naturally, Sisler pitched for the Collegians, and also for the Babcock & Wilcox team in Barberton. He went from Akron High School to the University of Michigan, and then directly to the St. Louis Browns, although not without a controversy which was in some ways reminiscent of Wise's plight in 1882 when he had signed contracts with both Cincinnati and Boston.

Sisler had signed a contract with Akron's Ohio and Pennsylvania League team while he was a 17-year-old high school senior. His father repudiated the contract and sent Sisler off to the University of Michigan. Meanwhile, Akron had sold Sisler's contract to Columbus of the American Association, and Columbus sold it to the Pittsburgh Pirates. When Sisler signed with the Browns, the Pirates also claimed him. The National Commission, which ruled professional ball before there was a commissioner, ruled in favor of the Browns.[15]

Sisler went to the Browns in 1915, and in a 15-year-career that was cut short by sinus trouble that impaired his vision, put up his Hall of Fame numbers as a first baseman. He posted a lifetime batting average of .340, including marks of .407 in 1920 and .420 in 1921. His Akron fans, however, remembered him as a pitcher and when he made his last playing appearance before a hometown crowd, the fans chanted, "Let George do it! We want Sisler." It was August 23, 1928, and the Boston Braves were playing the Akron General Tire team in an exhibition. Sisler, then in the twilight of his major league career, played his usual polished first base for the Braves and singled in five trips to the plate. With the Braves safely ahead in an eventual 11–4 victory, the fans' chants were rewarded. Sisler pitched a scoreless ninth inning.[16]

About the time that Akron was finishing its run of Ohio and Pennsylvania League championships, and Sisler was wrapping up his high school career, the city began a major transformation. Just as the little canal town had tripled in size during the 1860s, the quiet city of 70,000 again tripled in size during the second decade of the twentieth century. Spurred in part by World War I, the growth was almost entirely due to the rubber industry and the new demand for automobile tires. With a population that topped 200,000 in the 1920 census, the city was bursting with civic pride, which spilled over into baseball.

A group headed by lawyer Frank Doyle formed the Akron Exhibition Company, won the baseball territorial rights to Akron, and bought the defunct Binghamton, New York, franchise from the International League for $30,000. This was fast baseball company. The International League was just a step from the major leagues and included owners such as Baltimore's Jack Dunn, who had signed Babe Ruth off the Baltimore sandlots and later sold him to the Boston Red Sox.

In an age when minor league clubs had to sign their own talent, Akron managed to field a competitive team, including famed Indian athlete and Olympic hero Jim Thorpe. The Numatics, named for the newly developed pneumatic tire, finished a distant fourth behind Dunn's Baltimore club. Akron, however, was comfortably in the first division of the eight-team circuit, finishing more than 20 games ahead of fifth-place Reading.[17]

Akron also had ranked fourth in league attendance, but success on the field and at the gate did not keep the underfunded Akron Exhibition Company from having cash flow problems. The other International League owners were not about to help. Although Akron was on two main east-west railroad lines, the city was simply too far west to satisfy the other owners. They had taken steps to protect themselves from the start. Seven of the eight teams were required to pay visiting teams a $200 per game guarantee. Akron was required to pay visitors $300.

Toronto, Buffalo, Syracuse and Rochester made one fairly compact set of teams; Reading, Jersey City and Baltimore constituted another. There was no question that Akron was geographically isolated. It was not unreasonable for the other seven owners to want a change, but that didn't make it any more palatable to Akronites when the effort to oust the city from the league became public at a league meeting in New York City on Dec. 13, 1920.[18]

The immediate result was a desperate but unsuccessful effort to save the team. The Akron Exhibition Company was reorganized. To raise extra funds, Thorpe was sold to the Detroit Tigers. The Chamber of Commerce gave its support to an effort to sell 100,000 tickets for the 1921 season. The *Beacon Journal* held a contest to come up with a new team name.[19]

With the exception of George Sisler, Ralph Lattimore was the best known and most popular of Akron's homegrown ballplayers during the first two decades of the twentieth century. Akron's championship team in the Ohio and Pennsylvania League in 1911 had attempted to get Lattimore, a career minor leaguer, away from the Columbus club in the American Association. At the time, Akron was operating as a farm club for Columbus, which kept Lattimore for the entire season. In 1912, Columbus released Lattimore to Akron for its ill-fated club in the Class B Central League. With his playing days behind him, Lattimore had headed a group in 1920 that tried to bring a Class B Ohio League team to Akron, but was bested for the Akron territory by Doyle and the Akron Exhibition Company.

Now, in the reorganization, Joseph D. Thomas Sr., who once had taken Sisler into his home, was elected president. Lattimore was named manager and added to the board of directors of the Akron Exhibition Company. He traveled to New York for another league meeting on Feb. 17, 1921. Afterward he declared, "There is no question that the league is prepared to do everything in the world to oust Akron." He returned with a league-imposed deadline; Akron had 15 days to post a $15,000 bond. He also brought back a warning: Any sale of the team had to have league approval.[20]

With the end in sight, the Akron owners sought out a buyer for the franchise. By February 28, they believed a deal had been struck with a group from Montreal to sell the franchise for $42,000. The International League owners met again on March 3 in New York. The day of the meeting a headline in *The Sporting News* read: "Wish Akron Had Never Been Heard Of." *The Sporting News* was closer to the situation than the Akron owners. Before the meeting started the paper knew the Akron franchise was going to Newark, not Montreal.

Despite Akron's protests, the league awarded the franchise to Newark for $25,000. Akron threatened to sue for conspiracy and restraint of trade. In the end, Akron took its complaint to Baseball Commissioner Kenesaw

Mountain Landis in Chicago. He heard the arguments and on March 16, he ruled that the International League had control over its own franchises.[21]

The fight was over. Although Lattimore kept a Numatics team together for a time as an independent club, it was a far cry from an International League franchise. Akronites who had been involved in the battle were left with a bad taste that lingered for years. The city, however, was not without baseball. Sandlot ball had always been strong, and the growth of the rubber industry had been accompanied by the growth of equally competitive semipro industrial teams.

When the Numatics finished the 1920 International League season, they had scheduled two weekend exhibition games to honor the players and to let them split the gate receipts. The Numatics lost the Saturday game to the Firestone Non-Skids, and then pulled out a 2–1 win over an industrial league all-star team before a sparse Sunday turnout. That same day the Goodyear Wingfoots, playing at their own field before what was reported to be an enthusiastic crowd, swept a double-header from the Morgan & Wright team of Detroit to advance to the semifinals of the national industrial team tournament.[22]

Growth of industrial league baseball on a highly developed and competitive level was part of what was called "welfare capitalism," which reached its peak in the mid–1920s. It was an important part of the effort by industrialists to stave off organized labor by keeping their workers reasonably contented. Harold Seymour, in his *Baseball: The People's Game*, noted that "a survey of North Carolina plants made in 1926 showed that most of them contributed to the support of churches, 40 offered group insurance plans, 40 employed community workers; 28 supplemented school incomes— and 127 supported baseball teams." Baseball was, said Seymour, part of the manipulation of workers' leisure.[23]

He continued, "In keeping with the typical American organizational pattern, industrial leagues in 1921 formed an Association of Industrial Athletic Associations, or AIAA, to insure uniformity in eligibility and scheduling. Within a year the AIAA spread from Akron, Ohio, into five states, staged an intercity baseball series, and published its own monthly magazine, *Industrial Athletics*. Despite the organization's name, it focused on baseball."[24]

Indeed, for the first time since the 1881 Akrons had entertained major league teams regularly, major league exhibition games against the Goodyear, Firestone and General Tire industrial teams were a frequent feature of the city's baseball landscape. The east-west rail line wasn't enough to make Akron viable for the International League, but the city was an easy stopping point for major league clubs traveling in either direction. Not only did the industrial teams provide strong enough competition to be attractive opponents for the big leaguers, but they had their own ballparks.

That became an important consideration after 1923 when "old" League Park at Beaver and Carroll streets, east of downtown, was razed. The lack of playing sites for big time ball was remedied in 1925 when Firestone and General Tire opened new fields. Firestone Stadium, with its steel and concrete grandstand, was dedicated on July 18, 1925. Less than a week later the Cincinnati Reds took advantage of its short outfield dimensions to rout the Non-Skids 12–0.[25]

The likely high point of the matches between Akron industrial teams and the major leaguers came on August 22, 1926, when Charles E. Ketchum, a tall, thin, raw-boned right-hander, hurled a no-hitter for the Akron Generals against the defending world champion Pittsburgh Pirates at General Field. Eight days earlier Ketchum had hurled a no-hitter in an industrial league game.

Harold Sloop, an Akron high school athlete, was throwing batting practice for the Generals to strengthen his shoulder after a football injury, so he was on the field before the start of Ketchum's gem against the Pirates. "Ketchum had a glove with a hole in the middle. He worked chewing gum with emery dust in it to aid the break on his ball," Sloop recalled. "Before the game, the umpire told [Pirates manager Bill] McKechnie that Ketchum cheated, and asked if McKechnie wanted him to call it. McKechnie said let him throw."[26]

The Generals scored a run in the first inning and the game remained 1–0 until the bottom of the seventh, when the Generals scored two and added three more in the eighth for a 6–0 lead. The Pirates had three future Hall of Famers in their lineup that afternoon: the veteran Pie Traynor and rookies Paul Waner and Joe Cronin. With two outs in the top of the ninth inning, Ketchum decided to play the odds to protect his no-hitter. He walked the dangerous Waner intentionally to pitch to Cronin, who grounded out to end the game.

Ketchum's gem made him the target of big league scouts for about a week. The Boston Braves played the Generals at General Field on August 29, and Ketchum again was on the mound. The Generals led 4–0 and Ketchum had allowed only three hits when rain delayed the game after the top of the fifth inning. When play resumed, the Braves broke through for a 7–5 victory, although only one of the seven runs was earned.[27]

18

A Dawn of Fresh Glory

While the industrial teams and top-quality sandlot teams provided plenty of baseball for Akron, the city had been without a professional team for eight years when Walter Morris and Ike Sablosky, both of the Dallas club of the Texas League, put up the money to bring Akron a franchise in a newly formed Central League in 1928. The last barrier to Akron's participation was removed on January 4, 1928, when the city's Board of Zoning Appeals granted a permit for construction of a $100,000 ballpark on property at Crosier Street, Park Avenue and Long Street. The property was just east of Summit Lake and within sight of the Summit Beach Amusement Park.

Work on the ballpark was under way by January 14, but winter in northeast Ohio is not a great time for construction work. As the projected opening date approached, the ballpark work was 15 days behind schedule, and the home opener was delayed twice before finally taking place on April 30. The projected $100,000 cost also had climbed to $135,000.

While the construction was going on a contest was held to name the new team. The winning entry, announced on April 17, was the Tyrites. Like the earlier Numatics, Tyrites was a word play on Akron's rubber connection. The root of the name was tyre, the British version of tire, so the name was supposed to be pronounced "tyr-ites." To Akronites, however, it became "ty-rites," and remained so. In addition, it was announced that the new ballpark would be League Park, resurrecting the name of the old park that had been at Beaver and Carroll streets.[1]

Charlie Ketchum, of no-hit fame, pitched the Tyrites to victory in the opening game, but the Tyrites played .500 ball in 1928, fell to last place in 1929, and then the bottom fell out of the American economy. In retrospect, the entire enterprise appears to be the epitome of bad timing. Akron dropped out of the league in 1930, and in 1931 the league itself shut down. Both the league and the Tyrites attempted a comeback in 1932, but the Akron ownership gave up and moved the team to Canton early in the season. The

Canton incarnation of the team also folded later in the season, and the Central League finished 1932 with just four teams.

Nevertheless, the "new" League Park was there, and in 1933, when a new Negro National League was formed, it included the Akron Black Tyrites. They, too, folded before the close of the 1933 season, although their temporary presence was enough to get League Park listed in *Green Cathedrals* as a former major league ballpark.[2]

In the winter of 1934–35, the country was entering the sixth year of the Great Depression, and there was little sign of an economic turnaround. Akron was no exception to the general malaise, but there was an additional social dynamic at work in the area: widespread discontent with wages and working conditions by those rubber workers who still had jobs. At the beginning of June 1933, there had been fewer than 300 labor union members in Akron. Before the end of August, there were more than 12,000. By November, union membership in Summit County had reached 30,000. By the spring of 1935, major strikes loomed at the rubber plants.[3]

Such was the situation on January 11, 1935, when George Weiss and Paul Krichell of the New York Yankees arrived in Akron on a semisecret mission known only to sports editors Jim Schlemmer of the Akron *Beacon-Journal* and Ed Garman of the Akron *Times-Press*. The Yankees were looking to move their Middle Atlantic League franchise out of Wheeling, West Virginia, and Akron was one of three cities on their short list of possible replacement sites. Their tour revealed several problems.

Among the least of them were estimates of $2,500 for necessary repairs at the ballpark and $5,000 for new lights. In addition, the Yankees would have to pay off organized baseball's claims against the Akron territory. The claims, for unpaid salaries to Tyrite players in 1932, amounted to another $1,900. The big hurdle, however, was that there were two mortgages on the ballpark, which had been put in the hands of a court-appointed receiver. Wrote Schlemmer, "The park is disintegrating so rapidly that unless someone moves to check the decay this season, the court will have nothing to rent in another year."[4]

Lease negotiations on League Park opened on February 1. After daylong bargaining, the two sides were further apart. The key figure was Edyth Falor, who held the first mortgage on the ballpark. Since the park was in the hands of a receiver, the court could approve a lease without Mrs. Falor's agreement, but she also controlled all available parking space at the park. A ballpark lease without her approval would be of little value.

With talks at an apparent impasse, Bruce Bierce, Akron lawyer for the Yankees, let it be known that the team was ready to make an offer to Firestone for use of Firestone Stadium. By February 7, it appeared that agreement was near until Mrs. Falor told her lawyer that she wanted more time to think over the lease terms. Weiss told Bierce that if anything was changed, the deal was off and the Yankees would stay in Wheeling.

Final lease agreement was reached the next day, but then claims against the Akron territory by former Tyrite players became an issue. As the Yankees increased their efforts to move to Akron, the former players discovered additional money that was due them. Verifying the claims loomed as a major problem. Said Weiss, "We expect to pay off every legitimate claim organized baseball holds against the Akron territory. But we will not pay off a lot of imaginary claims. Rather than do this we will take the club to some other city."[5]

The Yankees made their move to Akron official on February 19 with spring training to start for the squad in Akron on April 16. Because of spring snow, the players were unable to get onto the League Park field until April 19. Two days later, about 5,500 Akron fans turned out to watch a free intrasquad game. The Yankees' move to Akron was predicated on attracting paying crowds. Referring to the surprise turnout for the exhibition, Eugene J. Martin, business manager for the team, said, "It was a grand demonstration. I have never seen anything comparable to it during the entire 17 years that I have been associated with the national game. Now we are convinced."[6]

But the key factor in the big turnout for the game was the fact that it was free. During the seven years that the Yankees kept their Middle Atlantic League franchise in Akron the relative lack of attendance was a bone of contention even though the team never turned in a losing season. In the last five of the seven seasons, the club made the league playoffs, and in 1940 it won the championship. It was the longest run of on-field success since Akron's seven seasons in the Ohio and Pennsylvania league 30 years earlier.

Generally, the only exceptions to the sparse crowds were for playoff games and for exhibitions with major league teams. The New York Yankees had been scheduled for an exhibition game with the Akron Yankees on May 2, 1935, but it was rained out. It was rescheduled for August 12, and the New Yorkers, behind two homers from George Selkirk and one by Lou Gehrig, beat their Akron farmhands 9–6.

The Akron Yankees also played an exhibition with the Cincinnati Reds in 1935, losing 5–2. In 1936 they played exhibitions with the New York Yankees, the St. Louis Cardinals, the Homestead Grays and the Pittsburgh Crawfords, beating the Cards 6–5 in 13 innings. On the final day of the season, Martin, the business manager, reflected on the fact that paid admissions had declined by 2,000 from the 1935 figures. "We promoted more this season than last," he mused. "We gave a car away, we put on special days, bargain prices, and what not, yet our attendance slumped terribly during regular games and only because we drew some 15,000 paid attendance at the exhibition games with the New York Yankees, St. Louis Cardinals, and for the Negro games are we able to present anything approaching a decent balance sheet for the campaign."[7]

Two examples standout to illustrate the Yankees' attendance problems, both reflecting, in part, the Depression ethos of Akron. In 1935, despite spotty paid attendance, the hill that rose above the right-center field fence at League Park was always packed with fans during games. Martin, the business manager, bought 200 feet of canvas fence to put atop the regular fence to screen off "Poverty Hill." Many rubber workers were suspicious of the team's perceived relationship with the Chamber of Commerce and chamber president Lisle Buckingham, a lawyer who represented the rubber companies in labor disputes. The canvas fence was viewed as a slap at poor working people. The canvas was stolen. A hole 4 feet long and 18 inches high was cut in the right-field fence. The clubhouse was robbed. The Akron police had no clues.[8]

In 1932 a group of neighborhood boys had constructed a baseball field for themselves on a vacant lot behind the Portage Township School at Copley Road and South Hawkins Avenue on Akron's west side. Eventually known as the Maple Valley Field, it became the home of two of Akron's best amateur teams, the Sohio A.C. (Athletic Club) and the National A.C. On Sundays, they would attract crowds of 2,000 to 3,000 people because the games had no admission charge, although a hat would be passed for donations. When the Yankees won the regular season Middle Atlantic League championship in 1941, they never drew as many as 2,500 fans until their final game of the season. During that same season the Sohio A.C. played a Youngstown team that had a one-armed outfielder. It attracted such a large crowd that Akron police had to block the adjacent streets.[9]

The last game for the Akron Yankees was on September 9, 1941, when they were eliminated from the championship playoffs in an 8–5 loss to the Canton Terriers. The team had drawn only about 40,000 spectators for the season. The parent Yankees had decided not to return to Akron in 1942 when world events intervened. Schlemmer, the *Beacon Journal* sports editor, wrote the epitaph in his column on December 10, 1941, three days after the Japanese attack on Pearl Harbor. He told Akron baseball fans not to kid themselves. The Yankees weren't coming back anyway. He wrote, "This is a move that cannot be blamed upon the war."[10]

When the New York Yankees pulled out of Akron, the city was without a professional team for 55 years until the Cleveland Indians located their AA Eastern League franchise in a new downtown Akron ballpark, Canal Park, in 1997. The old "new" League Park, however, survived the departure of the Yankees for many years. The field continued to be used for amateur baseball and for football. Eventually, it became known as St. Mary's Field from its use for football by the former St. Mary's High School. The site finally was acquired by the Akron Public Schools and is now home to a vocational education annex. Much of the old playing surface is now a soccer field. The light standards survived until the mid–1970s.[11]

The Yankees also left behind a namesake amateur team, the Yankee Juniors, which they had supported during their Akron tenure. The Juniors were managed by Speed Bosworth, an Akron sandlot legend. Deserted by their professional namesakes, the Juniors became the Akron Orphans in 1942. In 1945 Bosworth managed the Orphans to the National Amateur Baseball Federation championship. By 1950 he had posted a 456–110 record with the team. In the 1950s he became a part-time scout for the Cleveland Indians, and it was said that big-league scouts would never take a player from the Akron sandlots until they had conferred with Bosworth.[12]

And, despite the attendance problems, the Akron Yankees also left behind a legacy of accomplishment on the field. In their seven years in Akron, 43 future major leaguers played for the club. Some made the majors only briefly, but others made significant contributions. These included Joe Collins, first baseman on the 1941 Akron club, who went on to play eight seasons with the New York Yankees after World War II, playing on seven pennant winners and five World Series winners, and Hank Sauer, outfielder on the 1939 Akron team, who had a 15-year major league career and won the National League MVP award in 1952 when he hit 37 home runs and knocked in 121 runs for the Chicago Cubs.[13]

It was a long wait between September 9, 1941, and April 10, 1997, when the Akron Aeros, the new AA Eastern League team of the Cleveland Indians, inaugurated a dawn of new glory before a standing-room only crowd at Canal Park with a promising young pitcher named Jared Wright on the mound. The Aeros, or maybe it was the Akrons, beat the Harrisburg Senators 13–2.[14]

Appendix A: 1881 Calendar of Scores

All games at Akron unless noted

April 28: Clevelands (NL) 25, Akrons 1
May 6: Akrons 2, White Sewing Machine (Whites of Cleveland) 1
May 7: Akrons 10, Whites 3
May 13: Bostons (NL) 2, Akrons 1
May 16: Bostons 5, Akrons 1
May 23: Troys (NL) 9, Akrons 1
May 24: Whites 4, Akrons 3 (10 innings)
May 27: Worcesters (NL) 12, Akrons 3
May 30: Akrons 23, Beaver Falls (Pennsylvania) 4
June 4: Akrons 20, Cleveland Malleables 0
June 11: Akrons 13, Whites 3
June 18: Akrons 28, Picked Nine of Akron Amateurs 11
June 21: Akrons 9, Eclipse 1 (at Louisville)
June 22: Eclipse 11, Akrons 6 (at Louisville)
June 25: Akrons 10, Eclipse 5 (at Louisville)
June 26: Akrons 2, Eclipse 2 (19 innings at Louisville)
June 27: Akrons 14, Eclipse 5 (at Louisville)
Club reorganized
July 12: Akrons 6, Whites 6
July 15: Detroits (NL) 6, Akrons 1
July 18: Detroits 8, Akrons 7
July 21: Clevelands 4, Akrons 0
July 22: Akrons 10, Keystones (Meadville, Pennsylvania) 0
July 23: Akrons 29, Whites 1 (at Cleveland)
July 27: Akrons 13, Mercers 2 (at Mercer, Pennsylvania)
July 29: Akrons 15, Cleveland Red Stockings 0
Aug. 2: Akrons 24, Cantons 0
Aug. 4: Akrons 6, Eclipse 4 (at Louisville)
Aug. 6: Akrons 8, Eclipse 4 (at Louisville)
Aug. 7: Akrons 5, Eclipse 3 (at Louisville)
Aug. 8: Akrons 20, Louisvilles 5 (at Louisville)
Aug. 10: Akrons 9, Buffalos (NL) 4
Aug. 12: Buffalos 17, Akrons 4
Aug. 13: Akrons 26, Kent (Ohio) 4
Aug. 15: Detroits 4, Akrons 0
Aug. 17: Akrons 29, Crockery Citys 6 (at East Liverpool, Ohio)
Aug. 19: Akrons 8, Detroits 6
Aug. 27: Akrons 10, Brown Stockings 5 (at St. Louis)
Aug. 28: Browns 18, Akrons 14 (at St. Louis)
Aug. 29: Akrons 14, Browns 4 (at St. Louis)
Sept. 3: Akrons 14, Eclipse 2 (at Louisville)

Sept. 4: Akrons 3, Eclipse 2 (at Louisville)
Sept. 7: Akrons 14, Oberlin College 0 Club officially disbanded
Sept. 17: Browns 5, Akrons 3 (at St. Louis)
Sept. 18: Browns 10, Akrons 8 (at St. Louis)
Sept. 19: Akrons 13, Browns 11 (at St. Louis)

Appendix B: Box Scores of the Akrons

Nineteenth century baseball was largely a hitting and fielding game. Box scores tabulated batting (at bats, runs and hits) and fielding (putouts, assists and errors). Some abbreviations may look strange, and official scorers were unknown. Box scores printed in separate newspapers frequently varied; columns often did not balance; the home team did not always bat last. The team batting first generally was determined by a coin toss. Game stories frequently vary from the box scores, and often the only way to track extra-base hits is from the story, not from box scores.

Each game in the following 1881 box scores is identified by date and location, and the source or sources of the box score are indicated. In some cases, two box scores have been merged to give a more accurate representation, and errors are noted.

A blank column under "Innings" indicates that the team did not bat in that inning.

This listing also includes the Akrons' 1880 victory over the Chicagos.

Here are the abbreviations used: 1B — hits; A — assists; AB — at-bats; BH — base hits; E — errors; H — hits; PO — putouts; R — runs; SH — safe hits; T — times at bat; TB — times at bat.

Courier-Journal box scores copyright © 2001 *Courier-Journal* Louisville Times Co. Reprinted with permission.

Sept. 8, 1880 — Chicago at Akron

(New York *Clipper*, Sept. 18, 1880)

CHICAGO	T.	R.	1B.	P.O.	A.	E.
Dalry'ple, l.f.	4	0	0	2	1	0
Kelly, 3d b.	4	0	0	1	0	0
Will'on, c.,p.	4	0	0	2	3	1
Anson, p.,c.	4	0	0	1	3	2
Burns, s.s.	4	0	0	1	3	1
Golds'ith, 1b	3	0	0	10	0	0
Corcoran, c.f.	3	2	1	0	0	1
Flint, r.f.	3	0	0	3	0	0
Quest, 2b	3	1	1	4	4	0
Totals	32	3	2	24	14	5

AKRON	T.	R.	1B.	P.O.	A.	E.
J. Man'll, r.f.	4	1	1	0	0	0
Wise, 3d b.	4	0	1	1	4	0
Dorsey, 2b	4	0	1	3	3	1
M. Man'll, c.f.	4	0	2	1	0	0
Morton, s.s.	4	1	0	1	2	1
Green, 1b	4	1	1	16	0	1
Maskey, l.f.	3	0	0	1	0	1
Kemmler, c.	3	0	1	4	4	2
Mullane, p	3	1	1	0	11	0
Totals	33	4	8	27	24	6

| Chicago | 000 002 010 — 3 |
| Akron | 020 020 00 — 4 |

Run earned — Akron, 1.
Two-base hits — Green, 1; J. Mansell, 1.
Bases on errors — Chicago, 5; Akron, 2.
Struck out — Chicago, 6; Akron, 2.
Left on bases — Chicago, 1; Akron, 4.
Balls called — Anson, 47; Williamson, 31; Mullane, 67.
Strikes called — Anson, 4; Williamson, 2; Mullane, 22.
Wild pitches — Anson, 1; Mullane, 1.
Passed balls — Williamson, 1; Kemmler, 2. Umpire, Bradley.

Runs earned — Cleveland 11.
Two-base hits — Kennedy 1, Shafer 2, Nolan 1, Dunlap 1, Monyahan 1, Neagle 1, Swartwood 1, Morton 1.
Three-base hits — Phillips 1.
Home runs — Kennedy 1.
First-base on balls — Monayhan 1, Neagle 1, Swartwood 1, McPhee 1.
First-base on errors — Cleveland 10, Akrons 0.
Struck out — Neagle 1, Morton 1, Maskry 1.
Passed balls — Kemmler 1, Kennedy 1.
Wild pitches — Neagle 1.
Umpire — William Henry Edgar Purcell.

1881

April 28 — Cleveland at Akron

(Cleveland *Leader*, April 29, 1881)

CLEVELAND	A.B.	R.	1B.	P.O.	A.	E.
Clapp, c.f.	7	4	1	4	0	0
Dunlap, 2d b	7	2	1	1	1	0
Kennedy, c	7	3	3	6	1	0
Shafer, r.f.	7	2	3	2	1	0
Glasscock, s.s.	7	4	1	3	3	0
Phillips, 1st b	7	3	3	5	0	0
McCormick, p	3	1	0	0	3	0
Monayhan, l.f.	6	3	4	2	0	0
McGeary, 3d b	7	1	1	1	2	0
Nolan, p	3	2	2	0	2	0
Total	61	25	29	24	13	0

AKRON	TB.	R.	1b.	P.O.	A.	E.
Mansell, r.f.	4	0	1	1	1	1
Neagle, p.	3	0	1	0	0	1
Swartwood, 1st b.	3	0	1	8	1	4
Wise, 3d b.	3	0	0	2	3	2
Morton, s.s.	3	1	1	1	4	3
McPhee, 2d b.	3	0	0	4	2	3
Nolan, c.f.	3	0	1	4	0	1
Maskry, l.f.	3	0	0	4	0	0
Kemmler, c	3	0	0	0	2	2
McCormick, c.f.	0	0	0	0	0	0
Total	28	1	5	24	13	17

Innings	1	2	3	4	5	6	7	8	
Cleveland	5	0	3	1	0	0	8	8	—25
Akron	0	1	0	0	0	0	0	0	— 1

May 6 — Whites at Akron

(Cleveland *Leader*, May 7, 1881)

AKRON	A.B.	R.	1B.	P.O.	A.	E.
Mansell, c.f.	4	0	2	1	0	0
Swartwood, 1st b.	3	1	0	7	0	2
Wise, 3d b.	4	0	1	2	2	1
Green, r.f.	2	1	0	1	0	0
Morton, s.s.	4	0	1	1	2	1
Mullane, p.	3	0	1	0	16	0
Maskry, l.f.	3	0	1	0	0	0
McPhee, 2d b.	3	0	0	1	1	0
Kemmler, c	3	0	0	4	6	1
Total	29	2	6	17	27	5

WHITES	A.B	R.	1B.	P.O.	A.	E.
Sullivan, c	4	1	1	6	4	0
Atkinson, 1st b.	4	0	0	5	0	2
Nolan, s.s.	4	0	1	3	6	2
C. Bohn, r.f.	4	0	1	2	0	0
Strief, 2d b.	4	0	0	4	0	0
B. Bohn, 3d b.	4	0	0	4	2	1
West, c.f.	4	0	2	1	0	1
Arundel, p.	4	0	1	0	0	0
Keifer, l.f.	4	0	0	0	3	0
Total	36	1	6	24	15	6

Innings	1	2	3	4	5	6	7	8	9	
Akrons	1	0	0	0	0	0	0	1	—	2
Whites	0	0	1	0	0	0	0	0	—	1

Two base hits — Tony Mullane.
First base on balls — Akron 4.
Struck out — Akron 2, Whites 10.
Passed balls — Akron 2, Whites 3.

Wild pitches—Mullane 1.
Umpire—Dewey.

May 7 — Whites at Akron

(Cleveland *Leader*, May 9, 1881)

AKRON	A.B.	R.	1B.	P.O.	A.	E.
Mansell, c.f.	5	1	2	1	0	0
Swartwood, 1st b.	5	1	1	7	0	0
Wise, 3d b.	4	2	1	1	1	1
Green, s.s.	4	1	3	1	0	0
Neagle, r.f.	4	1	1	0	0	0
Mullane, p.	4	2	2	0	10	1
Maskry, l.f.	4	1	1	0	0	0
McPhee, 2d b.	4	0	3	4	1	1
Kemmler, c	4	1	0	7	2	1
Total	38	10	14	21	14	4

WHITES	A.B.	R.	1B.	P.O.	A.	E.
Sullivan, c	4	1	0	2	3	0
Atkinson, 1st b.	3	1	0	10	0	0
Nolan, s.s.	3	1	1	4	1	2
C. Bohn, rf & 3b	3	0	1	1	0	0
Strief, 2d b.	3	0	1	1	3	0
B. Bohn, 3b & p.	3	0	1	2	2	1
West, c.f.	3	0	1	0	0	2
Arundel, p & rf	2	0	0	1	5	1
Dewey, l.f.	3	0	0	0	0	1
Total	27	3	5	21	14	7

Innings	1	2	3	4	5	6	7	
Akrons	7	0	0	0	1	2	0	—10
Whites	0	0	0	0	0	3	0	— 3

Earned runs—Akrons 3.
Two-base hits—Wise, Green, Swartwood, Bohn.
First-base on balls—Whites 1.
Struck out—Akrons 2 Whites 5
Double plays—W. Bohn, Strief and Atkinson, Kemmler, McPhee and Swartwood.
Passed balls—Sullivan 2.
Umpire—McNaughton.

May 13 — Boston at Akron

(Cleveland *Leader*, May 14, 1881)

BOSTON	A.B.	R.	1B.	P.O.	A.	E.
Crowley, r.f.	4	0	1	0	0	0
Hornung, l.f.	4	1	1	2	0	0
Barnes, s.s.	4	0	1	4	2	0
Richmond, c.f.	4	0	1	1	0	0
Morrill, 1st b.	3	0	1	9	0	0
Burdock, 2d b.	4	1	1	3	1	1
Sutton, 3d b.	3	0	1	3	1	0
Bond, p.	3	0	1	0	1	0
Deasley, c.	2	0	1	5	2	1
Total	31	2	9	27	7	2

AKRON	A.B.	R.	1B.	P.O.	A.	E.
Mansell, c.f.	4	0	1	3	1	0
Swartwood, 1st b.	4	0	0	6	0	0
Wise, 3d b.	4	1	1	4	3	0
Neagle, cf & p.	3	0	1	0	2	0
Green, s.s.	3	0	0	0	4	1
Mullane, p & cf.	3	0	0	0	3	0
Maskry, l.f.	3	0	0	3	0	0
McPhee, 2d b.	3	0	1	3	0	1
Kemmler, c.	3	0	0	5	3	2
Total	30	1	4	24	16	4

Innings	1	2	3	4	5	6	7	8	9	
Boston	0	1	1	0	0	0	0	0		—2
Akrons	0	0	0	1	0	0	0	0	0	—1

Earned runs—Boston 1.
Two-base hits—Richmond, Burdock and Wise.
Total bases on clean hits—Boston 11, Akron 5.
Double play—Mansell and Wise.
Left on bases—Boston 4, Akron 1.
Struck Out—Barnes, Sutton 2.
Bases on called balls—Morrill and Deasley.
Fumbled grounders—McPhee.
Missed flies—Deasley 1.
Passed balls—Kemmler 4.
Balls called—On bond 42, Mullane 49, Neagle 41.
Strikes called—Off Bond 17, Mullane 16, Neagle 5.
Time of Game—One hour and 30 minutes.
Umpire—James O'Day, of Chicago.

May 16 — Boston at Akron

(Cleveland *Leader*, May 17, 1881)

AKRON	A.B.	R.	1B.	P.O.	A.	E.
Mansell, c.f.	4	0	2	0	0	0
Swartwood, 1st b	4	0	1	9	1	2
Wise, 3d b	4	0	1	2	1	1
Neagle, p	4	0	0	1	7	1
Green, s.s.	4	0	0	2	3	1
Mullane, c.f.	4	0	1	0	1	2
Maskry, l.f.	4	0	2	1	0	1
McPhee, 2d b	4	0	1	2	4	1
Kemmler, c	3	1	1	7	2	1
Total	35	1	9	24	19	10

BOSTON	A.B.	R.	1B.	P.O.	A.	E.
Crowley, r.f.	4	1	1	2	1	0
Hornung, l.f.	4	0	0	1	0	0
Barnes, s.s.	4	0	1	3	3	1
Richmond, c.f.	3	1	1	0	0	0
Morrill, 1st b	4	1	1	10	0	0
Burdock, 2d b	4	1	2	3	3	0
Sutton, 3d b	3	0	0	2	0	1
Bond, p	3	0	0	0	1	0
Deasley, c	3	1	0	6	3	0
Total	32	5	6	27	11	2

Earned runs— None.
Two-base hits— Wise 1.
Total bases on clean hits— Akron 10, Boston 6.
Double plays— Deasley and Morrill 2.
Left on bases— Akron 3, Boston 4.
Struck out— Barnes, Burdock, Deasley.
Bases on called balls— Richmond.
First base on errors— Akron 2, Boston 6.
Wild throws— Mullane 2, Neagle, Wise, Kemmler, Barnes.
Fumbled grounders— Green, McPhee, Sutton.
Missed flies— Swartwood, Maskry.
Passed balls— Kemmler 1.
Balls called— On Neagle 77, Bond 53.
Strikes called— Off Neagle 17, Bond 17.
Time of game— One hour and 25 minutes.
Umpire— Fulmer.

May 23 — Troy at Akron

(Cleveland *Leader*, May 24, 1881)

TROY	A.B.	R.	1B.	P.O.	A.	E.
Cassidy, c.f.	5	2	2	2	0	0
Connor, 1st b	5	0	1	12	0	0
Ferguson, 2d b	4	0	0	2	4	0
Gillespie, l.f.	5	1	1	2	0	1
Caskins, s.s.	5	1	2	1	1	0
Powers, c	5	0	2	6	2	0
Evans, r.f.	4	1	3	1	0	0
Hankinson, 3d b	4	2	2	0	5	0
Keefe, p.	3	2	1	1	4	0
Total	40	9	13	27	16	1

AKRON	A.B.	R.	1B.	P.O.	A.	E.
Mansell, r.f.	4	0	0	1	0	1
Swartwood, 1st b	4	0	2	9	0	0
Wise, 3d b	4	0	0	4	3	1
Neagle, p	4	0	0	0	4	2
Green, s.s.	3	0	0	1	5	1
Morton, c.f.	3	0	0	4	1	0
Maskrey, l.f.	3	1	1	1	1	1
McPhee, 2d b	3	0	1	3	0	0
Kemmler, c	3	0	0	4	4	2
Total	31	1	4	27	18	8

Innings	1	2	3	4	5	6	7	8	9	
Troy	3	0	0	2	0	4	0	0	0	—9
Akron	0	0	1	0	0	0	0	0	0	—1

Runs earned— Troy 1, Akron 1.
Two-base hits— Maskrey, McPhee, Gillespie, Connor.
Total bases on clean hits— Troy 15, Akron 6.
Left on bases— Troy 6, Akron 3.
Struck out— Mansell, Wise, Green, McPhee, Powers, Keefe.
Bases on balls— Ferguson, Keefe.
First base on errors— Troy 3, Akron 1.
Wild throws— Neagle, Kemmler 2.
Passed grounders— Maskrey, Wise.
Fumbled grounders— Green, Mansell.
Missed flies— Gillespie.
Muffed thrown ball— Neagle 1.
Passed balls— Kemmler 1.
Wild pitches— Neagle 1.
Ball called— On Neagle 101, on Keefe 52.
Strikes called— Off Neagel 20, off Keefe 19.

Box Scores of the Akrons 147

Time of game —1 hours and 23 minutes.
Umpire — Herman Boscher.

May 24 — Whites at Akron

(Cleveland *Leader*, May 25, 1881)

WHITES	A.B.	R.	1B.	P.O.	A.	E.
Sullivan, c	4	0	0	6	1	0
Atkinson, 1st b	4	0	0	6	1	0
Nolan, s.s	4	0	0	2	4	0
C. Bohn, p.	4	1	2	1	1	0
Strief, 2d b	4	1	0	3	2	0
W. Bohn, 3d b	4	0	0	2	2	0
West, c.f.	4	1	1	2	0	1
Maddoc, l.f.	4	0	0	6	0	1
Stockwell, r.f.	3	1	1	2	2	0
Total	35	4	4	30	13	2

AKRON	A.B.	R.	1B.	P.O.	A.	E.
Mansell, r.f.	5	0	0	0	0	2
Swartwood, 1st b	5	0	5	14	0	2
Wise, 3d b	4	0	0	0	0	2
Neagle, p.	4	0	1	0	12	0
Green, c	4	0	0	10	3	1
Morton, s.s.	4	2	2	0	3	0
Maskrey, lf.f	4	0	1	1	0	0
McPhee, 2d b	4	1	1	3	4	0
Kemmler, r.f.	4	0	1	1	0	0
Total	31	3	11	29	22	7

Innings	1	2	3	4	5	6	7	8	9	10
Whites	0	0	0	0	0	0	0	1	3 —	4
Akron	0	0	0	0	0	1	0	0	2 —	3

Earned runs— Akrons 1.
Two-base hits— Swartwood, Stockwell
Three-base hits— Stockwell.
First base on errors— Whites 5 Akron 1.
Struck out — Mansell, Bohn 2, Maddoc 3, Sullivan, Atkinson, Nolan.
Passed balls— Green 1, Sullivan 2.
Umpire — Andrews.

May 27 — Worcester at Akron

(Cleveland *Leader*, May 28, 1881)

AKRON	A.B.	R.	1B.	P.O.	A.	E.
Mansell, r.f.	4	0	3	1	0	0
Swartwood, 1st b	4	0	2	8	0	1
Wise, 3d b	4	0	0	2	2	1
Neagle, cf & p.	4	0	0	2	3	0
McPhee, 2d b	4	0	0	0	2	1
Maskrey, l.f.	4	2	2	2	0	0
Green, s.s.	4	1	2	2	2	2
Mullane, p & cf	4	0	2	1	1	3
Kemmler, c	4	0	1	9	2	0
Total	36	3	12	27	12	8

WORCESTER	A.B.	R.	1B.	P.O.	A.	E.
Stovey, 1st b	5	3	4	13	0	0
Dickerson, l.f.	6	1	3	2	0	1
Dorgan, r.f.	6	2	4	0	1	0
Irwin, s.s.	6	1	0	1	2	1
Carpenter, 3d b	6	0	1	2	2	2
Hotaling, c.f.	5	2	2	2	0	0
Corey, p.	5	1	3	0	8	0
Creamer, 2d b	5	1	1	2	4	0
Taylor, c	5	1	1	5	4	0
Total	49	12	19	27	21	4

Innings	1	2	3	4	5	6	7	8	9	
Akron	0	0	0	2	0	0	0	0	1 —	3
Worcester	0	7	2	0	2	0	0	1	0 —	12

Earned runs— Worcester 1.
First base on balls— Stovey.
First base on errors— Worcester 5, Akron 2.
Passed balls— Kemmler 2.
Wild pitches— None.
Umpire — Bradley.

May 30 — Beaver Falls at Akron

(Cleveland *Leader*, May 31, 1881)

AKRON	A.B.	R.	1B.	P.O.	A.	E.
Mansell, c.f.	6	3	3	0	0	0
Swartwood, r.f.	6	4	5	1	0	0
Neagle, p	6	4	3	0	16	0
Green, s.s.	6	3	2	0	1	1
Morton, 3d b.	6	2	4	0	3	0
McPhee, 2d b.	6	1	0	3	2	1
Maskrey, l.f.	5	4	2	0	0	0
Mullane, 1st b.	5	1	3	9	0	1
Kemmler, c	5	2	1	14	2	3
Total	51	23	23	27	24	6

BEAVER FALLS	A.B.	R.	1B.	P.O.	A.	E.
Feron, l.f.	3	1	0	0	2	1
Palmer, 2d b.	4	0	0	2	3	3

BEAVER FALLS (cont.)

Howard, c	4	0	0	3	0	1
West, c.f.	4	1	1	1	1	2
Baker, s.s.	1	0	0	3	4	1
Wise, s.s.	2	1	1	0	0	0
Williams, 1st b.	3	0	0	10	1	0
Hydon, 3d b.	4	1	0	3	0	3
Millin, r.f.	3	0	1	2	1	2
Baldwin, p.	3	0	1	1	5	3
Total	31	4	4	25	17	16

Innings	1	2	3	4	5	6	7	8	9	
Akron	5	2	2	1	2	2	4	5		—23
Beaver Falls	1	0	0	0	1	0	0	0	2	— 4

Two-base hits—Neagle, Kemmler, Mansell

First base on balls—Beavers Falls 3.
Struck out—Akron 1, Beaver Falls 14.
Double plays—Akron 1.
Time of game—2 hours and 15 minutes.
Umpire—James O. Day.

June 4 — Malleables at Akron

(Cleveland *Leader*, June 6, 1881)

MALLEABLES	A.B.	R.	1B.	P.O.	A.	E.
Sheets, 1st b.	4	0	1	10	1	0
Hardwick, c.f.	4	0	0	1	4	1
Bullis, c	4	0	0	1	3	0
Kelley, p.	4	0	0	1	7	0
Carroll, l.f.	3	0	1	2	0	2
Hudle, 2d b.	4	0	0	5	2	2
Snyder, c.f.	3	0	1	2	0	1
Chapman, r.f.	3	0	1	0	1	3
Bell, 3d b.	3	0	0	2	1	3
Total	32	0	4	24	19	13

AKRON	A.B.	R.	1B.	P.O.	A.	E.
Mansell, r.f.	5	4	2	0	1	0
Swartwood, c.f.	6	3	3	1	0	1
Wise, 3d b.	6	3	3	1	1	1
Neagle, p.	6	2	1	1	17	0
Morton, s.s.	5	2	2	1	0	0
McPhee, 2d b.	5	0	3	1	2	0
Green, c	5	0	0	14	1	1
Maskrey, l.f.	5	2	3	1	0	0
Mullane, 1st b.	4	4	3	7	0	1
Total	47	20	20	27	22	4

Innings	1	2	3	4	5	6	7	8	9	
Malleables	0	0	0	0	0	0	0	0	0	—0
Akrons	1	0	2	0	4	6	6	1		—20

Earned runs—Akron 10.
Two-base hits—Swartwood 2, Mullane.
Umpire—O'Day.

June 11 — Whites at Akron

(Cleveland *Leader*, May 13, 1881)

AKRON	A.B.	R.	1B.	P.O.	A.	E.
Mansell, r.f.	5	3	3	0	0	0
Swartwood, 1st b	5	1	1	10	1	2
Wise, 3d b	5	1	3	2	3	3
Morton, c.f.	5	1	1	1	1	0
Mullane, p.	5	2	2	0	7	1
Maskrey, l.f.	5	3	2	3	1	0
McPhee, 2d b.	5	1	2	3	3	1
Green, s.s.	5	1	1	0	3	2
Kemmler, c	4	0	1	8	3	0
Total	44	13	12	27	22	9

WHITES	A.B.	R.	1B.	P.O.	A.	E.
West, c.f.	5	0	1	1	0	2
C. Bohn, p.	4	0	0	0	6	1
Sullivan, c	5	1	2	5	1	1
Stockwell, r.f.	4	0	0	0	0	3
Nolan, s.s.	4	1	1	1	0	0
Strief, 2d b.	3	0	0	2	5	1
W. Bohn, 3d b.	4	0	0	1	2	1
Atkinson, 1st b.	4	1	0	12	0	1
Maddock, l.f.	4	0	1	2	1	1
Total	39	3	5	24	15	11

Innings	1	2	3	4	5	6	7	8	9	
Akrons	2	0	0	3	2	1	1	4		—13
Whites	0	0	0	1	0	0	0	1	1	— 3

Earned runs—Akrons 2.
Two-base hits—Mansell, Maskrey, McPhee 2, Sullivan.
First base on balls—Strief, C. Bohn.
Struck out—Whites 5.
Double plays—Maskrey and Swartwood.
Passed balls—Kemmler 1, Sullivan 1.
Wild pitches—Mullane 1, Bohn 1.
Umpire—O'Day.

June 21 — Akron at Louisville

(Louisville *Courier-Journal*, June 22, 1881)

ECLIPSE.	T.	R.	1B.	P.O.	A.	E.
Summers, s.s.	4	0	1	0	3	2
Burkalow, c.f.	4	0	0	4	0	2
J. Reccius, p.	4	0	1	0	8	1
Pfeffer, 2d b.	4	0	0	1	2	2
Crotty, c.	4	0	0	5	1	2
Zimmerman, r.f.	4	0	2	3	1	1
McLaughlin, 1st b.	4	0	0	10	0	1
P. Reccius, 3d b.	4	0	1	3	1	0
Dyler, l.f.	3	1	1	0	0	0
Totals	35	1	6	27	16	11

AKRONS	T.	R.	1B.	P.O.	A.	E.
Sullivan, c.f.	5	1	2	2	0	0
Swartwood, r.f.	5	2	1	0	0	0
Wise, 3d b.	5	0	1	0	2	0
Morton, s.s.	5	1	1	1	6	0
Mullane, p.	5	1	2	1	4	1
Maskrey, l.f.	4	1	0	2	0	0
McPhee, 2d b.	4	1	0	1	0	0
Green, 1st b.	4	0	1	14	0	1
Kemmler, c	4	2	0	6	1	0
Totals	41	9	8	27	13	2

SCORE BY INNINGS
Eclipse   0 0 0 0 1 0 0 0 0 — 1
Akrons   0 2 0 0 0 0 3 0 4 — 9

Runs Earned — Eclipse, one.
Left on Base — Eclipse, seven; Akrons, five.
Wild Pitch — Mullane, one.
Passed Balls — Crotty, three; Kemmler, two.
Struck Out — Eclipse, three, Akrons, three.
Two-base Hits — Summers, Zimmerman, Sullivan, Wise and Mullane.
Time of Game — One hour and forty-five minutes.
Umpire — Gus. Ruhl.

June 22 — Akron at Louisville

(Louisville *Courier-Journal*, June 23, 1881)

ECLIPSE	T.	R.	1B.	P.O.	A.	E.
Summers, 3d b.	5	2	2	1	2	1
Burkalow, c.	5	2	2	0	0	1
Browning, s.s.	5	1	1	1	3	1
J. Reccius, p	5	1	2	1	6	2
Pfeffer, 2d b.	5	2	2	5	3	2
Crotty, c	5	0	0	7	4	0
Zimmerman, r.f.	4	1	1	1	1	1
McLaughlin, 1st b.	4	1	2	11	0	1
Dyler, l.f.	4	1	2	0	0	0
Totals	42	11	14	27	19	9

AKRONS	T.	R.	1B.	P.O.	A.	E.
Sullivan, c.f.	5	0	1	2	0	0
Swartwood, r.f.	4	0	0	1	0	0
Wise, 3d b.	4	0	0	2	3	1
Morton, s.s.	4	2	2	1	1	4
Mullane, p.	4	1	0	0	4	0
Maskrey, l.f.	4	1	2	2	0	0
McPhee, 2d b.	4	1	1	3	1	2
Green, 1st b.	4	1	2	9	0	1
Kemmler, c.	4	0	0	4	3	1
Totals	37	6	8	24	12	9

SCORE BY INNINGS
Eclipse   1 0 5 1 0 3 1 0 — 11
Akrons   0 1 0 2 0 0 3 0 0 — 6

Earned Runs — Eclipse, six; Akron, three.
Two-base Hits — Reccius, McLaughlin and Morton.
Three-base Hits — McLaughlin and Maskrey.
Home Run — Pfeffer.
Struck Out — Eclipse, three; Akron, four.
Passed Balls — Crotty, one; Kemmler, three.
Umpire — Geo. Harrington.
Time of Game — One hour and fifty minutes.

June 25 — Akron at Louisville

(Louisville *Courier-Journal*, June 26, 1881)

ECLIPSE	T.	R.	1B.	P.O.	A.	E.
Sommers, s.s.	5	0	1	2	6	2
Burkalow, c.f.	5	0	0	3	0	2
J. Reccius, p.	5	2	3	1	3	0
Pfeffer, 2d b.	5	1	2	3	6	2
Crotty, c.	5	1	0	9	0	3
Zimmerman, r.f.	5	1	3	1	0	0
McLaughlin, 1st b.	4	1	1	5	0	1
P. Reccius, 3d b.	4	0	1	3	1	2
Dyler, l.f.	4	0	2	0	0	1
Totals	42	5	13	27	16	13

AKRONS	T.	R.	1B.	P.O.	A.	E.
Sullivan, c.f.	5	3	3	3	1	0
Swartwood, r.f.	5	1	2	0	0	0
Wise, 3d b.	5	0	1	0	3	2
Morton, s.s.	5	1	1	0	2	0
Mullane, p.	5	0	1	0	7	1
Maskrey, l.f.	5	0	1	1	0	0
McPhee, 2d b.	5	1	1	7	2	0
Green, 1st b.	5	2	0	10	0	1
Kemmler, c	5	2	1	5	4	0
Totals	45	10	11	26*	19	4

*McLaughlin hit by batted ball.

Earned Runs— Eclipse, two; Akron, five.
Two-base Hits— J. Reccius one, Zimmerman two, Swartwood one, Wise one, Kemmler one.
Three-base Hits— Sullivan one.
Struck Out — Eclipse four; Akron, three.
Double Plays— Sommers and P. Reccius, Pfeffer and McLaughlin.
Passed Balls— Crotty, one; Kemmler, two.
Wild Pitches— Reccius one.
Time of Game — Two hours.
Umpire— Geo. Harrington.

June 26 — Akron at Louisville

(New York *Clipper*, July 9, 1881)

ECLIPSE	T.	R.	1B.	PO.	A.	E.
Sommers, 3d b	8	1	2	4	4	0
Burkalow, c.f.	8	0	2	2	1	0
Browning, s.s.	8	0	1	0	3	0
Reccius, p.	8	0	0	1	15	1
Pfeffer, 2d b.	8	1	2	6	12	3
Crotty, c.	8	0	1	17	1	2
Zimmerman, r.f.	7	0	2	4	0	0
McLaughlin, 1st b.	7	0	2	19	0	4
Dyler, l.f.	7	0	0	4	0	0
Totals	69	2	12	57	36	10

AKRON	T.	R.	1B.	PO.	A.	E.
Sullivan, c.f.	8	1	3	1	0	1
Swartwood, r.f.	8	0	2	7	0	0
Wise, 3d b.	8	0	3	3	6	0
Morton, s.s.	8	0	1	3	6	0
Mullane, p.	8	1	2	1	16	0
Maskrey, l.f.	8	0	2	1	0	0
McPhee, 2d b.	8	0	1	5	5	1
Green, 1st b.	8	0	1	24	0	1
Kemmler, c	8	0	1	12	3	2
Totals	72	2	16	57	36	5

Earned runs— Eclipse, 2.
First base on errors— Eclipse, 2; Akron, 4.
Passed balls— Crotty, 4; Kemmler, 1.
Struck out— Eclipse, 11; Akron, 13.
Double-plays— Sommers, Pfeffer and McLaughlin; Crotty, Sommers, Pfeffer and McLaughlin; and Reccius, Pfeffer and McLaughlin; Kemmler, McPhee and Green. Two-base hits— Browning, 1, Pfeffer, 1; Swartwood, 1, Wise, 1.
Three-base hits— Pfeffer and Wise.
Umpire— Thos. Irwin of Cincinnati Ravens.
Time — 3h.5m.

June 27 — Akron at Louisville

(Louisville *Courier-Journal*, June 28, 1881)

ECLIPSE	T.	R.	1B.	P.O.	A.	E.
Sommers, 3b b & c.	5	0	1	3	1	2
Burkalow, c.f. & p.	5	0	2	0	2	3
Browning, s.s.	4	1	0	3	5	0
Reccius, p & c.f.	4	1	1	2	1	0
Pfeffer, 2d b.	4	0	1	3	3	0
Crotty, c & 3d b.	3	1	1	3	1	0
Zimmerman, r.f.	3	1	1	4	0	0
McLaughlin, 1st b.	3	1	1	9	1	0
Dyler, l.f.	3	0	0	0	0	0
Totals	34	5	8	27	14	5

AKRON	T.	R.	1B.	P.O.	A.	E.
Sullivan, c.f.	6	1	0	1	0	0
Swartwood, r.f.	5	2	2	1	0	1
Wise, 3d b.	5	5	4	4	2	0
Morton, s.s.	5	2	2	1	3	1
Mullane, p.	5	2	2	2	0	1
Maskrey, l.f.	5	2	3	1	0	0
McPhee, 2d b.	5	0	2	2	6	0
Green, 1st b.	5	0	0	13	0	2
Kemmler, c	5	0	0	2	2	1
Totals	46	14	15	27	13	6

SCORE BY INNINGS
Eclipse 2 0 0 0 0 0 3 0 0— 5
Akron   5 4 0 1 0 3 0 1 0—14

Time of Game— one hour and fifty-five minutes.

Passed Balls—Sommers, one; Kemmler, one.
Two-base Hits—Sommers one, McLaughlin one, Wise one, Mullane one.
Home-runs—Wise.
Wild Pitch—Burkalow.
Umpire—Thos. Irwin, of Cincinnati Ravens.

July 12 — Whites at Akron

(Combined from Akron *Daily Beacon* & Cleveland *Leader*, July 13, 1881)

AKRONS	A.B.	R.	H.	P.O.	A.	E.
Swartwood, r.f.	3	0	1	0	0	0
Wise, 3d b	3	1	1	2	5	0
Purcell, c.f.	3	2	1	1	0	0
Mullane, p.	4	1	1	2	7	0
Morton, s.s.	4	1	1	0	0	2
Maskrey, l.f.	4	0	1	1	1	0
McPhee, 2d b	3	0	2	2	4	0
Kemmler, c	4	0	0	11	2	2
O'Dea, 1st b	3	1	1	5	2	2
Total	31	6	9	24	21	6

WHITES	A.B.	R.	H.	P.O.	A.	E.
Sullivan, c	4	1	2	4	1	1
C. Bohn, 3d b	4	0	1	2	7	0
West, c.f.	4	0	2	3	2	1
Nolan, s.s.	4	1	2	1	2	1
Stockwell, r.f.	4	1	0	1	0	0
White, l.f.	4	1	1	2	0	0
Cullen, 2d b	4	0	0	0	1	1
Atkinson, 1st b	4	1	1	10	0	1
Jones, p.	3	1	2	1	2	1
Total	35	6	11	24	15	6

Innings	1	2	3	4	5	6	7	8	
Akrons	1	0	0	1	4	0	0	0	—6
Whites	0	5	0	1	0	0	0	0	—6

Earned runs—Akrons 2, Whites 2.
Two base hits—Sullivan.
First base on balls—Akrons 4.
Struck out—Morton, O'Dea, White, Bohn, Cullen, Jones, Stockwell, Atkinson.
Double plays—Bohn and Atkinson 2; Cullen and Atkinson; West and Sullivan; Bohn, West and Atkinson.

Passed balls—Sullivan 2, Kemmler 1.
Wild pitches—Mullane 1, Jones 2.
Umpire—Dewey.
Balls off Jones 80, strikes 25.
Balls off Mullane 70, strikes 46.
Time of game, 1 hr. 40 min.

July 15 — Detroit at Akron

(Cleveland *Leader*, July 16, 1881)

AKRON	A.B.	R.	H.	P.O.	A.	E.
Swartwood, r.f.	3	0	0	0	0	2
Wise, 3d b	4	0	0	0	1	0
Purcell, c.f.	4	0	0	1	0	0
Mullane, p.	4	1	1	0	6	0
Sullivan, 1st b	4	0	1	10	1	0
Maskrey, l.f.	4	0	1	3	1	0
McPhee, 2d b	3	0	0	1	5	1
Kemmler, c	3	0	0	9	1	1
Morton, s.s.	3	0	0	0	2	0
Total	32	1	3	24	17	4

DETROIT	A.B.	R.	H.	P.O.	A.	E.
Wood, l.f.	5	0	2	3	0	0
Knight, r.f.	5	1	2	0	0	0
Hanlon, c.f.	4	1	2	2	0	0
Powell, 1st b	4	1	3	15	0	0
Houck, s.s.	4	0	1	1	4	1
Mountain, p.	4	1	0	1	5	0
Whitney, 3d b	3	1	0	1	2	0
Gerhardt, 2d b	4	0	2	2	5	1
Rielly, c	4	1	1	2	0	0
Total	37	6	13	27	16	2

Innings	1	2	3	4	5	6	7	8	9	
Akron	0	0	0	0	0	0	1	0	0	—1
Detroit	2	0	0	1	0	0	0	1	2	—6

Runs earned—Detroit 2.
Three-base hits—Wood, Powell.
Total bases on clean hits—Akron 3, Detroit 15.
Double plays—Sullivan and McPhee; Morton, McPhee and Sullivan.
Left on bases—Akron 4, Detroit 5.
Struck out—Maskrey, Kemmler, Knight 2, Hanlon, Mountain, Whitney.
Bases on called balls—Swartwood, Whitney.
First base on errors—Akron 1, Detroit 4.

Missed catch of third strike — Kemmler.
Passed grounders — McPhee, Houck, Gerhardt.
Missed flies — Swartwood 2.
Passed balls — Kemmler 2, Rielly 2.
Wild pitches — Mullane.
Balk — Mountain.
Balls called — On Mullane 82, on Mountain 73.
Strikes called — Off Mullane 35, Mountain 29.
Time of game — 1 hour and 45 minutes.
Umpire — Bennett, of the Detroits.

July 18 — Detroit at Akron

(Akron *Daily Beacon*, July 19, 1881)

AKRONS	A.B.	R.	1B.	P.O.	A.	E.
Swartwood, r.f	5	1	2	2	0	0
Wise, 2d b	5	0	1	0	0	0
Purcell, p.	5	0	1	0	4	2
Sullivan, 1st b	5	1	1	10	0	0
Mullane, s.s.	5	2	1	3	6	1
Maskrey, l.f.	4	1	2	0	0	0
McPhee, 2d b	4	1	2	2	1	1
Kemmler, c	3	1	0	6	0	1
Morton, c.f.	4	0	0	1	0	0
Total	40	7	10	24	11	5

DETROITS	A.B.	R.	1B.	P.O.	A.	E.
Wood, l.f.	5	2	2	0	0	0
Knight, r.f.	4	1	2	2	0	1
Hanlon, c.f.	4	1	2	0	0	0
Powell, 1st b	5	1	1	11	1	1
Houck, s.s.	5	1	1	0	6	1
Gerhardt, 2d b	4	1	0	5	4	1
Whitney, 3d b	4	0	1	1	1	2
Mountain, p.	4	0	1	0	3	0
Rielly, c	4	1	0	8	1	1
Total	39	8	10	27	16	7

Innings	1	2	3	4	5	6	7	8	9	
Detroit	1	0	0	1	0	0	5	0	1	—8
Akron	0	5	0	0	0	0	0	2	0	—7

Earned runs — Detroits 1, Akrons 3.
Two-base hits — Purcell, Maskrey, Mullane.
Three-base hits — Wise.
Total bases on hits — Akrons 18, Detroits 10.

Home runs — Swartwood.
First base on balls — Akrons 1, Detroits 3.
Struck out — Detroits 4, Akrons 1.
Double plays — Mullane and Sullivan.
Passed balls — Kemmler 5, Reilly 1.
Wild pitches — Purcell 1.
Umpire — Descher.
Balls on Mountain, 92; strikes, 27.
Balls on Purcell, 108; strikes, 42.
Time of game — 2 hrs. 30 mins.

July 21 — Cleveland at Akron

(Cleveland *Leader*, July 22, 1881)

CLEVELAND	A.B.	R.	BH.	P.O.	A.	E.
Kennedy, l.f.	4	1	1	0	0	0
Shafer, r.f.	4	0	1	2	1	0
Clapp, c	4	2	3	8	2	0
Phillips, 1st b	4	0	1	7	0	0
Glasscock, 2d b	4	1	2	5	1	1
Nolan, p.	4	0	1	0	3	0
Bradley, s.s.	4	0	0	2	3	1
Moynahan, 3d b	4	0	0	1	0	0
Remsen, c.f.	3	0	0	2	0	0
Total	35	4	9	27	10	2

AKRON	A.B.	R.	BH.	P.O.	A.	E.
Swartwood, r.f.	4	0	1	0	0	0
Wise, 3d b	3	0	0	3	3	2
Purcell, s.s.	4	0	1	1	2	0
Sullivan, 1st b	4	0	1	9	0	0
Mullane, p	4	0	0	2	4	1
Maskrey, l.f.	4	0	0	3	1	0
McPhee, 2d b	3	0	0	3	1	0
Kemmler, c	2	0	0	3	0	0
Morton, c.f.	3	0	2	0	0	0
Total	31	0	5	24	11	3

Innings	1	2	3	4	5	6	7	8	9	
Cleveland	1	0	0	0	1	0	0	2		—4
Akron	0	0	0	0	0	0	0	0	0	—0

Runs earned — Cleveland 1.
Two-base hits — Nolan.
Total bases on clean hits — Cleveland 10, Akron 5.
Double plays — Clapps and Phillips; Shafer and Phillips; Maskrey and Sullivan.
Left on bases — Cleveland 6, Akron 2.
Struck out — Shafer, Bradley, Wise 3.
Bases on called balls — Wise, Kemmler.

First base on errors— Cleveland 3, Akrons 2.
Wild throws— Wise, Mullane.
Passed grounders— Glasscock.
Fumbled grounders— Wise, Bradley.
Passed ball— Kemmler.
Wild pitches— none.
Balls called— On Nolan 65, on Mullane 55.
Strikes called— Off Nolan 26, off Mullane 16.
Time of game— 1 hours and 14 minutes.
Umpire— Doscher.

July 22 — Meadville Keystones at Akron

(Cleveland *Leader* & Akron *Daily Beacon*, July 23, 1881)

AKRONS	A.B.	R.	H.	P.O.	A.	E.
Swartwood, 1b	5	0	2	7	0	2
Wise, c	5	1	2	10	0	2
Purcell, s.s.	5	1	1	2	4	1
Mullane, p.	5	2	3	1	8	0
Morton, 3b	5	2	1	1	2	0
Maskrey, lf	5	1	1	4	0	0
McPhee, 2b	5	1	3	2	4	0
Kemmler, rf	4	1	0	0	1	0
Weeks, cf*	5	1	1	0	0	0
Total	44	10	14	27	19	5

KEYSTONES	A.B.	R.	H.	P.O.	A.	E.
Pettis, s.s.	5	0	1	0	5	2
VanTassel, cf	5	0	1	3	0	0
Power, c	4	0	1	6	4	0
Sekins, 3b	4	0	1	4	0	1
Shaver, 1b	4	0	1	8	0	0
Rouche, rf	3	0	0	1	0	1
Hotchkiss, lf	4	0	0	1	0	1
McCullough, p	4	0	0	3	6	0
Wheeler, 2b	4	0	1	1	0	0
Total	37	0	6	27	15	5

Innings	1	2	3	4	5	6	7	8	9	
Akrons	1	1	4	2	0	0	2	0	0	—10
Keystones	0	0	0	0	0	0	0	0	0	— 0

Earned runs— Akrons 5.
Two-base hits— Wise 2, Mullane 2 and Maskrey.
Three-base hits— None.
Home runs— None.
First base on balls— Swartwood, Kemmler and Rouche.
First base on errors— Akrons 3, Keystones 4.
Struck out— Keystones 4, Akrons 2.
Double plays— Maskrey and McPhee.
Passed balls— Wise 2, Power 1.
Wild pitches— None.
Umpire— J. McNaughton, Akron.
Balls called off Mullane 67, strikes 33.
Balls called off McCullough 54, strikes 14.
Time— 1:30.
(*Cleveland *Leader* showed Morton playing third base and center field.)

July 23 — Akron at Cleveland Whites

(Cleveland *Leader*, July 25, 1881)

WHITES	A.B.	R.	BH.	P.O.	A.	E.
Nolan, s.s.	4	0	0	1	4	3
West, c	4	0	0	5	3	3
Strief, 2d b	3	0	0	1	3	1
White, 3d b	3	0	0	6	3	1
Stockwell, r.f.	3	1	1	1	0	2
Jones, p.	3	0	0	1	5	0
Atkinson, 1st b	3	0	1	12	0	0
Dewey, c.f.	2	0	0	0	0	3
Piercy, l.f.	3	0	0	0	1	2
Total	28	1	2	27	19	15

AKRONS	A.B.	R.	BH.	P.O.	A.	E.
Swartwood, r.f.	7	4	5	1	0	0
Wise, 3d b	5	4	4	0	0	0
Purcell, p.	7	4	4	0	12	0
Mullane, 1st b	7	6	3	9	0	0
Morton, c.f.*	7	4	5	3	0	0
Maskrey, l.f.	7	2	2	0	0	0
McPhee, 2d b	7	1	1	2	2	0
Kemmler, c	6	2	1	11	1	1
Morton, s.s.*	5	2	2	1	2	1
Total	58	29	27	27	17	2

Innings	1	2	3	4	5	6	7	8	9	
Akrons	4	1	4	3	0	0	7	6	4	—29
Whites	0	0	0	0	1	0	0	0	0	— 1

Runs earned— Akrons 14.
Two-base hits— Swartwood, Wise, Mullane, Morton, Maskrey.

(* Morton is listed as playing center field and shortstop.)

July 29 — Cleveland Red Stockings at Akron

(Cleveland *Leader*, July 30, 1881)

AKRON	A.B.	R.	B.H.	P.O.	A.	E.
Swartwood, r.f.	5	0	2	0	0	0
Wise, 3d b	5	2	2	1	2	0
Purcell, 1st b	5	3	2	13	0	0
Mullane, p	6	3	1	0	5	0
Morton, c.f.	5	2	1	0	0	0
Maskrey, l.f.	6	1	1	1	0	0
McPhee, 2d b	6	1	3	2	2	0
Kemmler, c	6	2	2	8	5	0
Piercy, s.s.	5	1	2	2	2	0
Total	49	15	16	27	16	0

RED STOCKINGS	A.B.	R.	B.H.	P.O.	A.	E.
Newell, 3d b	4	0	0	4	3	0
Thorne, 1st b	4	0	0	10	0	1
Waite, c	3	0	1	6	0	0
Burke, l.f.	3	0	1	1	0	0
Langell, s.s.	2	0	0	0	2	0
Brown, p.	3	0	0	1	1	1
Bailey, 2d b	3	0	1	3	5	3
Weiss, r.f.	2	0	0	0	0	0
Campbell, c.f.	3	0	0	2	0	1
Total	27	0	3	27	11	15*

(*Column totals only 6)

Innings	1	2	3	4	5	6	7	8	9	
Akron	0	1	0	0	4	4	2	3	1	—15
Red Stockings	0	0	0	0	0	0	0	0	0	— 0

Earned runs— Akrons 2.
Two-base hits— Wise and Swartwood.
First base on balls— Akrons 5
First base on errors— Akrons 8.
Struck out — Red Stockings 5.
Passed balls— Waite.
Umpire — John Criss.

Aug. 4 — Akron at Louisville

(Louisville *Courier-Journal*, Aug. 5, 1881)

ECLIPSE	T.	R.	1b.	PO.	A.	E.
Sommers, s.s.	5	1	1	0	3	3
Burgalow, c.f.	5	0	1	0	0	0
Browning, 3d.b	4	0	1	3	4	0
Reccius, p.	4	0	0	0	5	0
Pfeffer, 2d.b.	4	0	0	4	2	0
Crotty, c.	4	0	1	4	1	2
Wolf, r.f.	4	2	1	3	0	0
McLaughlin, 1.b.	4	1	2	9	1	2
Dyler, l.f.	4	0	0	1	0	0
Totals	38	4	7	24	16	7

AKRONS						
Swartwood, r.f.	4	1	3	0	1	0
Wise, 3d.b.	4	0	0	1	0	0
Purcell, 1b,cf,p.	4	0	0	8	1	2
Taylor, c.f., 1b	4	1	1	8	1	1
Mullane, p., c.f.	4	0	0	1	6	0
Maskrey, l.f.	4	1	1	2	0	0
McPhee, 2.b.	4	1	1	4	2	2
Kemmler, c.	4	1	1	3	4	0
Piercy, s.s.	3	1	1	0	2	0
Totals	35	6	8	27	17	5

Eclipse	0	1	0	3	0	0	0	0	0	—4
Akron	0	4	0	1	1	0	0	0	—	—6

Time of Game — Two hours.
Runs Earned — Eclipse, 3; Akron, 3.
First Base on Errors— Eclipse, 2; Akron, 3.
First Base on Called Balls— Eclipse, 4; Akron, 3.
Left on Bases— Eclipse, 7; Akron, 5.
Wild Pitches— Reccius, 1.
Passed Balls— Crotty, 2; Kemmler, 2.
Struck Out — Eclipse, 7; Akron, 3.
Double Play — McPhee and Taylor.
Two-base Hits— Burkalow, 1; Browning, 1; Swartwood, 2; Taylor, 1; Percy, 1.
Three-base Hits— McLaughlin, 1.
Umpire — Mike Walsh.

Aug. 6 — Akron at Louisville

(Louisville *Courier-Journal*, Aug. 7, 1881)

ECLIPSE	T.	R.	1B.	P.O.	A.	E.
Sommers, s.c.	4	1	1	1	3	3
Burkalow, cf, p.	4	0	2	1	0	0
Browning, 3d.b.	4	2	2	2	5	0
Reccius, p., c.f.	4	0	1	1	2	0
Pfeffer, 2d.b.	4	1	2	5	0	0
Crotty, c	4	0	0	5	0	3
Wolf, r.f.	4	0	0	3	1	0

ECLIPSE (cont.)

McLaughlin, 1b.	4	0	0	4	0	0
Dyler, l.f.	3	0	0	2	0	1
Totals	35	4	8	24	11	7

AKRONS

Swartwood, r.f.	5	0	0	1	0	0
Wise, 3d.b.	5	1	1	3	0	0
Purcell, c.f.	4	0	2	0	0	0
Taylor, 1b.	4	1	1	14	0	0
Mullane, p.	4	0	1	0	6	0
Maskrey, l.f.	4	2	1	1	1	0
McPhee, 2d.b.	4	3	2	4	4	1
Kemmler, c.	4	0	2	4	3	0
Piercy, s.s.	4	1	1	0	5	0
Totals	38	8	11	27	19	1

Eclipse   2 0 0 0 0 0 0 2 — 4
Akron   0 2 1 2 3 0 0 0 — 8

Time of Game — One hour and forty-five minutes.
Runs Earned — Akron 1.
First Base on Errors — Eclipse, 1; Akron, 4.
First Base on Called Balls — Eclipse, 2; Akron, 2.
Left on Bases — Eclipse, 4; Akron, 5.
Wild Pitches — Reccius, 1.
Passed Balls — Crotty, 2; Kemmler, 4.
Struck Out — Eclipse, 3.
Double Play — Kemmler, McPhee and Taylor.
Two-base Hits — Wise and Purcell.
Umpire — Mike Walsh.

Aug. 7 — Akron at Louisville

(Louisville *Courier-Journal*, Aug. 8, 1881)

ECLIPSE	T.	R.	1B.	P.O.	A.	E.
Sommers, s.s., r.f.	5	1	1	3	0	2
Browning, 3d.b.	4	0	1	2	3	0
Reccius, p.	4	2	1	0	2	0
Pfeffer, 2d.b.	4	0	1	3	2	1
Burkalow, c.f.	4	0	1	4	1	0
Wolf, r.f., s.s.	4	0	0	0	3	1
McLaughlin, 1b	4	0	0	9	0	1
Crotty, c.	4	0	0	1	3	1
Dyler, l.f.	4	0	0	1	0	1
Totals	37	3	5	24	14	7

AKRONS

Swartwood, r.f.	5	1	1	0	0	2
Wise, 3d.b.	4	1	2	2	2	2
Purcell, c.f.	4	2	2	0	0	0
Taylor, 1b	4	0	0	10	0	2
Mullane, p.	4	0	1	0	11	0
Maskrey, l.f.	4	1	1	0	0	0
McPhee, 2d.b.	4	0	1	2	3	2
Kemmler, c.	4	0	3	12	2	0
Piercy, s.s.	4	0	0	1	4	0
Totals	37	5	11	27	22	8

Eclipse   1 0 0 0 0 0 2 0 — 3
Akrons   1 0 0 0 0 3 1   — 5

Time of Game — Two hours.
Runs Earned — Akron, 2.
First Base on Errors — Eclipse, 5; Akron, 3.
First Base on Called Balls — Eclipse, 1; Akron, 1.
Left on Bases — Eclipse, 6; Akron 3.
Passed Balls — Kemmler, 4.
Struck Out — Eclipse, 10; Akron, 2.
Two-base Hits — Pfeffer, Wise, McPhee and Kemmler.
Three-base Hits — Purcell.
Umpire — Mike Walsh.

Aug. 8 — Akron at Louisville

(Louisville *Courier-Journal*, Aug. 9, 1881)

LOUISVILLES	T.B.	R.	1B.	P.O.	A.	E.
Huette, l.f.	4	0	1	5	0	2
Walker, c	4	1	2	2	2	4
Haideman, 1st b	4	0	0	8	0	3
Kennedy, 3d b	4	0	0	5	2	1
Robinson, c.f.	4	1	2	0	0	3
Avery, r.f.	4	0	0	0	0	0
Ferguson, s.s.	4	1	1	0	2	1
Bain, p	4	1	1	2	2	2
Ormsby, 3d b	3	1	0	2	1	2
Total	35	5	7	24	9	18

AKRON	T.B.	R.	1B.	P.O.	A.	E.
Swartwood, r.f.	4	4	1	1	0	2
Wise, 3d b	5	3	3	2	3	2
Purcell, p	5	2	3	5	7	1
Taylor, 1st b	6	0	3	8	3	0
Mullane, c.f.	6	2	1	1	0	0

AKRON (cont.)

	A.B.	R.	B.H.	P.O.	A.	E.
Maskrey, l.f.	6	2	1	0	0	0
McPhee, 2d b	6	2	2	4	1	1
Kemmler, c	5	2	1	6	2	0
Piercy, s.s.	5	3	2	0	3	1
Total	48	20	17	27	19	7

	1	2	3	4	5	6	7	8	9	
Louisvilles	0	0	0	1	0	0	0	2	2	— 5
Akrons	5	2	4	3	2	2	0	2	*	—20

Time of Game — Two hours.
Umpire — Fred Pfeffer, of the Eclipse Club.
Passed Balls — Walker, 3; Ormsby, 3; Swartwood, 3.
Wild Pitchers — Bain, 1; Taylor, 3.
Bases on Balls — Louisville, 1; Akrons, 4.
Left on Bases — Louisvilles, 4; Akrons, 8.
Double Plays — Kennedy and Haideman, and Huette, Bain and Walker.
Two-base Hits — Morton, Wise, Walker and Ferguson.
Three-base Hits — Swartwood, Wise and McPhee.

Aug. 10 — Buffalo at Akron

(Cleveland *Leader*, Aug. 11, 1881)

AKRON	A.B.	R.	B.H.	P.O.	A.	E.
Swartwood, r.f.	5	1	2	0	0	0
Wise, 3d b	5	0	1	2	4	1
Purcell, c.f.	5	2	2	4	0	0
Taylor, 1st b	5	1	4	10	0	0
Mullane, p	5	0	1	0	7	0
Maskrey, l.f.	5	1	1	2	0	1
McPhee, 2d b	4	2	2	3	2	1
Kemmler, c	4	1	1	5	1	0
Piercy, s.s.	4	1	1	1	1	1
Total	42	9	15	27	15	4

BUFFALO	A.B.	R.	B.H.	P.O.	A.	E.
Foley, 1st b & p.	5	1	1	4	4	1
O'Rourk, 3d b	5	0	1	2	2	2
Brouthers, lf & 1st b	4	2	2	7	0	1
Richardson, c.f.	4	1	1	0	1	0
White, 2d b	4	0	1	4	1	0
Rowe, r.f.	4	0	0	2	0	1
Peters, s.s.	4	0	1	1	4	1
Sullivan, c	4	0	0	7	1	0
Galvin, p	4	0	2	0	1	0
Total	38	4	9	27	14	6

Innings	1	2	3	4	5	6	7	8	9	
Akron	1	2	0	1	1	0	0	2	1	—9
Buffalo	1	0	0	1	0	0	2	0	0	—4

Earned runs — Akron 2, Buffalo 1.
Two-base hits — Taylor, Richardson.
Home runs — Taylor, Foley.
First base on balls — Akron 1.
Struck out — Akron 2, Buffalo 4.
Passed balls — Akron 1 Buffalo 3.
Wild pitches — Galvin, Mullane.
Umpire — Bradley.

Aug. 12 — Buffalo at Akron

(Cleveland *Leader*, Aug. 13, 1881)

BUFFALO	A.B.	R.	B.H.	P.O.	A.	E.
Foley, p & 1st b	5	2	2	0	1	0
O'Rourk, 3d b	5	3	4	5	1	0
Brouthers, l.f.	5	2	3	2	1	0
Richardson, c.f.	5	3	4	2	2	0
White, 2d b	5	0	0	2	0	0
Rowe, r.f.	5	2	3	1	0	0
Bradley, p & 1st b	5	2	3	8	0	0
Sullivan, c	5	1	4	6	0	1
Force, s.s.	5	2	3	1	5	0
Total	45	17	26	27	10	1

AKRON	A.B.	R.	B.H.	P.O.	A.	E.
Swartwood, r.f.	4	0	1	0	0	0
Wise, 3d b	4	1	2	1	2	1
Purcell, cf & p	4	0	1	4	4	1
Taylor, 1st b	4	0	1	5	1	0
Mullane, p & cf	4	0	1	0	0	0
Maskrey, l.f.	4	1	2	2	2	1
McPhee, 2d b	4	1	2	0	2	0
Kemmler, c	4	1	2	6	4	2
Piercy, s.s.	4	0	1	0	2	2
Total	36	4	13	24*	17	7

(*column totals only 18 outs)

Innings	1	2	3	4	5	6	7	8	9	
Buffalo	2	3	2	1	2	0	7	0	0	—17
Akron	0	0	0	0	0	1	2	0	1	— 4

Earned runs — Buffalo 11, Akron 4.
Two-base hits — Buffalo 1, Akron 3.
Three-base hits — Taylor, Brouthers.
Home runs — O'Rourke 2, Richardson.
First base on balls — Swartwood.

Struck out — Buffalo 4.
Double Plays — Piercy, McPhee and Taylor.
Passed balls — Kemmler.
Wild pitches — Mullane 2.
Umpire — Morton.

Aug. 15 — Detroit at Akron

(Cleveland *Leader*, Aug. 16, 1881)

DETROIT	A.B.	R.	B.H.	P.O.	A.	E.
Wood, 3d b	4	1	1	1	2	0
Knight, r.f.	4	1	0	1	1	0
Hanlon, c.f.	4	1	0	1	1	0
Powell, 1st b	3	0	1	13	0	0
Houck, s.s.	4	0	1	1	2	0
Bennett, c	4	0	1	8	0	0
Gerhardt, 2d b	2	0	0	2	6	0
Derby, p	2	1	0	0	7	0
Reilley, l.f.	3	0	1	0	0	0
Total	36	4	5	27	19	0

AKRON	A.B.	R.	B.H.	P.O.	A.	E.
Swartwood, r.f.	2	0	1	1	0	0
Taylor, 1st b	4	0	2	9	0	0
Morton, 3d b	4	0	0	2	4	0
Mullane, p	4	0	0	0	7	0
Maskrey, l.f.	3	0	1	1	0	1
McPhee, 2d b	3	0	0	3	2	2
Kemmler, c	3	0	1	6	1	0
Andrews, c.f.	3	0	0	2	1	0
Piercy, s.s.	3	0	1	0	3	3
Total	29	0	6	24	18	6

Innings   1 2 3 4 5 6 7 8 9
Detroit   1 0 0 0 1 0 1 1 — 4
Akron   0 0 0 0 0 0 0 0 0 — 0

Earned runs — None.
First base on balls — Detroit 2, Akron 4.
First base on errors — Detroit 4.
Struck out — Detroit 5, Akron 3.
Double plays — Knight and Powell.
Passed balls — Kemmler 3, Taylor 1.
Wild pitches — Mullane 4.
Umpire — Doescher.

Aug. 19 — Detroit at Akron

(Cleveland *Leader*, Aug. 20, 1881)

AKRON	A.B.	R.	B.H.	P.O.	A.	E.
Swartwood, r.f.	3	0	2	0	0	0
Wise, 1st b	4	0	1	9	0	1
Kemmler, c	4	2	1	1	4	0
Mullane, p	4	2	3	1	2	0
Maskrey, l.f.	4	0	1	0	1	1
McPhee, 2d b	4	1	1	7	3	1
Morton, 3d b	4	1	1	1	3	1
Andrews, c.f.	3	1	0	2	1	0
Piercy, s.s.	3	1	1	0	3	1
Total	33	8	11	21	17	5

DETROIT	A.B.	R.	B.H.	P.O.	A.	E.
Wood, p	4	0	1	0	2	0
Knight, 3d b	4	0	2	1	0	2
Hanlon, c.f.	4	0	0	2	0	1
Powell, 1st b	2	0	0	6	0	0
Bennett, l.f.	2	1	1	3	0	1
Houck, s.s.	3	2	3	3	2	3
Gerhardt, 2d b	3	1	1	4	3	1
Rielly, c	3	1	2	2	2	2
Foley, 3d b	3	1	1	0	2	0
Total	30*	6	11	21	11	10

(*column totals only 28; also note Detroit lineup includes two third basemen and no right fielder.)

Innings   1 2 3 4 5 6 7
Akron   0 0 0 2 0 6 0 — 8
Detroit   0 0 0 4 0 2 0 — 6

Earned runs — Akron 2, Detroit 2.
Two-base hits — Akron 2, Detroit 2.
Double plays — Wood, Gerhardt and Powell; Gerhardt and Powell; Andrews and Kemmler; McPhee and Wise.
Passed balls — Rielly 1.
Umpire — Doescher.

Aug. 27 — Akron at St. Louis

(combined box score — Missouri *Republican* and St. Louis *Globe-Democrat*, Aug. 28, 1881)

AKRONS	A.B.	R.	S.H.	P.O.	A.	E.
Swartwood, 1b	3	1	3	5	0	2
Wise, 3b	4	1	1	1	1	0

AKRONS (cont.)

Kemmler, c	4	1	2	5	2	2
Maskrey, l.f.	4	1	0	0	0	0
McPhee, 2b	3	2	0	6	2	0
Piercy, s.s.	4	1	1	1	2	1
Stockwell, r.f.	4	1	1	0	0	0
Andrews, c.f.	4	2	1	2	0	0
Jones, p.	3	0	0	1	2	1
Totals	33	10	9	21	9	6

ST. LOUIS	A.B	R.	S.H.	P.O.	A.	E.
J. Gleason, 3b	4	1	2	1	1	1
W. Gleason, s.s.	3	1	0	1	4	1
McCaffrey, c.f.	4	0	0	0	0	0
Seward, r.f.	3	1	3	1	0	0
Baker, c	3	0	1	8	2	0
McGinnis, p	4	1	1	0	1	1
Magner, l.f.	2	1	1	1	0	0
McDonald, 2b	3	0	0	4	2	0
Gault, 1b	3	0	1	5	0	0
Totals	29	5	9	21	10	3

Innings	1	2	3	4	5	6	7	
Akrons	0	0	6	0	1	0	3	—10
St. Louis	2	0	0	2	1	0	0	— 5

Three base hits — Swartwood 2, J. Gleason, Wise and Stockwell one each.
Two Base hits — Andrews and Seward.
Wild pitches — McGinnis 1.
Passed balls — Baker 1; Kemmler, 2.
Double plays — Kemmler and Wise; Piercy, McPhee and Swartwood.
Earned runs — Akron 4; Browns 3.
Base on balls — Akron 3 Browns 5.
Time of game — Two hours.
Umpire — Dan Devinney

Aug. 28 — Akron at St. Louis

(combined box score — Missouri *Republican* and St. Louis *Globe-Democrat*, Sept. 29, 1881)

ST. LOUIS	A.B.	R.	B.H.	P.O.	A.	E.
J. Gleason, 3d	5	3	4	2	0	1
W. Gleason, s.s.	4	2	2	2	5	0
McCaffrey, c.f.	5	1	2	2	0	0
Seward, r.f.	4	4	2	6	0	0
Baker, c.	5	2	4	5	2	2
McGinnis, p.	5	2	2	1	2	2
Magner, l.f.	3	2	0	1	0	1
McDonald and Levis, 2b	4	1	2	0	0	1
Gault, 1b.	5	1	2	8	1	1
Totals	40	18	20	27	10	8

AKRONS	A.B.	R.	B.H.	P.O.	A.	E.
Wise, 3d	4	2	3	2	0	1
Kemmler, c	5	2	0	5	1	0
Maskrey, l.f.	5	1	2	1	0	1
McPhee, 2b	4	2	2	2	1	2
Piercy, s.s.	5	1	1	1	4	2
Stockwell, r.f. & 1b	5	1	3	0	0	0
Andrews, c.f. & p.	5	0	0	1	0	0
Jones, p. & l.f.	5	2	3	4	3	1
Davis, 1.b.	5	3	1	8	3	1
Totals	43	14	15	24	12	8

Innings	1	2	3	4	5	6	7	8	9	
St. Louis	0	3	3	8	2	1	0	1		—18
Akrons	3	1	0	2	0	0	6	2	0	—14

Home Run — Levis.
Three-base Hits — Wise, Jones, J. Gleason, Maskrey and Davis.
Two-base Hits — Wise, Maskrey and J. Gleason.
Runs Earned — Browns, 5; Akrons, 5.
Bases on Balls — Browns, 5; Akrons, 3.
Passed Balls — Baker, 1; Kemmler, 4.
Wild Pitches — Andrews, Jones and McGinnis, one each.
Time of Game — Three hours.
Umpire — Mr. D. Devinney.

Aug. 29 — Akron at St. Louis

(combined box score — Missouri *Republican* and St. Louis *Globe-Democrat*, Aug. 30, 1881)

ST. LOUIS	A.B.	R.	S.H.	P.O.	A.	E.
J. Gleason, 3d	4	0	1	3	0	2
W. Gleason, s.s.	4	2	2	1	3	1
McCaffrey, 2b	4	0	0	3	3	0
Seward, c.	4	1	2	10	2	1
Baker, r.f.	4	1	1	0	0	0
McGinnis, c.f.	4	0	1	2	0	1
Magner, l.f.	4	0	1	1	0	0
Morgan, p.	4	0	0	0	2	0

ST. LOUIS (cont.)

	A.B.	R.	S.H.	P.O.	A.	E.
Gault, 1b	3	0	1	7	0	2
Totals	35	4	9	27	10	7

AKRONS	A.B.	R.	S.H.	P.O.	A.	E.
Swartwood, c.f.	5	1	1	0	0	0
Wise, 3b	5	3	3	1	1	1
Kemmler, c.	6	2	2	7	2	0
Maskrey, l.f.	5	2	0	4	0	1
McPhee, 2b	5	0	0	1	1	0
Stockwell, r.f.	5	1	2	2	0	0
Andrews, 1b	5	2	0	10	0	1
Morton, p & s.s.	5	1	1	1	4	0
Piercy, s.s. & p.	5	2	2	1	1	0
Totals	46	14	11	27	9	3

Innings	1	2	3	4	5	6	7	8	9	
Akrons	0	7	0	2	0	1	1	1	2	—14
St. Louis	1	0	0	3	0	0	0	0	0	— 4

Two-base Hits—J. Gleason and Swartwood.
Double play—McCaffrey and Gault.
Earned Runs—Akrons, 4; Browns, 2.
Passed Balls—Kemmler, 3; Seward, 3.
Time of game—Two hours and thirty minutes.
Umpire—Charles Davis. (*Globe-Democrat* lists umpire as Mr. Levis)

Sept. 3 — Akron at Louisville

(Louisville *Courier-Journal*, Sept. 4, 1881)

ECLIPSE	T.B.	R.	1B.	P.O.	A.	E.
Sommers, s.s., p.	4	0	2	2	5	2
Browning, 3d.b.	4	0	1	0	3	0
Reccius, p	4	0	2	1	3	0
Pfeffer, 2d.b	4	0	1	6	2	2
Burkalow, c.f.	4	0	0	1	0	2
Wolfe, l.f.	3	0	0	2	0	3
McLaughlin, 1b	3	1	1	11	0	0
Crotty, c	3	1	1	4	2	3
Zimmerman, r.f.	3	0	0	0	0	2
Totals	32	2	8	27	15	14

AKRONS						
Swartwood, r.f.	5	1	0	0	0	0
Wise, 3d.b.	5	4	2	1	2	0
Kemmler, c.	5	2	1	1	1	0
McPhee, 2d.b.	5	1	1	3	6	0
Maskrey, l.f.	5	1	2	1	1	0
Piercy, p.	5	2	1	5	2	2
Morton, s.s.	5	2	2	0	4	0
Andrews, 1b	5	1	2	13	1	0
Stockwell, c.f.	4	0	0	3	0	0
Totals	44	14	11	27	17	2

Eclipse	0	0	0	0	2	0	0	0	0	— 2
Akrons	2	1	5	3	0	1	2	0	0	—14

Time of Game—Two hours and fifteen minutes
Earned Runs—Akron 2.
First Base on Errors—Akron 5, Eclipse 1.
First Base on Called Balls—Akron 5.
Left on Bases—Akrons 3, Eclipse 3.
Wild Pitches—Reccis 1, Sommers 1, Piercy 1.
Passed Balls—Crotty 2, Kemmler 1.
Struck Out—Akron 2.
Two-base Hits—Wise, Andrews and McLaughlin.
Double Plays—Browning, Pfeffer and McLaughlin, Sommers and McLaughlin and Sommers, Pfeffer and McLaughlin; Wise, McPhee and Andrews, 2.
Umpire—Mr. Jones, of the Akrons.

Sept. 4 — Akron at Louisville

(Louisville *Courier-Journal*, Sept. 5, 1881)

ECLIPSE	T.B.	R.	1B.	P.O.	A.	E.
Sommers, s.s.	5	1	1	2	2	1
Browning, 3d.b.	5	0	1	1	2	1
Reccius, p.	5	0	1	0	2	1
Pfeffer, 2d.b.	5	0	0	3	5	1
Burkalow, c.f.	5	0	0	1	0	0
Wolfe, l.f.	4	0	1	3	0	0
McLaughlin, 1b	4	0	1	10	0	1
Crotty, c	4	1	1	6	2	3
Zimmerman, r.f.	4	0	1	1	1	0
Totals	41	2	7	27	14	8

AKRONS						
Swartwood, r.f.	4	1	1	3	0	2
Wise, 3d.b.	4	1	2	0	0	0
Kemmler, c.	4	0	0	3	1	1
McPhee, 2d.b.	4	0	0	5	2	0
Maskrey, l.f.	4	1	1	3	0	0

AKRONS (cont.)

Piercy, p.	4	0	2	0	3	0
Morton, s.s.	4	0	0	1	7	0
Andrews, 1b	4	0	0	9	0	1
Stockwell, c.f.	3	0	1	3	0	0
Totals	35	3	7	27	13	4

Eclipse	0 0 0 0 0 2 0 0—2
Akrons	0 0 0 2 0 0 1 0 —3

Time of Game — Two hours and fifteen minutes.
First Base on Errors — Eclipse 2, Akrons 2
First Base on Called Balls — Eclipse 4.
Left on Bases — Eclipse 11, Akrons 5.
Struck Out — Eclipse 1, Akrons 2.
Two base Hits — Swartwood 1 and Wise 1.
Three-base Hits — Crotty 1, Stockwell 1.
Double Plays — Crotty and McLaughlin 1, Zimmerman and Crotty 1, Sommers 1.
Umpire — Mr. Irvin.

Sept. 7 — Oberlin at Akron

(Akron *Daily Beacon*, Sept. 8, 1881)

AKRONS	A.B.	R.	H.	P.O.	A.	E.
Swartwood, r.f., p	5	1	3	2	4	0
Wise, 3b	5	3	3	1	3	0
Kemmler, c	5	1	0	5	1	0
Maskrey, l.f.	5	1	2	0	0	0
McPhee, 2b	5	3	3	4	2	0
Piercy, p, r.f.	5	3	4	1	2	0
Morton, ss	5	2	3	2	4	0
Andrews, 1b	4	0	0	12	0	0
Stockwell, c.f.	4	0	2	1	0	0
Total	43	14	20	27*	16	0

OBERLINS	A.B.	R.	H.	P.O.	A.	E.
Davis, l.f.	4	0	0	1	0	2
Derby, 1b	4	0	1	12	1	1
Brinsmaid, c.f., 3b	3	0	1	3	1	0
Thompson, c	3	0	0	2	2	2
Seiberling, ss	3	0	0	2	2	2
Spear, 2b	3	0	0	2	5	3
Breck, 3b, r.f.	3	0	0	0	0	3
Burket, p	3	0	1	0	7	1
Pounds, r.f., c.f.	3	0	1	2	2	2
Total	29	0	4	24	20	16

(*column totals 28)

Innings	1 2 3 4 5 6 7 8
Akrons	0 4 4 0 0 2 1 3—14
Oberlins	0 0 0 0 0 0 0 0— 0

Earned runs — Akron 11.
Two-base hits — McPhee.
Three-base hits — None.
Home runs — None.
First base on balls — None
First base on errors — Akron 4, Oberlin 0.
Struck out — Akron 2, Oberlin 4.
Double plays — Wise and Andrews; Swartwood, McPhee and Andrews.
Passed balls — Kemmler 2, Thompson 8.
Wild pitches — None.
Umpire — Mr. Jones, of the Akrons.

Sept. 17 — Akron at St. Louis

(combined box score — Missouri *Republican* and St. Louis *Globe-Democrat*, Sept. 18, 1881)

ST. LOUIS	A.B.	R.	S.H.	P.O.	A.	E.
J. Gleason, 3.b.	4	0	0	2	0	1
W. Gleason, s.s.	4	0	0	2	3	3
McCaffrey, 1b	4	0	1	9	0	1
Seward, r.f.	4	1	0	0	0	0
Baker, c	4	0	0	10	2	1
McGinnis, p	4	1	0	0	1	0
Magner, l.f.	4	2	0	1	0	0
Morgan, 2.b.	3	0	1	2	2	0
Levis, c.f.	4	1	1	1	0	0
Totals	35	5	3	27	8	6

AKRONS	A.B.	R.	S.H.	P.O.	A.	E.
Swartwood, r.f.	4	0	0	2	0	0
Wise, 3b	4	0	1	1	1	2
Kemmler, c	4	0	1	8	2	2
Maskrey, l.f.	4	0	0	2	0	0
McPhee, 2b	4	1	0	0	2	2
Piercy, s.s.	4	1	0	0	2	1
Morton, c.f.	3	0	1	1	0	0
Stockwell, 1b	3	1	0	13	0	1
Mountain, p.	3	0	0	0	4	1
Totals	33	3	3	27	11	9

Innings	1 2 3 4 5 6 7 8 9
St. Louis	0 0 1 3 0 0 0 0 1 — 5
Akron	0 0 0 0 0 1 2 0 0 — 3

Two-base Hits—Kemmler and Wise.
Sacrifice Hits—Levis.
Double Play—Kemmler and Stockwell.
Passed Balls—Baker, 1; Kemmler, 5.
Time of Game—Two hours.
Umpire—Mr. John Peters.

Sept. 18 — Akron at St. Louis

(combined box score — Missouri *Republican* and St. Louis *Globe-Democrat*, Sept. 19, 1881)

ST. LOUIS	A.B.	R.	S.H.	P.O.	A.	E.
J. Gleason, 3b	5	3	4	1	3	2
W. Gleason, s.s.	5	2	2	2	1	1
McCaffrey, 1b	5	0	2	7	0	1
Seward, r.f.	5	0	0	8	0	1
Baker, c.	5	0	0	6	0	5
McGinnis, p	5	1	1	0	12	0
Magner, l.f.	4	1	0	1	0	0
Morgan, 2b	3	2	0	0	1	2
Levis, c.f.	4	1	0	2	0	0
Totals	41	10	9	27	17	12

AKRONS	A.B.	R.	S.H.	P.O.	A.	E.
Swartwood, r.f.	5	1	0	2	0	0
Wise, 3b	5	0	1	2	1	1
Kemmler, c	5	1	0	4	0	1
Maskrey, l.f.	5	1	2	3	0	0
McPhee, 2b	5	1	0	6	1	1
Piercy, s.s. & p.	5	1	1	0	6	2
Morton, c.f. & s.s.	5	1	2	1	0	1
Stockwell, 1b	4	1	0	9	0	1(*)
Mountain, p. & c.f.	4	1	1	0	2	1
Totals	43	8	8	27	10	4

Innings	1 2 3 4 5 6 7 8 9
St. Louis	1 0 3 1 0 3 0 0 2 — 10
Akrons	2 1 0 2 2 0 0 0 1 — 8

Runs earned—Browns, 3; Akrons, 3.(**)
Home runs—Morton.
Three-base hits—J. Gleason and W. Gleason.(†)
Two-base hits—Levis and J. Gleason.(††)
Base on balls—Browns, 1; Akrons, 1.(§)
Passed balls—Kemmler, 2; Baker, 1.(§§)
Umpire—Mr. John Peters.(§§§)

Many differences in the box scores: (*) Missouri *Republican* shows Davis, not Stockwell; (**) *Globe-Democrat* shows Browns 4, Akrons 1; (†) shows only J. Gleason; (††) shows only J. Gleason with 2; (§) shows Morgan 1, Wise 1; (§§) doesn't show passed balls but shows wild pitch, McGinnis 1, Mountain 1; (§§§) shows umpire as Charlie Houtz.

Sept. 19 — Akron at St. Louis

(combined box score — Missouri *Republican* and St. Louis *Globe-Democrat*, Sept. 20, 1881)

ST. LOUIS	A.B.	R.	S.H.	P.O.	A.	E.
J. Gleason, 3b	4	1	1	0	4	0
W. Gleason, 1b and 2b	5	1	1	11	0	0
McCaffrey, s.s.	5	2	2	0	4	2
Seward, c	5	1	2	6	0	3
Cuthbert, c.f.	5	1	2	2	0	0
McGinnis, p and r.f.	5	2	2	1	1	1
Magner, l.f.	4	2	1	2	0	0
Morgan, 2b and p.	3	1	1	1	3	1
Levis, r.f. and 1b	4	0	2	1	0	0
Totals	40	11	14	24	12	7

AKRONS	A.B.	R.	S.H.	P.O.	A.	E.
Swartwood, r.f.	4	2	0	0	1	0
Wise, 3b	5	1	1	2	3	1
Kemmler, c	5	2	2	6	1	2
Maskrey, l.f.	5	2	1	2	0	0
McPhee, 2b	5	1	3	2	5	1
Piercy, p	4	2	1	1	2	1
Morton, s.s.	4	1	1	2	2	0
Stockwell, 1b	4	1	1	11	0	0
Arundel, c.f.	4	1	2	1	0	0
Totals	40	13	12	27	14	5

St. Louis	102 003 401 — 11
Akrons	110 218 000 — 13

Earned Runs—Browns, 6; Akrons 3.
Wild Pitch—McGinnis.
Passed balls—Kemmler, 2; Seward, 3.
Three-base hits—W. Gleason and Stockwell.
Two-base hits—Levis and Morgan. (*)
Double-plays—McPhee and Stockwell.
Umpire—Mr. John Peters.
(*) *Globe-Democrat* shows doubles by Levis and Magner, not Morgan; also shows time of game at 2 hours, 15 minutes.

Appendix C: 1881 Akrons Stats

The following statistics are compiled from the 40 available box scores and game stories. In several instances game stories and box scores do not agree. In some cases, published box scores do not balance and in other cases box scores in competing newspapers do not agree. Information which twenty-first century baseball fans take for granted was not tallied in the nineteenth century. What follows represents a good faith effort to achieve accuracy from the available sources.

Box scores for the following games could not be located: Akrons 28, Picked Nine 11; Akrons 13, Mercer 2; Akrons 24, Canton 0; Akrons 26, Kent 4; Akrons 29, Crockery Citys (East Liverpool) 6.

For batters, the following information appears with these abbreviations: G, games; AB, at-bats; R, runs; H, hits, 2b, doubles; 3b, triples; HR, home runs; BA, batting average; PO, putouts; A, assists; E, errors; FA, fielding average.

For pitchers, the following information appears with these abbreviations: AP, appearances; GS, games started; CG, complete games; W, wins; L, losses; IP, innings pitched; R, opponents' runs; ER, earned runs; H, hits surrendered; ERA, earned run average.

Batters and pitchers appear in alphabetical order.

Batters

	G	AB	R	H	2b	3b	HR	BA	PO	A	E	FA
Ed Andrews	7	30	6	3	2	0	0	.100	49	2	2	.962
Harry Arundel	1	4	1	2	0	0	0	.500	1	0	0	1.000
Jimmy Green	15	66	10	12	1	0	0	.182	101	22	15	.891
Daniel Jones	2	8	2	3	0	1	0	.375	5	5	2	.833
Rudy Kemmler	39	165	32	30	4	0	0	.182	223	71	31	.905
John Mansell	11	50	11	19	2	0	0	.380	8	3	4	.733
Leech Maskrey	40	179	40	50	6	2	0	.279	59	10	8	.896
Bid McPhee	40	174	31	48	5	1	0	.276	115	95	30	.875
Charlie Morton	28	127	31	39	4	0	1	.307	30	64	13	.879
Frank Mountain	2	7	1	1	0	0	0	.143	0	6	2	.750
Tony Mullane	28	129	33	39	10	0	0	.302	41	144	14	.929

Batters (cont.)

Jack Neagle	9	38	7	8	2	0	0	.211	4	61	4	.942
Andy Piercy	18	76	21	23	1	0	0	.303	14	49	17	.788
Blondie Purcell	13	59	16	20	2	1	0	.339	39	34	7	.913
Len Stockwell	9	36	6	10	0	2	0	.278	42	0	2	.954
Dan Sullivan	8	42	7	12	1	1	0	.286	38	2	0	1.000
Ed Swartwood	39	175	35	60	15	1	1	.343	116	9	27	.822
Bill Taylor	7	31	3	12	2	1	1	.387	64	5	3	.958
Sam Wise	38	171	42	56	19	4	1	.327	76	69	33	.815
Others	5	21	7	6	0	1	0	.286	18	7	5	.833
Akrons Totals	40	1584	340	450	76	15	4	.284	1050	669	217	.887
Opponents	40	1589	221	372	43	13	7	.234	1060	584	301	.845

Pitchers

	AP	GS	CG	W	L	IP	R	ER	H	ERA
Ed Andrews	1	0	0	0	0	4.2	6	2	10	3.91
Jimmy Green	1	1	0	0	1	5	7	3	9	5.40
Daniel Jones	2	2	1	1	1	10.1	17	6	19	5.24
Charlie Morton	1	1	0	1	0	5	4	2	5	3.60
Frank Mountain	2	2	1	0	1	14.2	12	8	9	4.93
Tony Mullane	22	21	17	13	6	177	81	34	171	1.73
Jack Neagle	8	6	6	2	4	64.2	55	14	78	1.95
Andy Piercy	6	4	3	4	1	39.1	18	6	38	1.37
Blondie Purcell	5	3	3	2	1	30	21	7	31	2.10
Ed Swartwood	1	0	0	0	0	4	0	0	2	0.00
Akron Totals	49	40	31	23	15*	354.2	221	82	372	2.08
Opponents	47	40	31	15	23	353	340	123	450	3.25

*two games were ties

Chapter Notes

All citations to the Louisville *Courier-Journal* are of copyrighted material: Copyright (c) 2001. Courier-Journal & Louisville Times Co. Reprinted with permission.

Introduction

1. Harold Seymour, *Baseball: The Early Years* (New York: Oxford University Press, 1960), pp. 3–12; Harold Seymour, *The People's Game* (New York: Oxford University Press, 1990), p. 3.
2. Harold Seymour, *Baseball: The Early Years*, p. 15; Jack Selzer, *Baseball in the Nineteenth Century: An Overview*, (Cleveland: Society for American Baseball Research, 1986), p. 4.
3. Seymour, *Baseball: The Early Years*, pp. 15, 20; Selzer, *Baseball in the Nineteenth Century*, p. 4; Tom Melville, *Early Baseball and the Rise of the National League* (Jefferson, NC: McFarland, 2001), p. 10.
4. Seymour, *Baseball: The Early Years*, p. 22; Selzer, *Baseball in the Nineteenth Century*, p. 5.
5. Seymour, *Baseball: The Early Years*, pp. 13–14, 31–32; Melville, *Early Baseball*, p. 11.
6. Seymour, *Baseball: The Early Years*, pp. 42, 45; Selzer, *Baseball in the Nineteenth Century*, p. 5.
7. Seymour, *Baseball: The Early Years*, p. 47; Melville, *Early Baseball*, p 10.
8. Seymour, *Baseball: The Early Years*, p. 18; Melville, *Early Baseball*, pp. 14, 24–26.
9. Melville, *Early Baseball*, p. 3.
10. Seymour, *Baseball: The Early Years*, p. 48; Selzer, *Baseball in the Nineteenth Century*, p. 6; Melville, *Early Baseball*, pp. 27, 31, 72.
11. Seymour, *Baseball: The Early Years*, p. 48; Melville, *Early Baseball*, p. 50.
12. Selzer, *Baseball in the Nineteenth Century*, p. 7; Greg Rhodes and John Erardi, *The First Boys of Summer* (Cincinnati: Road West, 1994), pp. 4, 7, 9.
13. Selzer, *Baseball in the Nineteenth Century*, p. 7; Rhodes and Erardi, *The First Boys*, pp. 130, 132–134; Melville, *Early Baseball*, pp. 42–43.
14. Selzer, *Baseball in the Nineteenth Century*, p. 7; Melville, *Early Baseball*, pp. 3, 20–21.
15. Selzer, *Baseball in the Nineteenth Century*, p. 7; Melville, *Early Baseball*, p. 49.
16. Selzer, *Baseball in the Nineteenth Century*, p. 9; Melville, *Early Baseball*, pp. 92–93, 96–97; Seymour, *Baseball: The Early Years*, pp. 91–92.
17. Selzer, *Baseball in the Nineteenth Century*, pp. 11, 18; Melville, *Early Baseball*, pp. 49, 110; Seymour, *Baseball: The Early Years*, pp. 76, 94, 135–136.
18. Seymour, *Baseball: The Early Years*, pp. 97–98, 100–103; Melville, *Early Baseball*, p 107.

1

1. *Summit County Beacon*, June 13, 1867.
2. Karl Grismer, *Akron and Summit County* (Summit County Historical Society, undated), pp. 76–84, 158, 217, 223.
3. Akron *Sunday Gazette*, May 4, 1879.
4. Akron *Sunday Gazette*, May 4, 1879.
5. *Summit County Beacon*, June 27, July 4, July 18, 1867; Akron *Sunday Gazette*, May 4, 1879.

6. *Summit County Beacon*, July 18, August 1, 1867; Akron *Sunday Gazette*, May 4, 1879.
7. Akron *Sunday Gazette*, May 4, 1879.
8. *Summit County Beacon*, August 22, 1867; Akron *Sunday Gazette*, May 4, 1879.
9. *Summit County Beacon*, July 18, August 1, August 22, September 5, 1867.
10. Grismer, *Akron and Summit County*, pp. 200, 665–666; Akron *Sunday Gazette*, May 4, 1879.
11. Akron *Sunday Gazette*, May 4, 1879.

2

1. Akron *Sunday Gazette*, April 13, 1879.
2. *Summit County Beacon*, April 16, 1879.
3. Akron *Sunday Gazette*, April 27, 1879.
4. *Summit County Beacon*, July 23, October 29, 1879.
5. Selzer, *Baseball in the Nineteenth Century*, pp. 9–11; Alvin K. Peterjohn, *Baseball in Akron, Ohio, 1879–1881, A Case Study*, undated paper in the Akron file at the National Baseball Hall of Fame Library; Grismer, *Akron and Summit County*, p. 166; *Summit County Beacon*, July 23, 1881.
6. *Summit County Beacon*, July 30, August 6, 1879.
7. *Summit County Beacon*, August 13, 1879.
8. *Summit County Beacon*, August 20, 1879.
9. *Summit County Beacon*, August 27, October 29, 1879; Peterjohn, *Baseball in Akron*.
10. *Akron City Directory 1879–1880* (Detroit: Burch, Potter & Co.); James A. Braden, ed., *A Centennial History of Akron* (Summit County Historical Society, 1925); Peterjohn, *Baseball in Akron*; *Summit County Beacon*, September 3, 1879.
11. Peterjohn, *Baseball in Akron*; Ivor-Campbell, Fredrick, Tiemann, Robert L., and Rucker, Mark, eds., *Baseball's First Stars*, (Cleveland: Society for American Baseball Research, 1996), p. 161; *Summit County Beacon*, September 24, October 29, 1879.
12. *Summit County Beacon*, October 1, 1879.
13. *Summit County Beacon*, October 29, 1879; Peterjohn, *Baseball in Akron*.

3

1. Akron *Sunday Gazette*, March 21, 1880.
2. Akron *Sunday Gazette*, April 11, 1880; Peterjohn, *Baseball in Akron*.
3. Akron *Sunday Gazette*, May 2, 1880; *Summit County Beacon*, May 5, 1880.
4. Braden, *A Centennial History*, p. 532; Grismer, *Akron and Summit County*, p. 661.
5. Akron *Sunday Gazette*, May 2, 1880.
6. Akron *Sunday Gazette*, May 9, May 23, 1880; Peterjohn, *Baseball in Akron*
7. *Summit County Beacon*, June 23, 1880.
8. New York *Clipper*, June 26, 1880, p. 107; Peterjohn, *Baseball in Akron*; John Thorn, Pete Palmer and Michael Gershman, eds. *Total Baseball*, 7th edition (Kingston, NY: Total Sports Publishing, 2001), p. 2431.
9. *Summit County Beacon*, June 23, 1880.
10. *Summit County Beacon*, June 9, 1880; July 7, 1880; Thorn, et al., *Total Baseball*, p. 1071.
11. Peterjohn, *Baseball in Akron*; *Summit County Beacon*, July 7, 1880; Akron *Sunday Gazette*, August 29, 1880.
12. *Summit County Beacon*, July 7, 1880; Akron *Sunday Gazette*, July 4, 1880.
13. New York *Clipper*, July 17, 1880, p. 130.
14. *Summit County Beacon*, July 14, 1880; July 21, 1880; Akron *Sunday Gazette*, July 11, 1880.
15. *Summit County Beacon*, July 21, 1880; Seymour, *Baseball: The Early Years*, pp. 98–103.
16. *Summit County Beacon*, July 21, 1880; *Akron City Directory 1879–1880*; Peterjohn, *Baseball in Akron*.
17. Thorn, et al., *Total Baseball*, p. 1033; Louisville *Courier-Journal*, June 26, 1881; *Spalding's Official Base Ball Guide*, 1884, pp. 60–66.
18. *Sporting Life*, September 30, 1893, p. 9; *Sporting Life*, December 15, 1894, p. 5; Akron *Beacon Journal*, December 10, 1921.
19. Peterjohn, *Baseball in Akron*; Thorn, et al., *Total Baseball*, p. 973; New York *Clipper*, September 4, 1880, p. 187; *Sporting Life*, September 24, 1883, p. 6; Seattle *Post-Intelligencer*, undated clipping in the Bid McPhee file at the National Baseball Hall of Fame Library, likely from late 1893 or early 1894; Akron *Sunday Gazette*, August 22, 1880.
20. Akron *Sunday Gazette*, July 25; Akron *Sunday Gazette*, August 29, 1880; *Summit County Beacon*, July 28, 1880.

21. Akron *Sunday Gazette,* August 29, 1880.
22. Akron *Sunday Gazette,* August 8, August 29, 1880; *Summit County Beacon,* July 28, August 11, 1880.
23. Akron *Sunday Gazette,* August 8, 1880; *Summit County Beacon,* August 11, 1880.
24. Akron *Sunday Gazette,* August 8, 1880; *Summit County Beacon,* August 11, 1880.
25. Akron *Sunday Gazette,* August 22, August 29, 1880; *Summit County Beacon,* September 1, 1880.
26. *Summit County Beacon,* September 1, 1880; Akron *Sunday Gazette,* September 5, 1880; Peterjohn, *Baseball in Akron.*
27. Peterjohn, *Baseball in Akron*; *Summit County Beacon,* October 6, 1880; Akron *Sunday Gazette,* September 5, 1880.
28. New York *Clipper,* September 18, 1880, p. 205.
29. Akron *Sunday Gazette,* September 12, 1880.
30. Akron *Sunday Gazette,* September 12, 1880; *Summit County Beacon,* September 15, 1880; New York *Clipper,* September 18, 1880, p. 205; Thorn, et al., *Total Baseball,* p. 2051.
31. Akron *Sunday Gazette,* September 12, September 26, 1880; *Summit County Beacon,* October 6, 1880; Peterjohn, *Baseball in Akron.*

4

1. *Summit County Beacon,* June 23, September 29, 1880; Peterjohn, *Baseball in Akron.*
2. *Summit County Beacon,* September 29, 1880; Peterjohn, *Baseball in Akron*; Grismer, *Akron and Summit County,* p. 229.
3. Akron *Sunday Gazette,* July 25, 1880.
4. Akron *Sunday Gazette,* August 15, 1880.
5. Akron *Sunday Gazette,* August 29, 1880; *Summit County Beacon,* September 22, 1880.
6. Grismer, *Akron and Summit County,* pp. 238–239.
7. *Summit County Beacon,* March 30, 1881.
8. Thorn, et al., *Total Baseball,* p. 1005; Seattle *Post-Intelligencer* undated McPhee clipping.
9. *The Sporting News,* August 9, 1886; Robert L. Tiemann and Mark Rucker, *Nineteenth Century Stars* (Cleveland: Society for American Baseball Research, 1989), p. 97; David L. Porter, ed., *Biographical Dictionary of American Sports: Baseball, Revised and Expanded Edition* (Westport, CT: Greenwood, 2000), pp. 1089–1091.

10. Thorn, et al., *Total Baseball,* p. 1651; *Sporting Life,* December 2, 1885, p. 3; *Sporting Life,* May 25, 1887, p. 1.
11. Thorn, et al., *Total Baseball,* pp. 571, 981, 1036, 1103, 1216, 1291, 1650, 1700, 1701.
12. Thorn, et al., *Total Baseball,* pp. 639, 703, 803, 990, 1002, 1088, 1112, 1165, 1191, 1623, 1707.
13. *Summit County Beacon,* October 29, 1879; Akron *Sunday Gazette,* September 26, 1880; Louisville *Courier-Journal,* June 23, 1881; St. Louis *Globe-Democrat,* September 19, 1881; Missouri *Republican,* September 19, 1881.
14. Bill James, *The Bill James Historical Baseball Abstract,* (New York: Villard Books, 1988), pp. 26, 43.
15. Louisville *Courier-Journal,* August 5, September 5, 1881; Cleveland *Leader,* July 23, 1881; Seymour, *Baseball: The Early Years,* p. 136; Missouri *Republican,* August 28, 1881; St. Louis *Globe-Democrat,* August 28, 1881.

5

1. *Summit County Beacon,* March 30, 1881.
2. *Akron City Directory, 1875–76; Akron City Directory, 1879–80.*
3. Peterjohn, *Baseball in Akron.*
4. Seattle *Post-Intelligencer,* undated McPhee clipping.
5. *Sporting Life,* December 2, 1899, p. 9, quoting from the Cincinnati *Post.*
6. Seattle *Post-Intelligencer,* undated McPhee clipping.
7. *Sporting Life,* April 28, 1894, p. 6, quoting from the Cincinnati *Times Star.*
8. Seattle *Post-Intelligencer* undated McPhee clipping.
9. Louisville *Courier-Journal,* June 26, 1881.
10. Thorn, et al., *Total Baseball,* p. 1005.
11. Ivor-Campbell et al., *Baseball's First Stars,* p. 25.
12. *Sporting Life,* April 17, 1889, p. 3.
13. *Sporting Life,* September 13, 1890, p. 4.
14. Thorn, et al., *Total Baseball,* p. 1005.
15. *Sporting Life,* April 12, 1890, p. 12.
16. Tiemann and Rucker, *Nineteenth Century Stars,* p. 91; *Sporting Life,* September 30, 1893, p. 2; October 10, 1896, p. 5.
17. Tiemann and Rucker, *Nineteenth Century Stars,* p. 91; *Sporting Life,* September 12, 1888, p. 2.
18. *Sporting Life,* July 3, 1889, p. 2.

19. Seattle *Post-Intelligencer*, undated McPhee clipping; *Sporting Life,* January 27, 1886, p. 3.
20. *Sporting Life,* July 31, 1897, pp. 1, 4; August 21, 1897, p. 5.
21. *Sporting Life,* March 31, 1900, p. 6.
22. *Sporting Life,* July 13, 1901, p. 5; September 28, 1901, p. 3.
23. Tom Simon, ed., *Deadball Stars of the National League* (Cleveland: Society for American Baseball Research, 2004), p. 49.
24. *Sporting Life,* July 19, 1902, Vol. 39, No. 18, p. 3; *Nineteenth Century Stars,* p. 91.
25. Ralph Moses, "Bid McPhee" (Web site of SABR BioProject, 2003, http://bioproj.SABR.org).

6

1. Peterjohn, *Baseball in Akron*; Cleveland *Leader,* April 27, 1881.
2. Cleveland *Leader,* April 27, 1881.
3. New York *Clipper,* May 7, 1881, p. 106; Cleveland *Leader,* April 28, 29, 1881.
4. Peterjohn, *Baseball in Akron*; Cleveland *Leader,* April 30, May 2, 7, 9, 1881; Akron *City Times,* May 11, 1881.
5. St. Louis *Globe-Democrat,* August 29, 1881; Porter, *Biographical Dictionary,* pp. 1089–1091.
6. Thorn, et al., *Total Baseball,* pp. 1037, 1651; Tiemann and Rucker, *Nineteenth Century Stars,* p. 97.
7. Porter, *Biographical Dictionary,* pp. 1089–1091.
8. Tiemann and Rucker, *Nineteenth Century Stars,* p. 97.
9. Tiemann and Rucker, *Nineteenth Century Stars,* p. 97; *Sporting Life,* December 2, 1885, p. 3.
10. *Sporting Life,* June 2, 1886, p. 5; David Nemec, *The Beer and Whisky League: The Illustrated History of the American Association—Baseball's Renegade Major League* (New York: Lyons & Burford, 1994), p. 36.
11. *The Sporting News,* August 9, 1886; Porter, *Biographical Dictionary,* pp. 1089–1091; Nemec, *Beer and Whiskey,* p. 36.
12. *Sporting Life,* February 6, 1889, p. 2.
13. *Sporting Life,* May 18, 1887, p. 9; May 20, 1893, p. 2
14. *Sporting Life,* May 25, 1887, p. 1.
15. *Sporting Life,* June 8, 1887, p. 10; June 15, 1887, p. 1; June 22, 1887, p. 3.
16. Ivor-Campbell, et al., *Baseball's First Stars,* p. 26; *Sporting Life,* August 8, 1888, p. 1.
17. *Sporting Life,* May 9, 1891, p. 1; May 30, 1891, p. 7.
18. *Sporting Life,* November 12, 1892, p. 3.
19. *Sporting Life,* May 13, 1893, pp. 1, 3; May 20, 1893, p. 1; May 27, 1893, p. 1; July 15, 1893, p. 1.
20. *Sporting Life,* July 1, 1893, p. 1; September 30, 1893, p. 2; January 20, 1894, p. 5.
21. Thorn, et al., *Total Baseball,* p. 1651; *Sporting Life,* April 13, 1895, p. 13; July 6, 1895, p. 6.
22. Tiemann and Rucker, *Nineteenth Century Stars,* p. 97; *Sporting Life,* December 26, 1896, p. 4; July 9, 1898, p. 5.
23. *Sporting Life,* August 20, 1898, p. 5; March 25, 1899, p. 4; October 28, 1899, p. 4; July 20, 1901, p. 13.
24. Tiemann and Rucker, *Nineteenth Century Stars,* p. 97.
25. Porter, *Biographical Dictionary,* pp. 1089–1091; death certificate in the Tony Mullane file at the National Baseball Hall of Fame Library.

7

1. Cleveland *Leader,* May 14, 1881.
2. Cleveland *Leader,* May 17, 1881; Akron *City Times,* May 18, 1881.
3. Worcester *Evening Gazette,* May 14, 28, 1881; New York *Clipper,* May 21, 1881, p. 138; *Summit County Beacon,* July 27, 1881; Cleveland *Leader,* May 14, 17, 24, 25, 28, 1881.
4. Cleveland *Leader,* May 24, 25, 27, 28, 1881; Akron *City Times,* May 25, 1881.
5. Peterjohn, *Baseball in Akron; Summit County Beacon,* June 15, 1881; Cleveland *Leader,* May 31, June 6, 13, 1881; East Liverpool *Tribune,* June 4, 1881.
6. Peterjohn, *Baseball in Akron*; *Summit County Beacon,* June 22, 1881; Akron *City Times,* May 18, June 22, 1881; Cleveland *Leader,* June 16, 1881.
7. *Summit County Beacon,* June 22, 1881; Akron *City Times,* June 22, 1881.
8. New York *Clipper,* July 2, 1881, p. 233.
9. Louisville *Courier-Journal,* June 22, 1881.
10. Louisville *Courier-Journal,* June 22, 1881.
11. Tiemann and Rucker, *Nineteenth Century Stars,* p. 19.

12. Louisville *Courier-Journal,* June 22, 1881.
13. Louisville *Courier-Journal,* June 26, 1881; Cleveland *Leader,* April 27, 1881.
14. Ivor-Campbell, et al., *Baseball's First Stars,* p. 161; *Sporting Life,* September 17, 1883, p. 6; December 19, 1891, p. 2.
15. Ivor-Campbell, et al., *Baseball's First Stars,* p. 161; Thorn, et al., *Total Baseball,* p. 1216.
16. *Sporting Life,* November 18, 1885, p. 1.
17. *Sporting Life,* October 27, 1886, p. 3; March, 16, 1887, p. 1.
18. *Sporting Life,* June 29, 1887, p. 3; Ivor-Campbell, et al., *Baseball's First Stars,* p. 161.
19. *Sporting Life,* March 28, 1888, p. 5; August 24, 1887, p. 5.
20. *Sporting Life,* May 9, 1888, p. 2; October 31, 1888, p. 2; February 6, 1889, p. 2; April 3, 1889, p. 4; Ivor-Campbell, et al., *Baseball's First Stars,* p. 161.
21. Ivor-Campbell, et al., *Baseball's First Stars,* p. 161; *Sporting Life,* February 26, 1890, p. 1.
22. *Sporting Life,* March 5, 1890, p. 4; Thorn, et al., *Total Baseball,* p. 1216.
23. *Sporting Life,* May 10, 1890, pp. 4, 7.
24. *Sporting Life,* October 31, 1891, p. 11.
25. Ivor-Campbell, et al., *Baseball's First Stars,* p. 161; *Sporting Life,* October 31, 1891, p. 11; September 24, 1894, p. 9.
26. Ivor-Campbell, et al., *Baseball's First Stars,* p. 161; *Sporting Life,* April 7, 1894, p. 1; April 27, 1895, p. 13.
27. *Sporting Life,* February 8, 1896, p. 6; February 22, 1896, p. 4.
28. *Sporting Life,* April 23, 1989, p. 5; May 13, 1899, p. 5.
29. *Sporting Life,* August 3, 1907, pp 1–2.
30. Thorn, et al., *Total Baseball,* p. 1216.

8

1. Louisville *Courier-Journal,* June 23, 1881.
2. Louisville *Courier-Journal,* June 23, 1881.
3. Louisville *Courier-Journal,* June 23, 1881.
4. Identification of Green used the research of Society for American Baseball Research members Richard Malatzky, Reed Howard, Joe Simenic, Vern Luse and Peter Morris; Peterjohn, *Baseball in Akron*; New York *Clipper,* May 1, 1880, p. 45; *Summit County Beacon,* July 21, 1880; *Sporting Life,* July 23, 1884; February 6, 1884; Columbus *Daily Times,* April 16, 1883; Dayton *Journal,* June 1, 1889; Cleveland death certificate.
5. Louisville *Courier-Journal,* June 23, 1881.
6. Louisville *Courier-Journal,* June 23, 1881.
7. Thorn, et al., *Total Baseball,* pp. 973, 981, 1212, 1216.
8. *Summit County Beacon,* June 22, July 20, 1881; Akron *City Times,* June 22, 1881.
9. Akron *Sunday Gazette,* July 4, 1880; New York *Clipper,* June 9, 1883, p. 189.
10. *Sporting Life,* April 12, 1890, p. 5; Thorn, et al., *Total Baseball,* p. 973.
11. Louisville *Courier-Journal,* June 26, 1881.
12. *Summit County Beacon,* June 29, 1881.
13. New York *Clipper,* July 9, 1881, p. 252.
14. *Sporting Life,* May 4, 1907, p. 1; November 4, 1893, p. 4.
15. *Summit County Beacon,* July 20, 1881.
16. *Sporting Life,* November 4, 1893, p. 4; New York *Clipper,* July 12, 1884.
17. New York *Clipper,* July 30, 1881; August 6, 1881; July 12, 1884.
18. Thorn, et al., *Total Baseball,* p. 1212; *Sporting Life,* July 21, 1886, p. 3; May 25, 1887, p. 10.
19. Louisville *Courier-Journal,* June 22, 23, 26, 1881; New York *Clipper,* July 9, 1881, p. 252.

9

1. Louisville *Courier-Journal,* June 28, 1881.
2. Louisville *Courier-Journal,* June 28, 1881.
3. Louisville *Courier-Journal,* June 28, 1881.
4. Louisville *Courier-Journal,* June 28, 1881.
5. Akron *Beacon Journal,* January 22, 1910, p. 1.
6. Louisville *Courier-Journal,* June 22, 23, 26, 28, 1881; New York *Clipper,* July 9, 1881, p. 252; Ivor-Campbell, et al., *Baseball's First Stars,* p. 173.
7. Thorn, et al., *Total Baseball,* p. 1291.
8. Ivor-Campbell, et al., *Baseball's First Stars,* p. 173.
9. Rochester *The Post Express,* May 26, 1898; Michael Benson, *Ballparks of North*

America (Jefferson, NC: McFarland, 1989), pp 189–190; Philip J. Lowry, *Green Cathedrals* (Reading, MA: Addison-Wesley, 1992), p. 164.

10. Ivor-Campbell, et al., *Baseball's First Stars*, p. 173.

11. Ivor-Campbell, et al., *Baseball's First Stars*, p. 25; New York *Clipper*, November 12, 1881, p. 555.

12. New York *Clipper*, January 28, 1882, p. 737.

13. Seymour, *Baseball: The Early Years*, pp. 140–141.

14. *Sporting Life*, October 29, 1883, p. 6.

15. *Sporting Life*, January 16, 1884, p. 3; November 14, 1883, p. 3.

16. Thorn, et al., *Total Baseball*, p. 1291.

17. *Sporting Life*, October 19, 1887, p. 3; January 18, 1888, p. 5.

18. *Sporting Life*, October 31, 1888, p. 2; November 7, 1888, p. 2.

19. *Sporting Life*, April 3, 1889, p. 1; April 24, 1889, p. 2.

20. *Sporting Life*, May, 22, 1889, p. 5.

21. *Sporting Life*, August 28, 1889, p. 1.

22. *Sporting Life*, November 20, 1889, p. 1; Thorn, et al., *Total Baseball*, p. 1291.

23. *Sporting Life*, April 25, 1891, p. 2; May 9, 1891, p. 2.

24. *Sporting Life*, April 25, 1891, p. 9.

25. *Sporting Life*, September 12, 1891, pp. 2, 4; October 17, 1891, p. 2.

26. *Sporting Life*, August 20, 1892, p. 2.

27. Rochester *Democrat and Chronicle*, September 7, 1892, p. 9.

28. *Sporting Life*, September 10, 1892, p. 2; September 17, 1892, p. 2; September 24, 1892, p. 9; October 8, 1892, p. 2.

29. Ivor-Campbell, et al., *Baseball's First Stars*, p. 173.

30. *Sporting Life*, April 30, 1892, p. 2; May 6, 1893, p. 2; November 19, 1892, p. 2.

31. Thorn, et al., *Total Baseball*, p. 1291; *Sporting Life*, May 20, 1893, p. 2; February 17, 1894, p. 2; March 24, 1894, p. 2; April 14, 1894, p. 3.

32. Ivor-Campbell, et al., *Baseball's First Stars*, p. 173; *Sporting Life*, December 15, 1894, pp. 1, 5; December 29, 1894, p. 2.

33. Ivor-Campbell, et al., *Baseball's First Stars*, p. 173; *Sporting Life*, June 6, 1895, p. 4; July 18, 1896, p. 5; September 26, 1896, p. 5; July, 10, 1897, p. 10.

34. *Sporting Life*, November 1, 1890, p. 4; February 14, 1891, p. 4; April 3, 1897, p. 5; April 30, 1898, p. 5; December 16, 1899, p. 5;
April 7, 1900, p. 3; October 6, 1900, p. 5; November 17, 1900, p. 4; March 31, 1906, p. 10; Akron *Beacon Journal*, January 22, 1910, p. 1.

35. Akron *Beacon Journal*, January 22, 1910, p. 1; *Sporting Life*, March 31, 1906, p. 10.

36. Akron *Beacon Journal*, February 1, 1909.

37. Mansfield *News*, May 21, 1906, p. 6; *Sporting Life*, July 7, 1906, p. 8; Akron *Beacon Journal*, February 1, 1909.

38. *Sporting Life*, August 27, 1898, p. 4; September 3, 1898, p. 5.

39. Akron *Beacon Journal*, January 22, 1910; death certificate in the Sam Wise file at the National Baseball Hall of Fame Library.

40. Braden, *A Centennial History of Akron*, pp. 532–533; Akron *Beacon Journal*, January 22, 24, 1910.

10

1. Louisville *Courier-Journal*, June 28, 1881; Peterjohn, *Baseball in Akron*; Akron *City Times*, June 22, 1881; Cleveland *Leader*, June 30, 1881.

2. Cleveland *Leader*, June 30, 1881; July 2, 1881.

3. Cleveland *Leader*, July 2, 1881; July 7, 1881.

4. Akron *Daily Beacon*, July 7, 1881.

5. Cleveland *Leader*, June 30, 1881; Worcester *Evening Gazette*, July 1, 1881.

6. Thorn, et al., *Total Baseball*, p. 910.

7. New York *Clipper*, September 4, 1880, p. 187; November 12, 1881, p. 555.

8. *Sporting Life*, September 24, 1883; November 18, 1885, p. 1; November 3, 1886, p. 1.

9. *Sporting Life*, May 18, 1887, p. 9; August 31, 1887, p. 6; September 19, 1888, p. 2; August 7, 1889, p. 4.

10. *Sporting Life*, September 11, 1889, p. 4; death certificate in the Rudolph Kemmler file at the National Baseball Hall of Fame Library.

11. *Summit County Beacon*, July 20, 1881; Cleveland *Leader*, July 13, 1881.

12. *Summit County Beacon*, July 20, 1881; Cleveland *Leader*, July 13, 1881; Akron *Daily Beacon*, July 13, 1881.

13. Peterjohn, *Baseball in Akron*; Cleveland *Leader*, July 16, 19, 1881; Worcester *Evening Gazette*, July 16, 1881; Akron *Daily Beacon*, July 19, 1881; New York *Clipper*, July 30, 1881.

14. Thorn, et al., *Total Baseball*, p. 1103, 1700–1701.

15. Thorn, et al., *Total Baseball*, p. 2433. *Sporting Life*, January 27, 1886, p. 2; June 6,

1886, p. 5; September 19, 1891; December 15, 1894, p. 2.
16. Thorn, et al., *Total Baseball*, p. 1103; New York *Clipper*, July 16, 1881, p. 266; *Summit County Beacon*, July 27, 1881; August 17, 1881; Cleveland *Leader*, April 29, 1881.
17. Cleveland *Leader*, July 22, 1881.
18. Akron *City Times*, July 20, 1881; Akron *Daily Beacon*, July 23, 1881; Cleveland *Leader*, July 23, 1881.
19. Akron *Daily Beacon*, July 14, 1881; Cleveland *Leader*, July 25, 1881.
20. Cleveland *Leader*, July 28, 1881.

11

1. Akron *Daily Beacon*, July 28, August 6, 1881.
2. Thorn, et al., *Total Baseball*, p. 981.
3. *Sporting Life*, July 30, 1883.
4. *Sporting Life*, August 26, 1885, p. 1; January 13, 1886, p. 3; June 2, 1886, p. 5; August 4, 1886, p. 5; *The Sporting News*, May 24, 1886, p. 5.
5. Ivor-Campbell, et al., *Baseball's First Stars*, p. 25; *Sporting Life*, December 14, 1887.
6. *Sporting Life*, December 14, 1887.
7. *Sporting Life*, August 31, 1887, p. 6; June 19, 1889, p. 1.
8. *Sporting Life*, March 26, 1890, p. 4; May 31, 1890, p. 1.
9. *Sporting Life*, May 31, 1890, p. 1; September 27, 1890, p. 9; *Spalding's Official Base Ball Guide 1891*, p. 36.
10. *Sporting Life*, February 14, 1891, p. 4; April 4, 1891; *Spalding's Official Base Ball Guide 1892*, pp. 110, 155.
11. *Sporting Life*, February 6, 1892, p. 1; Mercer *Dispatch and Republican*, April 7, 1922; August 22, 1930.
12. *Sporting Life*, June 25, 1892, p. 4.
13. *Sporting Life*, March 10, 1895, p. 13; February 29, 1896, p. 9; April 27, 1901, p. 3; Mercer *Dispatch and Republican*, April 7, 1922.

12

1. Cleveland *Leader*, July 30, August 3, 1881.
2. Thorn, et al., *Total Baseball*, pp. 1223, 1785; Worcester *Evening Gazette*, May 28, 1881; New York *Clipper*, August 27, 1881; September 1, 1883.

3. *Sporting Life*, July 11, 1891, p. 2; July 19, 1900, p. 7.
4. Thorn, et al., *Total Baseball*, p. 1092; Cleveland *Leader*, July 25, 30, 1881; *Sporting Life*, August 18, 1886, p. 5.
5. *Summit County Beacon*, July 27, 1881; New York *Clipper*, August 13, 1881, p. 330; Louisville *Courier-Journal*, August 5, 1881.
6. Louisville *Courier-Journal*, August 5, 7, 8, 9, 1881.
7. Akron *Daily Beacon*, August 11, 1881; Cleveland *Leader*, August 11, 1881.
8. Akron *Daily Beacon*, August 11, 1881.
9. Thorn, et al., *Total Baseball*, p. 1216; New York *Clipper*, August 20, 1881, p. 345; August 27, 1881, p. 362; *Summit County Beacon*, August 17, 1881; Cleveland *Leader*, Aug 13, 1881.
10. *Summit County Beacon*, August 17, 1881; Cleveland *Leader*, August 16, 1881.
11. East Liverpool *Tribune*, August 20, 1881; Cleveland *Leader*, August 20, 1881; New York *Clipper*, August 27, 1881, p. 362; the *Tribune* reported the score as 29–6 and 30–6 and had no box score.
12. East Liverpool *Tribune*, August 27, 1881.
13. Thorn, et al., *Total Baseball*, p. 1651; New York *Clipper*, August 13, 1881, p. 330; August 20, 1881, p. 345; Cleveland *Leader*, August 20, 1881.

13

1. Cleveland *Leader*, July 7, August 16, 1881; *Summit County Beacon*, August 17, 1881; October 6, 1880; *Sporting Life*, April 29, 1885, p. 7.
2. Thorn, et al., *Total Baseball*, p. 571; *Sporting Life*, January 25, 1888, p. 1.
3. *Sporting Life*, January 25, 1888, p. 1; Ivor-Campbell, et al., *Baseball's First Stars*, pp. 177–178.
4. *Sporting Life*, January 25, 1888, p. 1; Thorn, et al., *Total Baseball*, p. 571.
5. *Sporting Life*, January 25, 1888, p. 1; Thorn, et al., *Total Baseball*, p. 571.
6. *Sporting Life*, February 17, 1886, p. 5; January 4, 1888, p. 6.
7. *Sporting Life*, January 25, 1888, p. 1.
8. *Sporting Life*, November 16, 1895, p. 1.
9. *Sporting Life*, November 15, 1913, p. 2.
10. *Sporting Life*, November 15, 1913, p. 2.
11. *Sporting Life*, November 15, 1913, p. 2.
12. *Sporting Life*, November 22, 1913, p. 3.
13. *Sporting Life*, November 22, 1913, p. 3.

14. *Sporting Life,* November 22, 1913, p. 3.
15. *Sporting Life,* November 22, 1913, p. 3; November 29, 1913, p. 6.
16. *Sporting Life,* November 29, 1913, p. 6.
17. *Sporting Life,* October 17, 1891, p. 2; Palm Beach *Times,* August 13, 1934.
18. *Sporting Life,* July 13, 1895, p. 6; August 10, 1895, p.6; January 11, 1896, p. 5; March 14, 1896, p. 4; April 30, 1898, p. 4; June 17, 1899, p. 5; July 22, 1899, p. 5; Thorn, et al., *Total Baseball,* p. 2451.
19. Palm Beach *Times,* August 13, 1934.
20. *Sporting Life,* November 29, 1913, p. 16.
21. *Sporting Life,* November 29, 1913, p. 6.
22. *Sporting Life,* January 24, 1914, p. 2.
23. Palm Beach *Times,* August 13, 1934.

14

1. St. Louis *Globe-Democrat,* August 28, 1881; Missouri *Republican,* August 28, 1881.
2. St. Louis *Globe-Democrat,* August 28, 1881; Missouri *Republican,* August 28, 1881.
3. St. Louis *Globe-Democrat,* August 28, 1881; Missouri *Republican,* August 28, 1881.
4. Seattle *Post-Intelligencer,* undated McPhee clipping; *Sporting Life,* November 3, 1886, p. 1; New York *Clipper,* December 9, 1882; *Summit County Beacon,* July 27, 1881.
5. Thorn, et al., *Total Baseball,* p. 1206.
6. New York *Clipper,* December 9, 1882.
7. *Sporting Life,* January 6, 1886, p. 3; January 20, 1886, p. 2; February 3, 1886, p. 5; July 28, 1886, p. 5; August 25, 1886, p. 5; August 10, 1887, p. 5; December 10, 1892, p. 1; May 25, 1895, p. 4.
8. Thorn, et al., *Total Baseball,* p. 1550; *Spalding's Official Base Ball Guide,* 1884; Cincinnati *Commercial Gazette,* September 19, 1883; New York *Clipper,* September 15, 1883.
9. Thorn, et al., *Total Baseball,* p. 1623; St. Louis *Globe-Democrat,* August 28, 1881; Missouri *Republican,* August 28, 1881; *Summit County Beacon,* September 7, 1881.
10. St. Louis *Globe-Democrat,* August 28, 1881; Missouri *Republican,* August 28, 1881; *Summit County Beacon,* September 7, 1881.
11. St. Louis *Globe-Democrat,* August 29, 1881; Missouri *Republican,* August 29, 1881.
12. St. Louis *Globe-Democrat,* August 29, 1881; Missouri *Republican,* August 29, 1881.
13. St. Louis *Globe-Democrat,* August 29, 1881; Missouri *Republican,* August 29, 1881.
14. St. Louis *Globe-Democrat,* August 30, 1881.
15. Missouri *Republican,* August 30, 1881; St. Louis *Globe-Democrat,* August 30, 1881.
16. Louisville *Courier-Journal,* September 4, 1881.
17. Louisville *Courier-Journal,* September 5, 1881.
18. Akron *Daily Beacon,* September 8, 1881; *Summit County Beacon,* September 7, 14, 1881.
19. Thorn, et al., *Total Baseball,* p. 1322; *Summit County Beacon,* September 14, 1881; *Sporting Life,* April 16, 1904, p. 10; death certificate in the Harry Arundel file at the National Baseball Hall of Fame Library.
20. Thorn, et al., *Total Baseball,* pp. 1236, 1650; New York *Clipper,* October 14, 1882; Schenectady *Gazette,* November 20, 1939.
21. Schenectady *Gazette,* November 20, 1939; New York *Clipper,* July 2, September 17, 1881; October 14, 1882.
22. New York *Clipper,* October 14, 1882.
23. Thorn, et al., *Total Baseball,* pp. 1236, 1650.
24. Thorn, et al., *Total Baseball,* pp. 1236, 1650; Schenectady *Gazette,* November 20, 1939.
25. New York *Clipper,* October 14, 1882; *Sporting Life,* January 19, 1887, p. 3; February 16, 1887, p. 3; October 5, 1887, p. 6; May 30, 1888, p. 9; August 22, 1988, p. 2.
26. *Sporting Life,* October 17, 1888, p. 6; Schenectady *Gazette,* November 20, 1939.

15

1. Missouri *Republican,* September 18, 1881; St. Louis *Globe-Democrat,* September 18, 1881.
2. Missouri *Republican,* September 19, 1881; St. Louis *Globe-Democrat,* September 19, 1881.
3. Missouri *Republican,* September 19, 1881; St. Louis *Globe-Democrat,* September 19, 1881.
4. Missouri *Republican,* September 20, 1881; St. Louis *Globe-Democrat,* September 20, 1881.
5. Missouri *Republican,* September 20, 1881; St. Louis *Globe-Democrat,* September 20, 1881.
6. Missouri *Republican,* September 20, 1881; St. Louis *Globe-Democrat,* September 20, 1881.

7. Missouri *Republican*, September 20, 1881.
8. *Sporting Life*, January 13, 1886, p. 2; June 23, 1886, p. 8; April 2, 1892, p. 14; December 19, 1894, p. 5.
9. Akron *Beacon Journal*, December 10, 1921, p. 1; handwritten letter from Ralph Lin Weber of the Baseball Research Bureau in Toledo, Ohio, to S.C. Thompson, editor of *The Baseball Encyclopedia*, dated December 13, 1951, in the Charles Hazen Morton file at the National Baseball Hall of Fame Library.
10. Thorn, et al., *Total Baseball*, pp. 1033, 1649.
11. *Spalding's Official Base Ball Guide*, 1884; Ralph Lin Weber letter,*1951*.
12. Nemec, *Beer and Whiskey League*, pp. 27, 60, 68, 70, 73; Thorn, et al., *Total Baseball*, pp. 1651, 2431.
13. *Sporting Life*, November 18, 1885, p. 2; January 13, 1886, p. 2; March 3, 1886, p. 3.
14. *Sporting Life*, May 19, 1886, p. 5; June 23, 1886, p. 8.
15. *Sporting Life*, June 23, 1886, p. 8.
16. *Sporting Life*, June 30, 1886, p. 5; July 7, 1886, p. 5.
17. *Sporting Life*, September 8, 1886, p. 6.
18. *Sporting Life*, October 27, 1886, p. 3; November 24, 1886, p. 3; January 5, 1887, p. 3; January 12, 1887, p. 1; January 26, 1887, p. 1.
19. *Sporting Life*, February 16, 1887, p. 3; May 18, 1887, p. 9; May 25, 1887, p. 10.
20. *Sporting Life*, June 1, 1887, p. 3; August 24, 1887, p. 5.
21. *Sporting Life*, April 25, 1888, p. 4; October 17, 1888, p. 2.
22. *Sporting Life*, November 21, 1888, p. 3.
23. *Sporting Life*, March 6, 1889, p. 4; May 1, 1889, p. 4.
24. *Sporting Life*, March 5, 1890, p. 4; Thorn, et al., *Total Baseball*, pp. 2071, 2431.
25. *Sporting Life*, April 11, 1891; April 25, 1891, p. 2; May 30, 1891, p. 1; June 27, 1891, p. 1; July 11, 1891, p. 1; August 1, 1891, p. 9.
26. *Sporting Life*, April 2, 1892, p. 14; May 7, 1892, p. 2.
27. *Sporting Life*, September 16, 1893, p. 1.
28. *Sporting Life*, September 16, 1893, p. 2.
29. *Sporting Life*, September 1, 1894, p. 1.
30. *Sporting Life*, December 15, 1894, pp. 1, 5; December 29, 1894, p. 2; Ivor-Campbell, et al., *Baseball's First Stars*, p. 173.
31. *Sporting Life*, June 6, 1896, p. 1; July 4, 1896, p. 5.
32. *Sporting Life*, October 30, 1897, p. 2; November 13, 1897, p. 4; December 18, 1897, p. 2.
33. Rochester *Democrat and Chronicle*, May 21, 1898, p. 14.
34. Rochester *Democrat and Chronicle*, May 21, 1898, p. 14; May 22, 1898, p. 18.
35. *Sporting Life*, June 4, 1898, p. 10; Rochester *Post Express*, May 25, 1898, p. 10.

16

1. *Sporting Life*, June 18, 1898, p. 6; December 9, 1899, p. 6.
2. *Sporting Life*, March 11, 1905, p. 11; August 5, 1905, pp. 9, 15; August 12, 1905, p. 11; September 9, 1905, p. 12; *SABR Minor League Newsletter*, April 2003.
3. *Sporting Life*, October 21, 1905, p. 17; November 4, 1905, p. 2.
4. *Sporting Life*, December 16, 1905, p. 9; January 27, 1906, p. 5; March 24, 1906, p. 6; March 31, 1906, p. 6.
5. *Sporting Life*, June 2, 1906, p. 10; June 23, 1906, p. 13; Mansfield *News*, May 21, 1906, p. 6.
6. *Sporting Life*, January 5, 1907, p. 10; January 26, 1907, p. 2; November 16, 1907, p. 2.
7. *Sporting Life*, December 21, 1907, p. 9; January 18, 1908, p. 6.
8. *Sporting Life*, February 8, 1908, p. 10; September 19, 1908, p. 24.
9. *Sporting Life*, November 7, 1908, p. 10.
10. *Sporting Life*, October 31, 1908, p. 10.
11. Akron *Beacon Journal*, January 1, 2, 4, 6, 7, 8, 9, 11, 1909; *Sporting Life*, January 16, 1909, p. 10.
12. Akron *Beacon Journal*, January 13, 1909.
13. Akron *Beacon Journal*, January 13, 1909; *Sporting Life*, January 23, 1909, p. 8.
14. Akron *Beacon Journal*, January 16, 18, 22, 23, 28, 1909; *Sporting Life*, February 20, 1909, p. 7.
15. *Sporting Life*, November 14, 1908, p. 3.
16. Akron *Beacon Journal*, March 16, 1909; *Sporting Life*, March 19, 1909, p. 15.
17. Although Morton's infant son, Freddie, died in 1887, Morton had a second son, also named Fred.
18. *Sporting Life*, March 27, 1909, p. 15.
19. *Sporting Life*, March 27, 1909, p. 15; April 3, 1909, pp. 2, 7; June 19, 1909, p. 2.
20. Akron *Beacon Journal*, August 11, 1909; *Sporting Life*, August 28, 1909, p. 23.
21. Akron *Beacon Journal*, January 22, 1910, December 10, 1921; *Sporting News*, December 15, 1921; Massillon *Independent*, De-

cember 10, 1921; death certificate in the Charles H. Morton file at the National Baseball Hall of Fame Library.

17

1. *Sporting Life,* October 15, 1883, p. 3; October 29, 1883, p. 7.
2. Seymour, *Baseball: The Early Years,* pp. 151–152.
3. *Sporting Life,* February 13, 1884, p. 4.
4. *Sporting Life,* February 20, 1884, p. 2.
5. *Sporting Life,* March 12, 1884, p. 4; March 26, 1884, p. 3; April 2, 1884, p.3.
6. *Summit County Beacon,* April 9, 1884; *Sporting Life,* April 9, 1884, p. 6.
7. *Sporting Life,* April 9, 1884, p. 6; April 23, p. 5.
8. *Summit County Beacon,* May 14, 1884; *Sporting Life,* April 30, 1884, p. 6; May 7, 1884, p. 5.
9. *Sporting Life,* May 7, 1884, p. 5; May 28, p. 6; June 4, p. 6; June 18, p. 6.
10. *Sporting Life,* April 1, 1885, p. 5; May 6, 1885, p. 5; Akron *Beacon Journal,* May 14, 1935.
11. A.D. Sueshsdorf, "Honus Wagner's Rookie Year," *The National Pastime,* Winter 1987, Vol. 6, No. 1, pp. 11–17.
12. Lloyd Johnson and Miles Wolff, *The Encyclopedia of Minor League Baseball,* (Durham, NC: Baseball America, 1993), pp. 47, 109, 111, 114, 117, 120, 123, 126.
13. Johnson and Wolff, *Encyclopedia,* p. 47; Akron *Beacon Journal,* May 14, 1935.
14. Sherrill Leonard, "*Athletes in Akron Central,*" (Rooters Council of Akron Central High School, undated), pp. 34–36; Akron *Beacon Journal,* April 21, 1940.
15. Akron *Beacon Journal,* April 21, 1940.
16. Thorne, et al., *Total Baseball,* p. 1178; Akron *Beacon Journal,* August 24, 1928.
17. Johnson and Wolff, *Encyclopedia,* p. 47.
18. Akron *Beacon Journal,* December 13, 1920.
19. Akron *Beacon Journal,* January 6, January 13, January 14, February 9, 1921.
20. Akron *Beacon Journal,* February 17, 1921; *Sporting Life,* April 15, 1911, p. 12; April 22, 1911, p. 12; January 20, 1912, p. 10.
21. Akron *Beacon Journal,* February 28, March 4, March 11, March 17, 1921; *The Sporting News,* March 4, 1921.
22. Akron *Beacon Journal,* September 27, 1920.
23. Seymour, *Baseball: The People's Game,* pp. 236–237.
24. Seymour, *Baseball: The People's Game,* p. 248.
25. Akron *Beacon Journal,* July 28, 1981; July 14, 1925.
26. Akron *Beacon Journal,* August 16, 1926; interview with Harold Sloop, March 8, 1992.
27. Akron *Beacon Journal,* August 23, August 30, 1926.

18

1. Akron *Beacon Journal.*, January 5, January 6, April 11, April 17, April 18, April 19, 1928.
2. Akron *Beacon Journal.*, May 1, 1928; Johnson and Wolff, *Encyclopedia,* pp. 171, 173, 180; Dick Clark and Larry Lester, *Negro Leagues Book* (Cleveland: Society for American Baseball Research, 1994), p. 111; Lowry, *Green Cathedrals,* p. 93.
3. Ruth McKenney, *Industrial Valley,* (Ithaca, N.Y.: ILR Press, School of Industrial and Labor Relations, Cornell University, 1992), pp. 110, 122, 166–167, 196–199.
4. Akron *Beacon Journal,* January 12, January 14, 1935.
5. Akron *Beacon Journal,* January 30, February 2, February 5, February 9, February 11, 1935.
6. Akron *Beacon Journal,* February 21, April 17, 19, 20, 22, 1935.
7. Akron *Beacon Journal,* June 15, 16, July 8, August 18, September 7, 1936.
8. Akron *Beacon Journal,* July 6, 1935.
9. Richard McBane, "Field Days," *Beacon Magazine,* August 28, 1994, pp. 13–14.
10. Akron *Beacon Journal,* September 10, December 10, 1941.
11. Interview with William X. Walsh, December 29, 1988; interview with John Menesian, March 19, 1987.
12. Akron *Beacon Journal,* June 25, 1950.
13. Thorn, et al., *Total Baseball,* pp. 685, 1150–1151.
14. Akron *Beacon Journal,* April 11, 1997.

Bibliography

Books

Akron City Directory 1875–1876 and *1879–1880*. Detroit: Burch, Potter & Co.

Benson, Michael. *Ballparks of North America*. Jefferson, NC: McFarland, 1989.

Braden, James A., ed. *A Centennial History of Akron*. Akron, OH: Summit County Historical Society, 1925.

Clark, Dick, and Lester, Larry. *The Negro Leagues Book*. Cleveland: Society for American Baseball Research, 1994.

Grismer, Karl. *Akron and Summit County*. Akron, OH: Summit County Historical Society, undated.

Ivor-Campbell, Frederick, Tiemann, Robert L., and Rucker, Mark, eds. *Baseball's First Stars*, Cleveland: Society for American Baseball Research, 1996.

James, Bill. *The Bill James Historical Baseball Abstract*. New York: Villard Books, 1988.

Johnson, Lloyd, and Wolff, Miles. *The Encyclopedia of Minor League Baseball*, Durham, NC: Baseball America, 1993.

Lowry, Philip J. *Green Cathedrals*. Reading, MA: Addison-Wesley, 1992.

McKenney, Ruth. *Industrial Valley*. Ithaca, NY: ILR, 1992

Melville, Tom. *Early Baseball and the Rise of the National League*. Jefferson, NC: McFarland, 2001.

Nemec, David. *The Beer and Whisky League: The Illustrated History of the American Association — Baseball's Renegade Major League*. New York: Lyons & Burford, 1994.

Porter, David L. *Biographical Dictionary of American Sports: Baseball, Revised and Expanded Edition*. Westwood, CT: Greenwood, 2000

Rhodes, Greg, and Erardi, John. *The First Boys of Summer*. Cincinnati: Road West, 1994.

Selzer, Jack. *Baseball in the Nineteenth Century: An Overview*. Cleveland: Society for American Baseball Research, 1986.

Seymour, Harold. *Baseball: The Early Years*. New York: Oxford University Press, 1960.

_____. *Baseball: The People's Game*. New York: Oxford University Press, 1990.

Simm, Tom, ed. *Deadball Stars of the National League*. Cleveland: Society for American Baseball Research, 2004.

Spalding's Official Base Ball Guide. 1884, 1891 and 1892 editions.

Thorn, John; Palmer, Pete; and Gershman, Michael, eds. *Total Baseball*. 7th edition. Kingston, NY: Total Sports Publishing, 2001.

Tiemann, Robert L., and Rucker, Mark. *Nineteenth Century Stars*. Cleveland: Society for American Baseball Research, 1989

Periodicals

Akron *Beacon Journal*, 1909–10, 1920–21, 1925–26, 1928, 1935–41, 1950, 1981, 1997.
Akron *City Times*, 1881.
Akron *Daily Beacon*, 1881.
Akron *Sunday Gazette*, 1879–80.
Cincinnati *Commercial Gazette*, 1883.
Cleveland *Leader*, 1881.
East Liverpool *Tribune*, 1881.
Louisville *Courier-Journal*, 1881.
Mansfield *News*, 1906.
Massillon *Independent*, 1921.
McBane, Richard. "Field Days." *Beacon Magazine, Akron Beacon Journal*, Aug. 28, 1994.
Mercer *Dispatch and Republican*, 1922, 1930.
Missouri *Republican*, 1881.
Moses, Ralph, "Bid McPhee," Web site of Society for American Baseball Research BioProject, http://bioproj.SABR.org, 2003.
New York *Clipper*, 1880–84.
Palm Beach *Times*, 1934.
Peterjohn, Alvin K. "Baseball in Akron, Ohio, 1879–1881, A Case Study." Undated paper in the Akron file at the National Baseball Hall of Fame Library.
Rochester *Democrat & Chronicle*, 1892, 1898.
Rochester *Post Express*, 1898.
SABR Minor League Newsletter. April 2003.
Schenectady *Gazette*, 1939.
Sherrill, Leonard. "Athletes in Akron Central," Rooters Council of Akron Central High School, undated.
Sporting Life, 1883–1901, 1904–09, 1911–14.
The Sporting News, 1886, 1921.
St. Louis *Globe-Democrat*, 1881.
Sueshsdorf, A.D. "Honus Wagner's Rookie Year," *The National Pastime*, Vol. 6, No. 1, Winter 1987.
Summit County Beacon, 1867, 1879–81, 1884.
Worcester *Evening Gazette*, 1881.

Player Files, National Baseball Hall of Fame Library

Andrews, George Edward.
Arundel, Harry.
Dorsey, Jeremiah M.
Kemmler, Rudolph.
Mansell, John "Doc."
Maskry, Samuel Leech.
McPhee, Alexander "Bid."
Morton, Charles Hazen.
Mountain, Frank.
Mullane, Tony.
Wise, Sam.

Index

Aetna ball club (Warren, OH) 17
Akron Aeros ball club 139
Akron ballparks: Canal Park 139; in 1867 10; Maple Valley Field 138; new League Park 135–139; noisy children 27; old League Park 134; at Perkins & N. Union streets 22; Recreation Park 128; used as skating rink 33–34; viewing games from Union street 27, 78
Akron Base Ball Association 15, 22–23, 27, 33–34, 37, 53
Akron Bicycle Club 128
Akron Black Tyrites ball club 136
Akron City ball club 14
Akron Exhibition Co. 131–132
Akron High School 130
Akron Numatics ball club 131–133, 135
Akron Orphans ball club 139
Akron Recreation Commission 130
Akron Steam Forge Works 13
Akron Tyrites ball club 135–137
Akron Yankees ball club 137–139
Albany, NY: ball club 54, 61–62
All-American ball club 69
Allegheny (Pittsburgh American Association club) 56, 87, 110
Allegheny County 59
Allentown, PA 72
Alliance, OH 14, 126
Altoona, PA 126
American Association 7, 8, 23, 25, 34–35, 39–40, 47, 56–58, 62, 64, 67–69, 71, 87, 104, 110, 113, 126, 130
Andrews, Ed 31, 35, 46, 70, 92–99, 102, 104
Angel, E.B. 10
Anson, Cap 29–30, 63
Anthracites ball club (Pottsville, PA) 61
Ardner, Joe 104

Arundel, Harry 104, 108
Ashland Anchors ball club 17
Ashtabula County 109
Association of Industrial Athletic Associations 133
Association Park (Kansas City) (The Pit) 66
Aston Villa of Birmingham (English club) 84
Atlanta: Southern League club 79, 85
Atlantic & Great Western Railroad 13
Atlantic League 73
Atlantics ball club (Brooklyn) 2, 6, 62
attendance figures 36, 137–138
Auburn, NY 23
Aultman, Miller & Co. 21
Austinburg, OH 14

B.F. Goodrich Co. 13, 21
Babcock, Will 10
Babcock & Wilcox Co. 130
Baker, George 103
Baltimore, MD 35, 131; American Association club 66, 71; International League club 131; National League club 50–51
Barberton, OH 65, 130
Base Ball Players Fraternity 95
Beaver Falls, PA: ball club 53
Bierce, Bruce 136–137
Binghamton, NY 131; Eastern League club 58, 72, 114
Birmingham, AL: Southern League club 110
Blue Stockings ball club (Akron) 14
Bohn, William 128
Boston, MA 70–71; ball club 7, 8, 28–29, 32, 35; National League club 52, 68–70, 72–73, 75, 92, 130–131, 134
Bosworth, Speed 139

Braddock, PA: Ohio & Pennsylvania League club 118
Bradford, PA: ball club 87
Brady, Billy 115
Brooklyn, NY: American Association club 56; Players League club 93, 95–96
Brown, John 15
Browning, Louis Rogers (Pete) 55, 63
Brush, John T. 43, 96
Buchtel, J.D. 10
Buchtel College 21, 34
Buckeye ball club: Akron 12, 14; Cincinnati 6
Buckeye Mower & Reaper Works 21, 34, 73, 130
Buckingham, Lisle 138
Buffalo, NY 73, 113–114; Eastern League club 72–74; International League club 131; National League club 25, 30, 32, 56, 80, 89, 108; Players League club 66, 70
Buffalo Street Railway Co. 73
Burkalow, Ike Van 63, 65
Butler Bros. ball club 78
Butte, MT 50

California 88
Canton, OH 33, 90, 122, 126, 135–136; ball club 12, 87–88; Buckeye League club 130; Central League club 130; Interstate League club 129–130; Middle Atlantic League club 138; Ohio & Pennsylvania League club 117, 120–121; Tri-State League club 61
Carter, W.H. 20–22
Cartwright, Alexander 1
Cass ball club (Detroit) 87
Caylor, Oliver Perry (O.P.) 40, 67–68, 77, 83–84
Central League 118, 120, 132, 135–136
Chadwick, Henry 49–50
Champion, Aaron 6
Chandler, Dr. A.F. 20
Chicago, IL 2, 51, 78, 122–124, 133; National League club 24, 29–30, 32, 50, 58, 69, 75, 88, 105, 139
Cincinnati, OH 5–7, 41, 51, 83, 120, 127; American Association club 39–40, 47–50, 67–68, 77, 82–83, 96, 127, 130; National League club 26, 30, 32, 50, 79, 93, 95, 134, 137; Red Stockings club 92; reserve club 128
Cincinnati Gun Club 38
Civil War 2–3, 5, 9, 13, 15
Clepper, Ed 121
Cleveland, OH 2, 9, 33, 60, 64, 68, 77, 80–81, 87, 89, 91–93, 104, 119–123, 126–128; American League club 138–139; National League club 18, 21, 23, 28, 30, 32, 45–46, 51, 77, 80, 87, 89, 100, 127–128; reserve club 127–128
Cleveland Grays 27
Cleveland Malleables 53
Cleveland Red Stockings 87–88
Clymer, Billy 116
Collegians ball club 130
Collins, Joe 139
Colorado League 38
Colorado Springs, CO 38
Columbus, OH: American Association club 26, 35, 58, 78, 105–106, 127, 130, 132; reserve club 127; Tri-State League club 61
Connecticut 60
Cooke, Frank 112
Cordova, IL 100
Council Bluffs, IO: ball club 100
Cratty, R.A. 123
Crescent City ball club 69
Cripple Creek, CO 58
Crockery City ball club 90
Cronin, Joe 134
Crouse, George W. 20–21, 34, 45
Cushman, Ed 112–113
Cuthbert, Ned 108
Cuyahoga Falls, OH 9

Darrow, E. 15, 23
Davenport, IO 38–39, 78; ball club 99–100, 112
Dayton, OH 126; Ohio League 127; Tri-State League club 61
Denver, CO 38; ball club 87
Derby (English club) 84
Des Moines, IO 4; Western Association club 56–57, 84, 112
Detroit, MI 2, 94, 133; American League club 132; International Association club 57; National League club 25, 34, 46, 64, 66, 79–80, 90–92, 99, 101, 105, 110
Diamond Tire & Rubber Co. 73
Dorsey, Michael 17, 18, 20, 23, 25, 29, 31, 34, 37
Doyle, Frank 131
Dreyfoos, Al 38
Dubuque, IO 3; Northwest League club 87
Duluth, MN 78
Dunlap, Fred 40
Dunn, Jack 131

Index

Eagle ball club: Hudson 12; New York 2
East, Walter 73–74, 118
East Liverpool, OH 90, 120, 126; Ohio & Pennsylvania League club 120, 130
Eastern League 25, 51, 58, 71–72, 114–115, 139
Easton, Jack 58
Eau Clair, WI: Northwestern League club 100
Eckford ball club (Brooklyn) 2
Electric Light 34
Elyria, OH 126; ball club 17, 21–23, 25, 27, 33, 36, 53, 92
Empire ball club (New York) 2
England 82, 84–85
Enterprise ball club (Hudson) 12
Erie, PA 34; Central League club 130; Eastern League club 113–114; Ohio & Pennsylvania League club 120–121
Ewing, Buck 97
Excelsior ball club (Brooklyn) 2–3

Faber, Margaret (Mrs. Charles H. Morton) 110, 122
Falor, Edyth 136–137
Farrell, J.H. 117–119
Findlay, OH: ball club 21, 27, 33, 53, 104
Firestone Non-skids ball club 133, 134
Firestone Stadium 134, 136
Flagler, Henry M. 97
Florida 96–98
Florida East Coast Hotel Co. 97
Forest City ball club: Cleveland 9, 12, 18, 28, 29, 33; Ft. Madison, IO 100
Fort Edward, NY 105
foul bound rule 61, 108
Franklin, James 25, 115
Fultz, David 95

Gaffney, John 94–95
Galesburg, IL: ball club 101
Galvin, Pud 89
Garman, Ed 136
Garrettsville, OH: ball club 14, 16–18, 21, 27
Gehrig, Lou 137
General Electric 106
General Railway Supply Co. 122
General Tire ball club 131, 133–134
Geneva, OH 35
Germany 110
Glasscock, Jack 70, 96
Glick, Abe 15, 17

Goff, Olive (Mrs. Samuel Leech Maskrey) 85
Good, Jacob 16
Goodrich, Dr. B.F. 21; *see also* B.F. Goodrich Co.
Goodwin, Wendell 96
Goodyear Wingfoots ball club 133
Gore, George 68
Gotham ball club (New York) 2
Grand American Handicap 38
Grand Avenue ball grounds (St. Louis) 99, 102–103, 107
Green, Dowling 59
Green, James (Jimmy) 17, 18, 20, 25, 28, 37, 45–46, 60–62, 76
Greenville, PA 86
Gumpert, Addison C. 59
Guy, Richard 123

Hamilton, Ontario: ball club 57
Hanford, Fred 10, 12
Hanlon, Ned 97
Hanscom, Ace 9, 12
Harrington, D. 15
Harrisburg, PA 126; Eastern League club 139
Hart, Jim 85
Hartford, CN 7
Haverly's Mastadon Minstrels 105
Haynes, M.R. 20–22
Herrmann, August 95
Holyoke, MA: ball club 64
Homestead, PA: Ohio & Pennsylvania League club 117
Homestead Grays ball club 137
Hoover, Billy, 71
Huber, Joe 58
Hudson, J.W. 9–10
Hudson, Nat 78
Hulbert, William 7

Illinois-Iowa League 101
Independent Association of Base Ball Clubs 117
Indianapolis, IN: American Association club 127; National League club 93, 95–96; Western League club 115
International Association 8, 57, 112
International League 131, 133
Interstate League 120, 127, 129
Iowa League 101
Iredell, Robert S. 17, 22, 25
Ireland 34
Iron & Oil League 85

Jackson Iron Co. 92
Jacksonville, FL 87
Jamestown, NY: ball club 113
Jersey City, NJ: International League club 131
Johnson, William (Ed) 15, 18, 20, 23–24, 28
Johnson's Corners, OH 65
Johnstown, PA 126, 128
Jones, Charley 67, 77
Jones, Daniel Albion (Jumping Jack) 99, 101–104
Jones, L.K. 21–22

Kansas City, KS: ball club 26, 77; National League club 66; Western Association club 112
Keithsburg, IL 38
Kelly, Mike (King) 96
Kemmler, Rudy 26, 28, 30, 37, 52, 67, 77–78, 80, 88, 100, 102, 107–108
Kent, OH 90; ball club 18, 90
Kenyon College 3
Ketchum, Charles E. 134, 135
Keystones (Meadville, PA) 80–82
Kingsville, OH 109
Knight, Clarence 17, 20–22, 25, 52
Krichell, Paul 136

Ladies Day 48
Lake ball club (Uniontown) 12
Lake Erie 9, 109
Lancaster, OH: Ohio & Pennsylvania League club 117–120
Landis, Kenesaw Mountain 132–133
Lattimore, Ralph 132–133
Law & Order League 119
League Alliance 8, 25
Lilly, Jim (Grasshopper) 66–67
Litchfield, CN 101
Long, D.J. 21
Los Angeles, CA: ball club 57
Louisville, KY 7, 35, 54–55, 60–66, 76–77, 83, 88, 99, 103, 109, American Association club 36, 46, 82–83, 100
Louisville Eclipse 35–36, 39, 54–55, 60–65, 69, 76–77, 85, 88, 99, 103
Louisville Slugger bat 55
Louisvilles ball club 88

Mansell, John (Doc) 23, 28, 30, 37, 45, 54, 61–62
Mansell, Michael 26, 30, 71
Mansfield, OH 10–11; ball club 11–12, 18; Interstate League club 129; Ohio & Pennsylvania League club 73–74, 118–120
Marion, OH: Ohio & Pennsylvania League club 119–120
Marshall, Tom 38
Martin, Eugene J. 137
Marvin, Judge U.L. 16
Maskrey, Harry 85
Maskrey, Samuel Leech 26, 28, 35, 37–39, 46, 61, 76, 79, 82–86, 100, 102, 108
Maskrey, William 85
Massachusetts 68
Massillon, OH 125; Ohio & Pennsylvania League club 117
Massillon State Hospital for the Insane 125
Mathews, C.H. 17
McCaffrey, Harry Charles 103
McCormick, Jim 45
McGinnis, George (Jumbo) 101–103, 107–109
McKechnie, Bill 134
McKeesport, PA 120; Ohio & Pennsylvania League 120
McPhee, John Alexander (Bid) 34–35, 37–45, 55, 67, 76–77, 89, 100–101, 108, 129
Meadville, PA 81, 85, 128
Mechanics ball club (Middlebury) 9, 10
Meckey Opera Company 41
Memphis, TN: Southern League club 64
Mercer, PA 82, 85, 87; ball club 82
Michigan (University of) 130
Middle Atlantic League 136–137
Middlebury, OH 9
Miller, Thomas & Co. 37
Milwaukee, WI: ball club 100; Northwestern League club 84, 111
Minneapolis, MN: Western Association club 113
Mobile, AL: ball club 85
Montana State League 50
Montreal, Que. 132
Monumental ball club (Twinsburg) 12
Moran, John 15, 20, 23, 37
Morgan, Dan 103
Morgan & Wright ball club 133
Morrill, John 68
Morris, Walter 135
Morton, Aaron D. 109
Morton, Charles Hazen (Charlie) 17, 18, 20, 22–23, 25–26, 28, 30–31, 37–38, 45, 47–48, 52, 55–57, 63, 73, 76, 79–80, 88, 91–92, 99, 103–105, 107–125, 129

Index

Morton, Fred 124
Morton, Freddie 111–112
Morton, Harry U. 122–124
Morton, John F. 109
Mount Union College 14
Mount Vernon, OH: Ohio & Pennsylvania League club 117
Mountain, Frank 35, 79, 104–107
Mulford, Ren, Jr. 43
Mullane, Anthony John (Tony) 26, 28–31, 34–35, 38, 45–53, 60–61, 63, 65, 67, 76, 79–80, 87–91, 99, 103, 110
Mutes of Columbus 24

Nallin, Dick 73–74
Nancy Hanks (race horse) 113
Nash, Billy 73
National A.C. ball club 138
National Amateur Baseball Federation 139
National Association (minor league organization) 117, 119–120, 122
National Association of Base Ball Players 2–3, 6
National Association of Professional Base Ball Players (National Association) 6–8, 57
National Baseball Hall of Fame 34, 130
National Commission 130
National League 7–8, 14, 25, 32–35, 51, 53, 58–59, 61, 66, 68, 77, 80, 87–93, 97, 99, 101, 104–105, 108, 110, 126, 139
National Resort and Training Park Co. 97–98
Neagle, Jack 17, 18, 20, 23–24, 27–28, 30, 37, 52–54, 64
Negro National League 136
New Castle, PA 120, 126; Ohio & Pennsylvania League club 118–122
New Jersey 91
New Orleans, LA 68
New York (state) 91
New York, Chicago & St. Louis Railroad 76
New York City 7, 49, 68, 105–106, 132
New York Knickerbockers 1–3
New York Metropolitans 8, 54, 64
New York Mutuals 7
New York Yankees 136–138
Newark, NJ 132; Atlantic League club 73
Newark, OH: Ohio & Pennsylvania League club 117–120; Ohio State League 129
Niles, CA 100

Nolan, Edward (The Only) 45, 80
Northern Ohio Base Ball League 126
Northwestern League 25, 64, 84, 92, 100–101, 110
Norwalk, OH: ball club 21, 27–28, 33, 53

Oberlin, OH 126
Oberlin College ball club 104
Ohio 126
Ohio & Erie Canal 9
Ohio League 127, 129, 132
Ohio-Michigan League 129
Ohio-Pennsylvania League 25, 73, 117–125, 129–132, 137
Ohio River 9
Ohio State League 129
Oil & Iron League 128
Ormsby, Fred R. 124
O'Rourke, Orator Jim 80
Orrville, OH: ball club 15, 16
Osterhout, Charles H. (Charlie) 23–24, 28, 71

Pacific Northwest League 38, 51, 85
Painesville, OH 92
Parks, W. 15
Parrott, Jiggs 113
Pennsylvania 82, 91, 126
Pennsylvania State League 72
Peoria Reds 87
Perkins, Col. George Tod 12–13
Perkins, Tom 10
Peters, John 108–109
Pfeffer, Fred 40, 63, 88
Philadelphia, PA 7, 68, 94, 97, 104; American Association club 62, 79, 101, 105; National League club 35, 79, 92–94, 96, 98
Philadelphia Athletics 2, 7
Piercy, Andrew J. 88, 90, 99, 102–104, 108
Pinewood Deep Springs Water Co. 97
Pittsburgh, PA 56, 59, 121–122, 126; American Association club 64, 77, 104–106; National League club 50, 58, 75, 113, 130, 134; reserve club 128
Pittsburgh Crawfords 137
Players League 67, 70, 73, 93, 95–96
P.O.M. (Pennsylvania, Ohio, Maryland League) 120, 123
Portage Township School 138
Porter, C. 15
Portsmouth, OH 9
Powell, Abner 57
Powers, Phil 50

Preston North End (English club) 84
Pritchard, Joe 41
Protective Association of Independent Clubs 117
Providence, RI 64; ball club 64; Eastern League club 58, 72; National League club 68, 77, 92, 104
Purcell, William Aloysius (Blondie) 35, 78–82, 88–89, 99
Putnams ball club (Brooklyn) 2

Radbourn, Charles Gardner (Old Hoss) 87
Ravenna, OH: ball club 18, 27
Rawson, Ed 10, 12
Reach, Al 94
Read, Ralph 122
Reading, PA: International League club 131
Reccius, John 63, 65
Red Stockings ball club: Akron 14; Cincinnati 6
reserve clause 68, 70, 93, 96, 126
reserve teams 126–129
Resolutes ball club (Cincinnati) 5
Richter, Francis 120
Riversides ball club (Portsmouth, OH) 61
Robinson, Wilbert 41
Robinson, Yank 40
Rochester, NY: Eastern Association club 113; Eastern League club 58, 71–72, 115–116; International League club 131
Rockwell, W.E. 37–39
Romulus, NY 62
Ruth, Babe 131
Rutland, VT 49

Sablosky, Ike 135
Sage, Corwin 43
Sage, John B. 32
St. Louis, MO 2, 7, 99, 101, 104–105, 107, 109, 125; American Association club 46–47, 58, 64, 69, 78, 110; American League club 130; National League club 137–138; reserve club 128
St. Louis Brown Stockings or Browns 35, 76, 99, 101–103, 107–109
St. Louis Reds 54
St. Paul, MN: ball club 100, 112; Western League club 51
San Francisco, CA: ball club 87
San Jose, CA 88
Sauer, Hank 139
Savannah, GA: Southern League club 64, 100, 110–112

Schenectady, NY 105–106
Schlemmer, Jim 136
Schmelz, Gus 49
Seattle: Pacific Northwest League club 85
Selkirk, George 137
Seville, OH: ball club 17, 18
Seward, George 103, 108
Sharon, PA 120; Ohio & Pennsylvania League club 74, 119–121
Shaw, W.C. 114
Shelby, OH 74, 119
Shorb, Adam 121–122
Sioux City, IO: ball club 58
Sisler, George Harold 130–132
Sloop, Harold 134
Smith, Elmer 58
Smith, E.S. 10
Sohio A.C. ball club 138
Southern League 110–111, 113
Spalding, A.G. 69, 82, 84–85
Spokane, WA 51
Springfield, OH: Ohio League club 127–128
Star ball club (Ravenna, OH) 12
Stars ball club (Dallas, TX) 100
Stern, Aaron 49
Steubenville, OH: Interstate League club 129; Ohio & Pennsylvania League club 130
Stockwell, Len 99–101, 108
Stoke (English club) 84
Stoneham, MA: ball club 64
Sullivan, Daniel (Link) 30, 46, 54, 61–64, 79
Sullivan, John L. 75
Summit ball club (Akron) 12
Summit Beach Amusement Park 135
Summit Lake 135
Sunday, Billy 74–75
Sunday baseball 2, 74, 118–119
Swartwood, Cyrus Edward (Ed) 17, 18, 20, 35, 37, 45, 52–59, 60–61, 63, 72, 76, 79, 88–90, 101–102, 104, 108, 113
Syracuse, NY 71, 106, 112, 115; International League club 131; National League club 23, 79

Tacoma, WA: Pacific Northwest League club 85
Taylor, William Henry (Bolicky Bill) 53, 87–91, 99
Tebeau, Patsy 97
Texas 100
Texas League 135

Thomas, Col. D.W. 37
Thomas, Joseph D., Sr. 130, 132
Thorpe, Jim 131–132
Tiffin, OH: Ohio State League club 129
Toledo, OH 48, 110, 112–113; American Association club 23, 25, 46–47, 57, 110, 113, 127; ball club 106; International Association club 112; Northwestern League club 25, 92, 101, 110, 113
Topeka, KS 26
Toronto, Ontario: Eastern League club 51; International League club 131
Traynor, Pie 134
Tri-State League 106, 129
Trowbridge, Charles 15
Troy, NY: National League club 24, 32, 52–53, 105
Tuholsky, Nate 122

uniforms (of the Akrons) 16, 28
Union Association 47, 126–127
Union Classical Institute 105
University of Michigan 130
Utica, NY 71

Valley Railroad 33, 81
Vermont 49
Voltz, W.H. 128–129
Von der Ahe, Chris 47, 69, 129

Wagner, Honus 129
Walker, George R. 24
Walker, Moses Fleetwood 23, 47, 104, 110
Walker, Welday 104
Waner, Paul 134
Ward, John Montgomery 70, 95–96
Warren, OH: ball club 14, 21, 23
Warren, PA 128; ball club 85
Washington, DC 87; National League club 35, 66, 69, 70, 72, 75, 113; Union Association club 60–61

Washington Nationals 5
Weiss, George 136–137
West Palm Beach, FL 97–98
Western Association 51, 56, 58, 84, 112
Western League 51, 115
Western Reserve ball club (Western Reserve College, Hudson, OH) 10, 12, 18, 21, 29, 31
Western Reserve College 92
Westerns ball club (Topeka, KS) 100
Wheeling, WV 136–137; Tri-State League club 61
White Sewing Machine (ball club) (Whites) 27–28, 30, 32, 46, 52–54, 63, 76, 78–81, 88, 99, 128
Wiedner, F. 15, 18
Williams, Harry 124
Williamson, Ned 24, 29–30
Windsor, John T. 121–124
Wise, Samuel Washington (Sam) 15–17, 20–21, 23, 30, 35, 37–38, 52–53, 58, 65–75, 78–80, 88–89, 102, 107–108, 114, 119, 125, 130
Worcester, MA: National League ball club 15, 25, 28, 32, 52–53, 77, 87, 105
Wright, Harry 92–94
Wright, Jared 139
Wright, Sam 119, 121–122

Yale University 101
Yankee Juniors ball club 139
Yonkers, NY: Eastern League club 72
Young, Nick 50–51
Youngstown, OH 14, 75, 117, 120–121, 126–127, 138; Central League club 130; Ohio & Pennsylvania League club 117–121; Ohio State League club 129

Zanesville, OH 118; Ohio & Pennsylvania League club 117–118

www.ingramcontent.com/pod-product-compliance
Ingram Content Group UK Ltd.
Pitfield, Milton Keynes, MK11 3LW, UK
UKHW042013140426
5217IPUK00015B/1148